Joshua First is the Croft Assistant Professor of History and International Studies at the University of Mississippi. He has published on a variety of topics related to Soviet cinema after Stalin, ranging from film audience research to melodrama to Ukrainian cinema during the 1960s–1980s. He teaches courses on modern Russian and Soviet history, and on contemporary Russian politics and culture.

GW00775920

Published and forthcoming in *KINO: The Russian and Soviet Cinema Series*

Series Editor: Richard Taylor

Advisory Board: Birgit Beumers, Julian Graffy, Denise Youngblood

Performing Femininity: Woman as Performer in Pre-Revolutionary Russian Film
Rachel Morley

The Russian American Hero in Soviet Film: Cinema's Role in Shaping the Early Culture of the USSR
Marina Levitina

Through a Russian Lens: Representing Foreigners in a Century of Russian Film
Julian Graffy

Cinema in Central Asia: Rewriting Cultural Histories
Edited by Gulnara Abikeyeva, Michael Rouland and Birgit Beumers

The Cinema of Tarkovsky: Labyrinths of Space and Time
Nariman Skakov

The Cinema of Alexander Sokurov
Edited by Birgit Beumers and Nancy Condee

Eisenstein on the Audiovisual: The Montage of Music, Image and Sound in Cinema
Robert Robertson

Sergei Eisenstein Selected Works
Edited by Richard Taylor

Cinema and Soviet Society: From the Revolution to the Death of Stalin
Peter Kenez

Dziga Vertov: Defining Documentary Film
Jeremy Hicks

Film Propaganda: Soviet Russia and Nazi Germany (second, revised edition)
Richard Taylor

Forward Soviet: History and Non-Fiction Film in the USSR
Graham Roberts

Propaganda and Popular Entertainment in the USSR: The Mezhrabpom Studio
Jamie Miller

Real Images: Soviet Cinema and the Thaw
Josephine Woll

Russia on Reels: The Russian Idea in Post-Soviet Cinema
Edited by Birgit Beumers

Savage Junctures: Sergei Eisenstein and the Shape of Thinking
Anne Nesbet

Soviet Cinema: Politics and Persuasion under Stalin
Jamie Miller

Vsevolod Pudovkin: Classic Films of the Soviet Avant-Garde
Amy Sargeant

Queries, ideas and submissions to:
Series Editor: Professor Richard Taylor – richtea21@hotmail.com
Cinema Editor at I.B. Tauris: Anna Coatman - acoatman@ibtauris.com

Ukrainian Cinema

Belonging and Identity during the Soviet Thaw

Joshua First

BLOOMSBURY ACADEMIC
LONDON • NEW YORK • OXFORD • NEW DELHI • SYDNEY

BLOOMSBURY ACADEMIC
Bloomsbury Publishing Plc
50 Bedford Square, London, WC1B 3DP, UK
1385 Broadway, New York, NY 10018, USA
29 Earlsfort Terrace, Dublin 2, Ireland

BLOOMSBURY, BLOOMSBURY ACADEMIC and the Diana logo
are trademarks of Bloomsbury Publishing Plc

First published in 2015 by I.B. Tauris & Co Ltd
Paperback edition published by Bloomsbury Academic in 2022

Copyright © Joshua First, 2015

Joshua First has asserted his right under the Copyright,
Designs and Patents Act, 1988, to be identified as Author of this work.

For legal purposes the Acknowledgements on pp. x-xi constitute
an extension of this copyright page.

All rights reserved. No part of this publication may be reproduced or
transmitted in any form or by any means, electronic or mechanical,
including photocopying, recording, or any information storage or retrieval
system, without prior permission in writing from the publishers.

Bloomsbury Publishing Plc does not have any control over, or responsibility for,
any third-party websites referred to or in this book. All internet addresses given
in this book were correct at the time of going to press. The author and publisher
regret any inconvenience caused if addresses have changed or sites have
ceased to exist, but can accept no responsibility for any such changes.

A catalogue record for this book is available from the British Library.
A catalog record for this book is available from the Library of Congress.

ISBN: HB: 978-1-7807-6554-9
PB: 978-1-3503-7149-1
ePDF: 978-0-8577-2670-4
ePUB: 978-0-8577-3626-0

Series: KINO – The Russian and Soviet Cinema

To find out more about our authors and books visit
www.bloomsbury.com and sign up for our newsletters.

CONTENTS

LIST OF ILLUSTRATIONS

Chapter 1

Chapter 2

Chapter 3

Chapter 5

Chapter 6

Chapter 7

KINO: THE RUSSIAN AND SOVIET CINEMA SERIES

General Editor's Preface

Cinema has been the predominant art form of the first half of the twentieth century, at least in Europe and North America. Nowhere was this more apparent than in the former Soviet Union, where Lenin's remark that 'of all the arts, cinema is the most important' became a cliché and where cinema attendances were until recently still among the highest in the world. In the age of mass politics Soviet cinema developed from a fragile but effective tool for gaining support among the overwhelmingly illiterate peasant masses during the civil war that followed the October 1917 Revolution, through a welter of experimentation, into a mass weapon of propaganda through the entertainment that shaped the public image of the Soviet Union – both at home and abroad for both elite and mass audiences – and latterly into an instrument to expose the weaknesses of the past and present in the twin processes of *glasnost* and *perestroika*. Now the national cinemas of the successor republics to the old USSR are encountering the same bewildering array of problems, from the trivial to the terminal, as are all the other ex-Soviet institutions.

Cinema's central position in Russian and Soviet cultural history and its unique combination of mass medium, art form and entertainment industry have made it a continuing battlefield for conflicts of broader ideological and artistic significance, not only for Russia and the Soviet Union, but also for the world outside. The debates that raged in the 1920s about the relative merits of documentary as opposed to fiction film, of cinema as opposed to theatre or painting, or of the proper role of cinema in the forging of post-revolutionary Soviet culture and the shaping of the new Soviet man, have their echoes in current discussions about the role of cinema *vis-à-vis* other art forms in effecting the cultural and psychological revolution in human consciousness necessitated by the processes of economic and political transformation of the former Soviet Union into modern democratic and industrial societies and states governed by the rule of law. Cinema's central position has also made it a vital instrument for scrutinizing the blank pages of Russian and Soviet history and enabling the present generation to come to terms with its own past.

This series of books intends to examine Russian, Soviet and ex-Soviet films in the context of Russian, Soviet and ex-Soviet cinemas, and Russian, Soviet and ex-Soviet cinemas in the context of the political history of Russia, the Soviet Union, the post-Soviet 'space' and the world at large. Within that framework the series, drawing its authors from both East and West, aims to cover a wide variety of topics and to employ a broad range of methodological approaches and presentational formats. Inevitably this will involve ploughing once again over old ground in order to re-examine received opinions but it principally means increasing the breadth and depth of our knowledge, finding new answers to old questions and, above all, raising new questions for further enquiry and new areas for further research.

The current monograph is our second book on the Thaw period and our first to examine the cinema of a single union republic other than the Russian Federation. The study of Ukraine and its cinema during the Thaw period poses particular problems, politically, historically, geographically, linguistically and culturally and these are ably addressed throughout the book, beginning with the author's note on transliteration.

The continuing aim of this series is to situate Russian, Soviet and ex-Soviet cinema in its proper historical and aesthetic context, both as a major cultural force and as a crucible for experimentation that is of central significance to the development of world cinema culture. Books in the series strive to combine the best of scholarship, past, present and future, with a style of writing that is accessible to a broad readership, whether that readership's primary interest lies in cinema or in broader political history.

Richard Taylor
Swansea, Wales

ACKNOWLEDGEMENTS

Several individuals and institutions deserve my gratitude for help-ing me to complete this project. First and foremost, William G. Rosenberg provided me with unconditional support at the University of Michigan and, equally important, the confidence to pursue such an unusual topic for a historian of the Soviet Union. Most importantly, I hope that his way of approaching intellectual problems has worn off to some degree on my own thinking. Johannes von Moltke, a brilliant film historian, has shown me the importance of taking film analysis seriously. Ronald Suny and Valerie Kivelson have shown patience in reading and listening to my frequently illegible ramblings. Professor Kivelson, in particular, has been a good friend and, deservedly, a tough critic. Of course, I would not be asking questions about Soviet nationalities policy if not for the pioneering work of Professor Suny. I was fortunate enough to spend a year at the Havighurst Center for Russian and Post-Soviet Studies at Miami University of Ohio as a research fellow, where Steve Norris, Vitaly Chernetsky and Karen Dawisha, in particular, helped me re-conceptualize the project and transform it into a more mature piece of scholarship.

Within the field of Soviet film history, I owe a huge debt to Denise Youngblood for her pioneering work. She defined the field for me with her seminal monograph, *Movies for the Masses: Popular Cinema and Soviet Society in the 1920s*. Without this book, I might have never thought to work on a film-related topic. In Ukraine, the prolific work of Larysa Briukhovets'ka and Serhii Trymbach were instrumental in pointing me in the right direction.

I am grateful to the many institutions that helped facilitate my research and writing during graduate study. At the University of Michigan, the Center for Russian and East European Studies funded my study of the Ukrainian language, in addition to my first research trip to Kyiv. The departments of History and Screen Arts and Cultures, in addition to the Rackham School of Graduate Studies, aided me immeasurably at key moments in my research and writing. I conducted the bulk of my research in Kyiv and Moscow for this book on an IREX Individual Advanced Research Opportunities fel-lowship during the 2004–2005 academic year. While such support was essential for completing this project, all views expressed in it are entirely my own. At the University of Mississippi, I received two

Summer Research Grants that allowed me to do additional research at the Davis Center at Harvard, and to complete revisions to the book manuscript.

In Kyiv, I would like to thank the staff at the Central State Archive Museum of Literature and Art of Ukraine for going above and beyond the call of duty in getting essential research materials to me. Thanks to Irina Fomenko at the Oleksandr Dovzhenko National Film Centre for screening a number of films unavailable through other means. I am grateful to have met Svetlana and Miron Petrovskii, who shared not only their flat during part of my research but also their personal recollections about the period and subject of my project.

I am also grateful to have met a number of wonderful people while working on this project – colleagues, friends and my wife – who positively contributed to my intellectual development and influenced this book. Conversations and arguments at Michigan, Miami and Mississippi have all enriched the period of my life that I dedicated to realizing my first book. My wife, Sara Babcox First, deserves more gratitude than I could express in such a formulaic declaration, but I thank her most recently for postponing her own goals to help me complete this book.

NOTE ON TRANSLITERATION

Transliteration from the Cyrillic to the Latin alphabet is a perennial problem for writers on Russia and the Soviet Union. I have opted for a dual system: in the text we use the Library of Congress system, but I have departed from this system when a Russian or Ukrainian name has an accepted English spelling (e.g. Sergei Paradjanov instead of Sergei Paradzhanov; Alexander Dovzhenko instead of Oleksandr Dovzhenko), or when names are of Germanic origin.

However, there is a further complication to the transliteration in this study. During the Soviet era, places and names associated with Ukraine were usually transliterated into English in their Russian variant. It is now accepted practice in scholarship to render these using the Library of Congress system for Ukrainian. Thus, Kiev is here rendered as Kyiv, Lvov as Lviv and Sergei as Serhii, etc. Of course, when names are primarily known in Russian, or the nationality of the person in question is not Ukrainian, I render their name in the Russian transliteration.

INTRODUCTION

Soviet cinema was an immense and costly cultural and industrial project, the medium's novelty striving to assist the work of
constructing new Soviet workers, patriots, men and women, while
establishing a space for collective amusement. While prior scholarship has examined Soviet cinema in terms of its role in reproducing
class, state and gender identities, this book, in its focus on cinema's
attempts to define 'national character', expands upon the very definition of that goal: what was 'national character' and how could it
be rendered in Soviet art?[1] In affirmation of the complex relationship between the 'nations' that composed the USSR and the centralized state, authorities instructed their loyal servants in the film
industry to create scenes of national belonging that did not contradict the goals of a highly centralized and Russian-dominated political and cultural system. But how did cultural producers like film
directors, screenwriters and actors understand their relationship to
the national categories that were codified under a Soviet nationalities policy? Ukrainian film-makers during the 1960s, in particular,
assumed key roles in re-imagining a core Soviet concept – multinationality (*mnogonatsional'nost'*) – shifting its emphasis from incorporation, assimilation and modernization to difference, authenticity
and tradition.

Despite this unique emphasis on cultural federalism, the practice of filmmaking and the consumption of movies in the Soviet
Union after Stalin shared many characteristics with film industries
in Western Europe and even Hollywood. Authorities gave directors
considerable leeway to develop their own projects as *auteurs,* or to
accept assignments originating from other screenwriters. Directors
and studios competed with each other to attract and hire the biggest

stars, and the star system that developed in the Soviet Union looked similar to celebrity culture in the West. Moreover, studios and the administration for film distribution marketed films within familiar genre categories like comedy, melodrama, adventure and science fiction. The industry even hired its own 'sociologists' to conduct market research to determine which kinds of genres different sub-sections of the population enjoyed most. When citizens went to the movies, as they frequently did (20 times per person during 1968, on average), they had a wide variety of choices.[2] During a typical week in Kyiv during the late 1960s, one could catch a light comedy, a film about the World War II in a theatre outfitted with wide-screen technology, an 'art film' and several foreign options from France, Poland, Mexico, India and even the United States.[3] Cinema was both an important aspect of cultural life in the USSR and highly profitable.

At the same time, the practice of film-making and the consumption of movies in the Soviet Union were profoundly different from their counterparts in the West. The state funded film production, and the construction and maintenance of film studios and movie theatres; state functionaries determined 'thematic plans' for all the studios, reviewed screenplays, viewed unedited footage, determined salaries and bonuses for casts and crews, castigated theatre managers for showing too many foreign films and took a keen interest in audience opinions. And while overtly political themes receded in Soviet cinema after Stalin, the Communist Party of the Soviet Union maintained constant vigilance over studios and film-makers for ideological deviation. After all, the CPSU never backed away from Stalin's notion of cultural producers as 'engineers of the human soul'. Most notably, the party frequently ordered particular films into production to celebrate important anniversaries (Lenin's birthday, the Revolution, Victory Day, etc.) and political projects (the Virgin Lands campaign, persecution of bourgeois nationalists, etc.), thus asserting ideological objectives over audience desires. From available evidence, we know that spectators understood these *zakaznye fil'my* (ordered films) to be artistically bankrupt and unentertaining, and avoided them whenever possible.[4]

The establishment of national film studios in the Union Republics emerged as part of the political project of Soviet cinema beginning in the mid-1920s. The Bolsheviks believed that the development of national cinema was the mark of modern nations, and should be pursued in Ukraine, Georgia, Uzbekistan, etc. alongside the development of national literatures, theatre, visual art, dance and music. This fixation on cultural nation-building was enmeshed in features unique not only to the formation of the Soviet state in the 1920s as a multinational federation but also to ideological conflicts between Central and East European nationalism and Marxism during the late-nineteenth century. Marxist internationalists rejected the ahistorical conception of the nation state, and believed that nationalist interests were merely a ruse by national bourgeoisies to erode workers' consciousness of how capitalism functioned.[5] At the same time, other Communists and Social Democrats attempted to engage with nationalism in a variety of ways, which suggested that principles of national autonomy and protection of national minorities' political rights could be incorporated into a socialist agenda. As historian Yuri Slezkine argues, culture became the essential space for defining the importance and function of nations in a socialist polity. According to the framers of Soviet nationalities policy, nations needed languages, native subjects and native teachers in order to 'polemicize with "their own" bourgeoisies...and to banish the virus of nationalism from their proletarian disciples and their own minds'.[6] Hence, Ukrainian films were needed to transform Ukrainians into Communists. In Stalin's 'Marxism and the National Question', however, he distinguished such a national community as Ukraine from 'state communities' like Russia. In a future socialist state, there could be no such thing as 'Russian cinema' due to the imperialist connotations of such terminology. Thus, the project of building 'national cinemas' in the republics became removed from the broader project of Soviet cinema, with related but unique goals for the former.

Film studios were built in most republican capitals by the end of the 1930s, but conflicts immediately arose over different definitions of national cinema.[7] Film-makers at the Georgian and Ukrainian studios in particular asserted thematic ownership over 'their own' national material, and made films about pre-revolutionary cultural and political icons that celebrated unique national pasts and cultural traditions. Industry and party authorities in Moscow, however, aimed for more homogeneous cultural production in the national republics, and accused these film-makers of bourgeois nationalism. This conflict between making films *about* Ukraine and Georgia and making films about the Soviet Union *in* Ukraine and Georgia had fatal consequences during the national purges of 1931–2 and the Terror of 1936–8. After all, Stalin and his coterie were not so much interested in what we now call 'identity politics' as they were with the seemingly simpler question of language rights for non-Russians. While Ukraine's most famous director, Alexander Dovzhenko, escaped with his life and his career intact, authorities forbade him from making another film in Kyiv after 1932, thus removing him from his 'nationalist' influences and impulses.

Republican studios further declined after the war, with even the sizeable facilities in Kyiv making between zero and two films annually. While changing its name to the Dovzhenko Feature Film Studio during the late 1950s to draw attention to its glorious past, the studio in Kyiv nonetheless suffered from an ageing staff of directors who had made their most recognizable films under Stalin, and a management fearful of the implications of de-Stalinization. Moreover, few in Ukraine or the rest of the USSR wanted to see Ukrainian films. Movie theatre managers reported that they had to black out the name of the studio to entice viewers to watch them.[8] In the midst of a vibrant film-going culture and renewed international interest in Soviet cinema by the late 1950s, the Kyiv studio seemed to be operating according to old principles, and was duly ignored.

By 1963 however, the Ukrainian studio took the lead in re-examining the core intentions of a multinational film industry: what did it mean to make Soviet *Ukrainian* cinema? Was this merely an aesthetic problem, or did it also encompass issues of studio personnel, the context of production, promotion and reception? Could a Ukrainian national cinema – a cinema *about* Ukrainians and Ukraine – actually attract a mass audience in the Soviet Union, or even in Ukraine? Could film, the 'most democratic' of the arts, as Trotsky once called it,[9] help transform national identity from a problem, something considered and discussed by elites, into the everyday, something felt and understood by ordinary citizens? Anthony Smith writes that the great potential of cinema is that while the 'message is certainly addressed to the imagination of the elite, [it is] even more to the moral will, the emotions and the shared memories of the masses'.[10] While case studies on national formations investigate the ideologies of certain politicians and intellectuals, they rarely address the politics of representation: In the present case, this includes questions of what Ukrainians looked like, what Ukrainians sounded like and what kinds of spaces Ukrainians inhabited, especially as they took shape in popular imagery. Cinema functioned to establish a vivid connection between national space and the natural landscape. Film, moreover, provided a means to move away from the association of nationality and the 'national question' exclusively with national rights, and language rights in particular, an area of politics which dominated the earlier efforts of Soviet Ukrainian intellectuals.[11]

The problem of identity did not materialize at Dovzhenko Studio simply because Ukrainian filmmakers were able to speak more freely after Stalin's death; rather, it emerged from broader social, political and cultural problems of the 1960s. During this decade, Ukraine underwent several important changes, some which were characteristic of the Soviet Union as a whole and others which were unique to its own internal development. Ukraine emerged during this decade as predominantly urban, only the third Soviet republic to make this demographic shift from a rural and agricultural economy. With urbanization came more widespread Russification in the republic. Educated Ukrainians came to rely on Russian in their daily communication, while Ukrainian language and identity was associated with the domestic sphere, as a 'kitchen language'. Thus, Ukrainian filmmakers, like other members of the Ukrainian intelligentsia, were confronted by a sense of loss, a sense that Ukrainian difference was neither recognized nor easily identifiable.

In 1963, Nikita Khrushchev appointed Petro Shelest as First Secretary of the Ukrainian Communist Party (CPU). While Moscow considered Shelest to be a loyal technocrat, his interests in the republic increasingly intersected with the concerns of film-makers, writers and other intellectuals. During the same year, Dovzhenko Studio also came under a new managing director, the Ukrainian literary critic and World War II partisan commander, Vasyl' Tsvirkunov, who set a cautious agenda for the Ukrainianization and modernization of the studio. Tsvirkunov rejuvenated creative personnel at Dovzhenko Studio, and reintroduced Ukrainian as a film language; he defined its core objective as the reproduction of cinematic knowledge about the republic and its people, demanded that film-makers seek new methods of representation that were in line with the aesthetic principles of the Thaw and promised industry authorities that Ukrainian cinema would become profitable for the state.

Identity remained at the centre of Tsvirkunov's attempts to rebuild Kyiv Studio, but it existed alongside, and in concert with, questions about artistry and marketability. After all, films are unique cultural products, both for their representational ability to combine images, motion and sound in the process of telling stories, and for their incredible cost to produce, towards which a paying customer's desires must be considered in order to ensure a return on the initial investment. In a letter addressed to the studio, one writer expressed his displeasure about a film experience by taking the role of a 'consumer (*potrebitel'*)' of a 'product (*produktsiia*)', noting, 'The spectator never forgets that he sits in the theatre, in a comfortable chair, with his wife, friend or somebody else, and that he is the spectator'.[12] In other words, the customer has a right to entertainment, over and above the political projects to create new Soviet men and women or to create national cinema. Thus, while the processes of the Thaw gave voice to a wider diversity of cultural interests in Ukraine, which led to renewed interest in identity politics at Dovzhenko Studio, the dual threat of ideological authorities and empty movie theatres made these emergent concerns fragile at best.

*   *   *

As scholars have argued for decades, nations are 'imagined' and ideologically 'constructed' sites of political and cultural action, emerging, in their present form, only under the conditions of modernity, which include a mass press, industrial economy, compulsory education and conceptions of participatory politics.[13] More pertinently, people had to 'invent' Ukraine as a nation and Ukrainians as a nationality before these ideas became political facts.[14] This book proceeds from such scholarship, but offers an interpretation of how 'Ukraine' and 'Ukrainian' functioned as constructs after the Soviet Union supposedly had solved the 'national question'. Not surprisingly, most scholarship on the Soviet Union as a 'nation-building' state deals with the 1920s-1930s, that is, the period when Soviet leaders defined nationalities policy and its intended goals.[15] While cinema has remained in the background of this extensive scholarship on Ukraine's position within the early USSR, George Liber's biography of Alexander Dovzhenko demonstrates how the most recognizable Ukrainian film-maker negotiated Ukrainian and Soviet identities within the context of ethnic federalism and Stalinist repression.[16]

Only recently have historians begun exploring how Soviet nations continued to be reproduced after the death of Stalin. Sergei Zhuk and William Jay Risch have offered compelling examinations of the meanings attached to Ukrainian identity in two highly different cities in Soviet Ukraine (Dnipropetrovsk and Lviv, respectively) after Stalin. Like many recent scholars on the Thaw and the Brezhnev era,[17] they highlight the role of everyday experience over the designs of party and state authorities, and place greater importance on regional over national identities.[18] This historiographical shift from nationalities policy to experience not only reflects academic trends, but also the availability of a different source base and hence the necessity of different methodological tools for understanding the USSR after Stalin.

These recent works on post-Stalinist Ukraine nonetheless lend credence to Ron Suny's observation in his classic text *Revenge of the Past* that party and state officials continued to employ a flexible and differentiated approach to nationalities policy, which took into account questions of security, economics and demographics, in addition to the demands (or lack thereof) of national elites.[19] The situation in Belorussia, with its absence of native language schools in cities, coexisted with that in Georgia and Estonia, where national elites resisted Russian-language instruction.[20] And, as Zhuk and Risch demonstrate, Lviv and Dnipropetrovsk, while located in the same Ukrainian Soviet socialist republic, were subjected to widely varying policies regarding language, education and support for cultural institutions. In my own research, I found that, despite the rules which mandated dubbing all motion pictures into Ukrainian for release within the republic, organs of distribution refused to comply in areas they knew contained few Ukrainian speakers, such as the east Ukrainian cities of Kharkiv, Donetsk and Dnipropetrovsk.[21] While such deliberate flouting of nationalities policy was accepted in this case, similar actions in the west Ukrainian cities of Lviv, Chernivtsy or Ivano-Frankivsk would not have been tolerated.[22]

Yet we also find a general trend in that most of the republics emerged at the end of the 1960s as 'more national in character, not only demographically, but politically and culturally as well', according to Suny.[23] This situation emerged from a renewed commitment from the late 1950s through the 1970s to promote native elites within the republican state and Communist Party apparatuses. Many of these up-and-coming national elites spoke of promoting national culture and cultural autonomy in their republics. By and large, party authorities in Moscow only took notice of such language if it appeared definitively anti-Soviet or it dovetailed with poor economic decisions.[24] First Secretaries of the Ukrainian Communist Party throughout this period vigorously defended the republic's economic interests, occasionally entering into disputes with Moscow. And, with the appointment of Shelest in 1963, cultural interests joined the economy on centre stage in a jockeying for cultural authority between Moscow and Ukraine.

Nationality, in fact, became a site of contestation in several of the national republics, both from dissidents and from individuals working inside the system, just as did notions of socialist legality and cultural authority more generally. Along with the processes of postwar Soviet modernity, moreover, came a certain malaise among many artists, intellectuals and students, leading to nostalgia for a pre-Stalinist and, indeed, pre-Soviet past. Among Ukrainians in the 1960s, such a past seemed all the more tangible in the western regions of the republic – Galicia and Bukovyna, in particular – which had only recently been incorporated into the USSR, and which had been a focus for Ukrainian nationalism since the nineteenth century. For the Kyiv intelligentsia, the discovery and exploration of western Ukraine became a means to reject the homogenization of contemporary Soviet life as they attempted to articulate a more organic, authentic – and less Russian – Ukrainian space. In this sense, nationality became a question of self-discovery, an experiential rather than rights-based discourse that resembled what British and American commentators would call 'identity politics' in the 1970s. Intellectuals in the Republic were becoming disaffected with the language and practice of duplicitous non-discrimination contained in the oft-repeated slogan, 'Friendship of Peoples', suggesting instead that it masked conscious attempts to destroy minority cultures through assimilation. While dissident intellectuals certainly appealed to political rights in their writings, more often they highlighted problems of media and popular representation, stereotyping and the everyday and unofficial acts of discrimination that self-conscious Ukrainians experienced. The appeal to Ukrainian culture worked in tandem with a sense that the 'Soviet way of life' under 'developed socialism' was being stripped of its humanist intimations. Thus, the hope was that national culture could breathe life into the banal affirmations of official discourse. This does not mean that the appeal to 'national culture' was deliberately or always oppositional; rather, it was a search for personal and collective meaning under the peculiarly bland conditions of post-Stalinist modernity.

Perhaps because the appeal to national culture was tied into a broader malaise with contemporary life in the USSR, ethnic Ukrainians (those whose official documents identified them as such) were not the only ones who worked within the idiom of promoting national culture within the republic. Despite efforts to

'Ukrainianize' Dovzhenko Studio during the 1960s, one of the dominant figures there was the Tbilisi-born, Russian-speaking Armenian Sergei Paradjanov. His film, *Shadows of Forgotten Ancestors* (*Tini zabutykh predkiv*), released in 1965, established the Carpathians as an exotic and yet quintessentially Ukrainian space. In this sense, nationality functioned as an alternative to conformist notions of 'contemporaneity (*sovremennost'*)' and the 'Soviet image of life (*sovetskii obraz zhizni*)'. Instead of a question of national rights or the assimilationist language of the 'Friendship of Peoples', the intelligentsia in Ukraine imagined the Soviet concept of multinationality (*mnogonatsional'nost'*) as a creative affirmation of cultural diversity. While the Soviet state never ceased to ascribe nationality to its citizens, artists and intellectuals in the 1960s began to explore what it meant to possess a particular nationality, and thus challenged Soviet attempts to deny difference.

Many Ukrainian filmmakers participated in this project of national self-discovery, although not in an openly oppositional manner. They crossed paths with Ukrainian dissidents, but did not enter their world entirely, principally because to do so would mean the end of their careers as film-makers. Still, even while working squarely within the field of cultural bureaucracies and remaining subject to economic plans and the desires of audiences, filmmakers attempted to establish a more or less popular imagery and narrative of what it meant to be Ukrainian, both in the past and within the contemporary USSR. Yet cinema, like music, the theatre and architecture, is an inherently collaborative art form, and thus subject to the interests, goals and intentions of a diverse and dispersed network of writers, directors, cinematographers, actors, studio and industry officials, Communist Party and government authorities, critics and the administration of film distribution. Many of these groups, and many individuals within each of these groups, had little interest in promoting Ukrainian culture. Others objected to what they labelled Ukrainian cinema's 'ethnographic' conception of 'national character' during the 1960s, suggesting, also from the perspective of defending Ukrainian culture, that such a 'fetishistic' and essentializing imagery denied Ukrainians' position within the contemporary world and as beneficiaries of socialist modernity. Nonetheless, the Dovzhenko Studio leadership made a conscious decision to support a group of predominantly young film-makers in developing a decidedly different image of Ukraine than the assimilationist concept of a 'Friendship of Peoples' could contain.

Many film-makers and writers in Ukraine were concerned with the problem of revealing national difference, of coming to terms with what it meant to be Ukrainian in the absence of any project for achieving political sovereignty. As such, the nationality question in the 1960s was tied to the problem of artistic, rather than political, representation. In unintentional conformity with Canadian theorist Charles Taylor's definition of multiculturalism, the Ukrainian intelligentsia sought recognition for a culturally sophisticated notion of Ukrainian nationality, one that was not dependent on deterministic categories such as language, nor either erased or reduced to clichéd folkloric spectacle.[25] At the same time, most sought such recognition without engaging in open conflict with central authorities, as dissidents did during this time.

Apart from the general malaise about the 'Soviet way of life', two other factors contributed to the shift of nationality from a question of political rights to one of artistic representation and a striving for recognition of ethnic difference. First, in an attempt to overcome the effects of Stalinism in the arts, literary critics in particular demanded that authors look into themselves to find truth and authenticity in representation. Khrushchev, moreover, gave tacit approval for this project of exposing 'real life' in his critique of Stalin's 'personality cult' during the Twentieth Party Congress in February 1956. According to such reasoning, artists and authors possessed power to create meaning, rather than simply being charged with the responsibility to interpret and 'propagandize' a political theme. Ukrainian film-makers saw the basis of national cinema located, not within a system of production based on a Stalinist imagery of non-Russians, but as a function of the artist's/author's personal expression. Consequently, film-makers and writers were engaged in questioning the categories of national representation that the Stalinist system of cultural production had established with the 'Friendship of Peoples' mythology. In turn, the artist gained new credibility and importance as the producer of nationality itself, precisely because more authorities were willing to view art as an autonomous field after Stalin, and as a transcendent site where genius could be revealed. Thus, a collective understanding of nationality during the 1960s was predicated on the resolution of particularly personal aesthetic concerns.

A second factor influencing the development of the nationality question during the 1960s emerged from the first: if nationality had become a problem of artistic representation, the ways the Soviet culture industry structured reception of cultural products was of key importance. The spectator was no longer exclusively the 'object of reshaping', as Evgeny Dobrenko characterized early Soviet reception theory, but an active consumer of an increasingly diversified amount of media.[26] Artists had to consider who would be interested in their work on self-consciously national subject matter. On the one hand, this revision of Soviet reception theory that took place in the 1960s intended to forge more particularized relationships between artists and media consumers, but it also aimed to market particular types of 'products' to specific segments of the population, in order to maximize financial returns on them. Thus, in cinema, melodrama would be directed towards women, adventure films towards young men, art films towards intellectuals (at home and abroad) and, at least potentially, national films towards members of those nationalities they claimed to represent. In practice, however, the increasing commercialization of the film industry during the following decade meant that authorities were most interested in the desires of the most active segments of the film-going public. Ukrainian film-makers had to compete for the same spectators as Moscow film-makers, rather than for 'their own'.[27] Thus, cinema provides us not only with a method to examine the new representational context of the nationality question, but also allows us to investigate the new ways that cultural producers were conceptualizing a 'national' public.

Much of the negotiation between a Stalinist system of national representation and an author-centred vision, and between different conceptions of the media consumer, was common to many republican cinemas during the 1960s. Nonetheless, Ukraine posed unique challenges to Soviet nationalities policy, even as the central government and the CPSU subjected the republic to similar policies of establishing socialist nationhood common throughout the country. Ukraine was the most populous of the national republics that constituted the USSR, as Russia was itself a non-national federated republic composed of multiple national territories. Moreover, Ukrainians were the second largest 'nationality' in the country, after Russians. As such, they were the largest 'national minority' in the 1960s with approximately 40 million people in the Republic and elsewhere in the country.[28] More importantly, Ukraine was the only site in the USSR of continued conflict between Communists and Nationalists from the revolution to the end of the 1940s.

Because of Ukrainians' status as a majority-minority and the uniquely chequered past of the republic, the common Soviet epithet of 'bourgeois nationalism' was frequently applied to them in particular. This suggested an inherent quality that they possessed, and against which authorities always had to maintain strict vigilance in order to detect the subtleties of dangerous expression. One example of the conflation of Ukraine with anti-Soviet nationalism occurred when Kyrgyz writer Chinghiz Aitmatov spoke 'on the problems of national cinemas' at a 1967 conference. After listening to the speech, industry functionary Aleksandr Karaganov stated that it contained a 'small manifestation of nationalism', which could 'bring a Ukrainian under the yellow banner [of national independence]'.[29] Despite Aitmatov's discussion of larger inequalities in the Soviet film industry that prevented the further development of cinema in the republics, Karaganov read such complaints as a provocation and an attempt to sway impressionable Ukrainians. To a degree, Soviet authorities already understood the nationality question within a Ukrainian context.

While affirming an inherent connection between Ukraine and nationalism, central authorities also considered Ukrainians as one of the groups most easily assimilated into a Russian – that is, non-national – Soviet identity.[30] Thus, Soviet conceptions of Ukrainian identity present us with an interesting paradox: Ukrainians were inclined towards 'bourgeois nationalism' while also marked for easy assimilation, partly to spread the civilizing mission to the more 'backward' Soviet nations of Central Asia. To many, the Ukrainian language itself constituted a degree of cultural excess, something that lacked practical necessity and thus possessed potentially dangerous connotations. Leonid Brezhnev indicated as much during a 1969 discussion of the 'nationality question' with Petro Shelest, the latter a Russian-speaking Ukrainian who learnt his 'native' language after assuming his post in Ukraine. Brezhnev asked Shelest why publishers needed to print materials in Ukrainian when almost all Ukrainians also knew Russian. Offended, Shelest responded in his diary that Brezhnev would never ask a similar question of party leaders in the other republics.[31] To him, mere knowledge of Russian was not equivalent to the absence of a separate national identity rooted in language itself. The problem of Ukrainian language related less to the needs of comprehension, and pointed more towards the recognition of cultural difference.

Within this context, the project for artists and intellectuals became a justification for the maintenance of a Ukrainian cultural identity, and a defence of a conception of cultural difference within the framework of a predominantly bilingual population. A fairly typical and mundane argument that emerged during the professional discussion in July 1968 of a now-forgotten Ukrainian film demonstrates the everyday political significance that film-makers placed on the minutiae of artistic representation. One member of Dovzhenko Studio's Artistic Council, the group that workshopped early footage before the studio sought final state approval, asked director Volodymyr Dovhan whether his latest film would be released in Ukrainian or Russian. The latter replied that he would shoot the material in Russian and immediately dub it into Ukrainian for republican release. Dovhan's interrogator continued, apparently unsatisfied with his answer:

> You understand, we have a lot of enemies right now who position themselves against our activity. Even among our brother Republics such people appear, who come here sometimes, and say it all into the microphone, particularly about the language that we speak here. Thus, [our] material works as propaganda.[32]

The very existence of a Ukrainian-speaking public was fragile at best, necessitating the work of 'propaganda' to generate recognition from potential 'enemies' outside Ukraine.

Like Dovhan himself, most of the younger film-makers who came to work at Dovzhenko Studio during the 1960s were Russian-speaking Ukrainians, and consequently perceived less meaning in representing Ukraine as linguistically pure. While individuals like Dovhan's critic promoted their political rights to speak Ukrainian in conducting party and state business, the younger generation found little incentive to learn a language that they had lost while being raised in an urban and cosmopolitan environment. In coming to work at Dovzhenko Studio, an institution that promoted Ukrainian national identity, younger film-makers butted heads with earlier conceptions of the nationality question, while attempting to forge a new politics of artistic representation that incorporated their interest in modernism. Thus, language would not remain the sole dimension of the nationality question for Ukrainians, despite what Brezhnev indicated to Shelest.

Film-makers during the 1960s pushed for other forms of recognition of Ukrainian difference, principally located in a modernist exploration of Ukrainian folklore, but one which rejected the stereotypical images of non-Russians contained in a Stalinist system of folkloric representation. In part, this new interest in folklore was a means to play with the canonical forms of 'Ukrainianism', but it also suggested that folklore remained the idiom through which Soviet citizens, including the film-makers themselves, understood the republic and its people. Non-Russians in Soviet cinema could be readily identified through hats, hairstyles and clothing. Here, the physical and material quality of non-Russians possessed a dual nature: they were at once modern Soviet subjects and pre-modern ethnic objects. Negotiating between these two necessary components of Soviet visual culture required both political skill and artistic talent. Many film-makers during the 1960s, however, demanded that cinema reveal the authentic character of Ukrainian folklore rather than its ideological function as justifying the Soviet political system. In contrast to the Stalin-era mobilization of a 'folklore of consensus',[33] such film-makers relied on representations of exceptional Ukrainian spaces, ones which were unfamiliar and thus outside of the 'Friendship of Peoples' canon of national characters, landscapes and thematic tropes.

During the 1960s, film-makers at Dovzhenko Studio would discover an exceptional and unfamiliar space of Ukrainian authenticity in the Western oblasts, an authenticity they believed had been lost in the East to Soviet modernity and Russian cultural hegemony. While not all of the film-makers that I examine in this book set all their films in the Western oblasts, they approached Ukraine as unfamiliar territory, a territory that required re-exploration and a re-imagining of its landscape and principle historical tropes. In itself, this assertion of difference constituted a form of resistance because the Soviet state imaged national territories as necessarily unitary, and constructed a nationalities policy that reflected this principle of homogeneity.[34] Yet a notion of Ukraine as exceptional, heterogeneous and *different* was predicated on the continued existence of the Soviet Union itself, not only as an image of a conformist and Russo-centric dystopia, but also as a state whose policies demanded (at times) that non-Russians explore their own national themes.

*   *   *

The nationality question emerged anew during the 1960s within the tensions outlined above: first, in the articulation of national difference against a supposedly conformist notion of Soviet culture and 'way of life', and second, between conceptions of elite and popular publics. Chapter 1 of this work explores shifts in representational strategies from the 1930s through the early 1960s, focusing on how

Ukrainians fit into an image of the 'Friendship of Peoples'. Under Stalinism, I identify a folkloric mode of viewing the Ukrainian in popular cinema, whereby they became generically identifiable through costumes, moustaches, hats and hairstyles, in addition to the identification of certain non-essential concerns (nature, the past) revealed within poetic monologue, song and dance. Contained within and above such a 'colourful' national spectacle was a narrative of overcoming backwardness combined with political union that typically contained a strong component of Russian leadership. The important shift in post-Stalinist modes of representing Ukrainians was the reconstitution of ethnic difference. When film-makers appealed to folklore after Stalin, they frequently rejected the homogenizing narrative of the Stalinist folkloric, adopting an ethnographic view, whereby principles of national identification were linked to an exoticized image of essential differences. This chapter grounds this shift in representational strategies within both Thaw-era nationality politics and film-making practices within the Soviet Union as a whole.

Chapter 2 explores several interlocking phenomena related to the emergence of a viable film studio in Ukraine after Stalin: as part of Khrushchev's efforts at the devolution of authority to local enterprises, film studios were given some degree of autonomy. Along with this partial devolution of authority came an increase in funding for republican studios and a spurt in production. Now the Kyiv studio had to attract a new base of creative personnel, and this posed several problems. While committed to indigenizing the staff of directors, screenwriters and actors, Ukraine lacked a viable means to educate 'its own' people. Under its new leadership, however, which was conversant with both Ukrainian national discourse and broader Thaw-era aesthetic questions, Dovzhenko Studio began to recover from its reputation in the Soviet Union as a provincial studio that continued to represent the world according to Stalinist aesthetic principles.

Chapter 3 focuses on the production of Sergei Paradjanov's *Shadows of Forgotten Ancestors*, shot on location in the Ukrainian Carpathians with the participation of local peasants. The studio marketed the film as a revival of 'Alexander Dovzhenko's poetic traditions' and appealed to the authenticity of 'real Hutsuls', untouched by modernity, on display therein. Paradjanov's film became the largest influence on Ukrainnian cinema into the mid-1970s, with its ethnographic thematic orientation and its outlandish visual style. Paradjanov and cinematographer Iurii Illienko emphasized the strange, fairy-tale quality of the landscape and its people, even as it broke from realist dramatic conventions. The film's cast and crew presented the Carpathians as a site of authenticity and purity through an aestheticized ethnoscape.[35]

When *Shadows of Forgotten Ancestors* first screened publicly on 4 September 1965, as part of Kyiv's annual 'Cinema Days' festival, literary critic Ivan Dziuba interrupted the event with an unscheduled speech about the arrest of several Ukrainian intellectuals implicated in a supposed nationalist conspiracy. The event at the premiere sparked the Ukrainian dissident movement and Ukrainian cinema's intersections with this movement. Common to certain Ukrainian filmmakers and dissident nationalists was a conception of personal authorship, whereby individuals could embody not some Romantic notion of the 'national spirit', but the ability to see and articulate the 'authentic' self. In examining Ukrainian cinema's politics of personal authorship in Chapter 4, I explore how Paradjanov's largely aesthetic problems generated concerns about the unfulfilled promises of Soviet nationalities policy in the 1960s.

Chapter 5 examines how this later engagement with a new nationalist politics in the republic resulted in a number of films also set in the Carpathians. An exploration of two of these films, directed by Iurii Illienko and Vasyl' Illiashenko, demonstrate how Ukrainian cinema increasingly embarked on impressionistic and stylistically eclectic filmmaking. Both films were shelved, largely because cultural authorities, who themselves professed concerns about national identity, believed that they 'failed' to 'correctly' represent Ukraine and its people. This conflict over Illienko's and Illiashenko's films revealed that a broader consensus over the need for cultural revival in the republic did not preclude disagreements over the substance and style of national representation. This conflict, furthermore, was grounded in broader disagreements about the meanings of de-Stalinization and the Thaw.

Chapters 6 and 7 examine the political and cultural transformations in Ukraine during the early 1970s by comparing the later work of the 'poetic' directors with that of the more 'establishment' film-makers. During this time, Petro Shelest's successor as CPU First Secretary from 1972, Volodymyr Shcherbytskyi, called for the complete repression of the 'Ukrainian poetic school', which he believed 'fetishized' the Ukrainian national character. Their modernist sensibilities and thematic focus on a west Ukrainian ethnography provoked a political scandal by the middle of the decade, largely because the new party leadership no longer supported the notion of essential differences between Ukrainian and Russian culture.

Nationalist politics aside, other tensions were emerging in the early 1970s that also jeopardized 'Ukrainian poetic cinema'. Authorities in the film industry were fed up with what they labelled an 'elite' cinema, and began to view republican studios as financial liabilities. These final chapters explore the economic factors implicated in the movement away from the nationalist politics of the 1960s. Over the next decade, Goskino (the state film committee) demanded a return to comprehensible and 'realist' understandings of 'national character' instead of the 'difficult' aesthetic of Paradjanov and his followers in Ukraine. The growing field of film audience research demonstrated that central studios were the only ones that continued to make money during the industry's economic downturn of the 1970s. Despite the political excision of 'poetic cinema', many Kyiv film-makers attempted to work within popular genres without abanodoning Ukrainian subject-matter. It was only at the end of the decade that Goskino abandoned the very idea of a 'national theme' due to its scientifically-determined economic liability. By 1980, Ukrainian films came to be associated with a 'B movie' aesthetic in the Soviet Union, but otherwise resembled the generic and thematic conventions of central productions. The question of Ukrainian difference had been resolved and, from the perspective of film-makers, industry officials and critics alike, the era of 'national cinemas' in the Soviet Union had ended.

* * *

While such concepts as 'nationality', the 'nationality question' and 'national cinema' were familiar terms to the individuals that interest me in this book, I also draw on the admittedly problematic notion of 'identity', which became a concept in Russia and Ukraine only through Anglo-American cultural studies during the 1990s. More recently, some scholars have advocated getting 'beyond identity' altogether, largely because 'identity' functions merely as a 'place holder' rather than as a useful analytical category.[36] Here, I nonetheless use 'national identity' as one of many accepted models for knowing oneself in relation to those around oneself in the Soviet Union. Although I will speak frequently of 'nationalism' in this context, I insist on 'national identity' for its greater 'multidimensionality'. As Anthony Smith writes, whereas 'national*ism*' refers exclusively to an 'ideology or movement', identity as a concept extends 'to include a specific language, sentiments and symbolism'.[37] I do not suggest that everyone need internalize an 'identity', but that national identity was available for individuals and groups to employ for political, social, cultural, or sentimental purposes. Moreover, the films and film-makers that appear in this study did not perform the impossible role of constructing a uniform national identity in Ukraine, but they did help to define the parameters for discussing national identity in Ukraine.

Every Ukrainian knew they were 'Ukrainian' in the USSR, largely because of the legal certainty of line four on Soviet internal passports. Some others identified with a common Ukrainian past or a contemporary ethno-linguistic community that transcended Soviet Ukraine. This study, however, examines the uncertainties of national identity, a space where individual film-makers attempted to make sense of, and propagate, what it meant to be 'Ukrainian' and what 'Ukraine' was, apart from a territory with fixed borders that were determined largely by non-Ukrainians.

My selection of films has had to be extremely limited in order to engage in both formal analysis and historical interpretation. But I followed certain principles in this selection process that I believe conform to the methodology employed herein and the questions I am interested in resolving. First, I look at only one of the several film studios operating in Ukraine during the 1960s and 1970s, Dovzhenko Studio in Kyiv, which was established in 1929 as the seat of the Soviet Ukrainian film industry. Another notable site was Odessa Studio, which constituted a vibrant showcase for young talent, with Soviet *auteurs* Marlen Khutsiev and Kira Muratova getting their start there during the Thaw. In the 1960s and 1970s, the identity of Odessa Studio shifted to one that was at the forefront of production in popular genres like adventure and comedy. Odessa Studio thus made a significant transition from the politics of film authorship (which I explore in Chapter 4) that characterized the Thaw, to a politics of audience demand and mass culture, which characterized the post Thaw moment (examined in Chapter 7). Nonetheless, film-makers at Odessa did not participate in the specifically Ukrainian cultural politics that pervaded Dovzhenko Studio during this period. The *Odessity* did not, like the *Dovzhenkovtsy*, consider themselves 'Ukrainian film-makers', nor did they consider their work to be emblematic of 'Ukrainian national cinema'. Therefore, I feel it necessary to exclude this studio from analysis in this book, believing that film production in Odessa would best be examined in relation to central studios like Mosfilm and Gorky. Documentarists working in Kyiv (at the Kyiv

Studio of Documentary Films and Newsreels), however, did participate in the cultural politics that emerged in Ukraine during the
early 1960s, yet the aesthetic assumptions behind documentary are
quite different from feature film production. Moreover, documentary was largely divorced from both *auteurism* and audience politics
of the 1960s and 1970s, two issues that shed considerable light on the
new conditions of nationality politics during the Thaw.

Because this book deals overtly with the confluence of cinema,
mass culture and nationality politics in Ukraine, Dovzhenko Studio
is the site of my examination. This one Ukrainian studio alone produced a daunting number of films to examine, which also would
have made it impossible for me to accomplish the kind of rigorous
analysis of such texts that I thought necessary. Therefore, I have had
to be selective in my choice of films, and have chosen those directors who made movies about the Carpathians, largely because so
much of the discussion of 'national character' and 'national culture'
centred on the small portion of this Eastern European mountain
range located in Ukraine. Alongside a number of films generally
considered artistic achievements for the 1960s and 1970s, I explore
an assortment of genre films that dealt with similar themes. I demonstrate throughout this book how the Carpathian film was part
of a generic system of film and literary production in Ukraine. At
the same time, the cycle of Carpathian films during the 1960s and
1970s were in many cases conceived as 'author-driven' expressions,
and were highly modernist in their aesthetic outlook.

Apart from the films, I wanted to tell the story behind them,
principally about the people who made them, but also about the
authorities who put so many restrictions on film production in the
Soviet Union yet, perhaps more importantly, made these films possible. I spent close to a year putting these stories together, from
largely unused documents found in Ukrainian archives, mainly at
the Central State Archive Museum of Literature and Art of Ukraine,
but also in the Ukrainian Party Archive and the Ukrainian State
Archive. In Moscow, I completed my research at the Russian State
Archive of Literature and Art and the Russian State Library. In addition to following debates about nationality and cinema in the central
press, I read its much more extensive coverage in the Ukrainian-
language press. Ukraine was the only republic to have its own
mass-circulation film monthly, which emphasized and promoted
Ukrainian cinema. This magazine, *Novyny kinoekrana* (*Screen News*)
has been a largely unexplored source for examining how one of the

Union republics possessed its own culture industry even into the 1970s. I find it particularly interesting that the Union of Ukrainian Cinematographers, who operated the magazine, clearly perceived *Novyny kinoekrana* as a means to promote a vernacular mass culture, with its emphasis on light reviews, full-colour images of Ukrainian actors and actresses and the promotion of their localized celebrity status. Roman Szporluk has argued that Ukrainian-language newspapers dealing with art and culture were restricted in their coverage of high culture and folk culture, but neglected to articulate a Ukrainian mass culture.[38] Yet this is precisely what we see presented in *Novyny kinoekrana*, the circulation of which reached 500,000 in the mid-1970s.

In examining film-makers' attempts to create a Ukrainian mass culture through cinema, I also wanted to tell the story of those who watched these films, people who participated in the discursive construction of nationalistic value. While I occasionally address reception in this study, data about audiences does not tell us how individuals understood their relation to such nationalist texts. For an understanding of audience subjectivities, I have relied largely on the words of those few who wrote letters to Ukrainian newspapers, magazines and Dovzhenko Studio itself, but I cannot generalize about their words. Instead, I view such rare texts as ways in which 'ordinary spectators' (as they typically called themselves) self-consciously placed themselves within the larger discourses that are typically defined and understood through the much more readily available words of cultural and political elites. Despite the absence of the much-fetishized 'voice of the people', the longevity and vitality of Carpathian imagery becomes obvious when we consider the tone of cultural nationalism during Ukraine's brief yet vibrant Yushchenko era. Ukrainian Carpathia continues to represent a more organic model of national development, one in clear opposition to both Russo-Soviet modernity and Western mass culture, and yet located securely in the very centre of Europe.

Chapter 1

STALINISM, DE-STALINIZATION AND THE UKRAINIAN IN SOVIET CINEMA

During the late 1950s and early 1960s, Soviet cinema was experiencing a new rise to global prominence, the likes of which had not been experienced since the 1920s *avant-garde*. At home, cinema was part of the Thaw narrative of dismantling the Stalinist culture industry by questioning the Communist Party's absolute control over film-makers' aesthetic decisions, and by advancing a new conception of realism more in touch with a pan-European New Wave than with the one advanced by Maxim Gorky in 1934.[1] Moreover, the number of films released on Soviet screens in 1960 was six times greater than a decade earlier. Attendance for films rose dramatically during this decade – a Soviet citizen, for example, on average, went to the movies 20 times in 1968.[2] Yet this was primarily a phenomenon centred in Moscow, and around the productions of one film studio in particular, Mosfilm. Among the several films that either won international awards or became so-called 'leaders in distribution' at the turn of the decade, Mosfilm was represented in excessive disproportion to what one would expect from a single studio.[3]

In Kyiv, 1960 was a depressing year for film production, both in terms of ticket sales and acclaim. Ukrainian film critics and the film-makers themselves lamented how theatres showing Ukrainian films stood empty. Party and state authorities, while at times highly critical of the now-classic works of Mikhail Kalatozov, Grigorii Chukhrai, Marlen Khutsiev and others, called Dovzhenko Studio's best films 'mediocre' and 'clichéd'.[4] During the Twenty-Second Congress of the Communist Party of Ukraine in October 1961, First Secretary Mykola Pidhornyi singled out Ukrainian cinema for particular criticism, but not for ideological mistakes. Instead, he called the studio's films 'outwardly correct', but without 'inspiration'.[5] They lacked specificity and brand recognition within the larger Soviet film industry during the Thaw. In many ways, the productions of 1960 offered little that was new or attention-grabbing, and a little controversy such as that generated by Pidhornyi's comments had the potential to reinvigorate Ukrainian cinema. Several of the great directors of the Thaw got their start at Kyiv Studio during the 1950s, but left for Mosfilm when they could. According to an 'open letter' printed in *Komsomol'skaia pravda* in January 1962, the studio management categorically refused to accept new 'cadres' from the All-Union Film Institute (VGIK) in Moscow, instead affirming the creative authority of local directors and screenwriters, who were educated during the Stalin era.[6] A young Sergei Paradjanov, who began working at the studio in 1952, wrote to *Literaturna Ukraina* in the late 1950s decrying the 'lack of trust in people' prevalent among the leadership during this time, which deliberately drew attention to the degree to which the Ukrainian film industry was out of touch with the cultural transformations of the Thaw.[7] According to these critics of the studio, there seemed to be an intentional effort at the studio to remain 'provincial' and outside of the main currents of Thaw-era cultural discourse.

This problem however was not only one of leadership and 'cadres', although these were certainly important issues during the early 1960s. Another predicament touched on the very project of developing 'national cinemas' in the Soviet Union, which appeared more in line with the folkloric clichés of Stalinist cinema and the mythology of a 'Friendship of Peoples' than with the 'sincerity' and 'authenticity' that Thaw-era critics and film-makers advanced.[8] As Alla Zhukova and Heorhii Zhurov noted in the second volume of their 1959 history of Ukrainian cinema (*Soviet Ukrainian Film Art: Essays*), 'In Ukrainian cinema, folklore frequently lies at the basis of the work itself, and is one of the sources, which express its ideological content'.[9] Without folklore, the authors implied, Ukrainian cinema would not exist as a national cinema. Yet this continued insistence on a 'national' subject contributed to Ukrainian cinema's poor reputation. The films about Ukraine and Ukrainians produced at the studio were, according to contemporaries, filled with 'sociological schemas' and the 'dominance of stereotypes'. Oleh Babyshkin, a prominent Kyivan film scholar at the beginning of the 1960s, wrote in *Literaturna Ukraina* that Dovzhenko Studio's productions represented a 'forgery of the national form that appears in the external attributes, in which directors endow their characters based on the recipes of old, "little-Russian", vagrant, *hopak*-dancing, *horilka*-swilling musicians'.[10] In a speech before the Ukrainian Union of Cinematographers in 1962, First Secretary Tymofii Levchuk (himself far from innocent in this respect) concurred, saying that Ukrainian films were 'in the language of backwards clichés about a tedious and bland people ... Instead of a living peasant (*kolhospnyk*) ... a half-witted old man looks at us from our screen with drunken eyes'.[11] The trope of folksy backwardness was still alive and well within notions of what 'Ukrainian national cinema' meant at the turn of the decade. For Soviet movie-goers too, Ukrainian cinema brought to mind historical films populated by Cossacks with their characteristic hair locks and droopy moustaches, or *kolkhoz* comedies featuring fat peasants in embroidered shirts, singing about a material abundance, which was in fact absent from real life. In their insistence on folklore as the basis for Ukrainian national cinema, film-makers in Kyiv seemed to be ignoring Nikita Khrushchev's directives to seek out reality, to reflect that which was already present in Soviet life.

As Richard Taylor shows, Ivan Pyr'ev's late Stalinist film *Kuban Cossacks* (*Kubanskie kazaki*, 1949) became highly emblematic during the Thaw for its 'varnish of reality [*lakirovka deistvitel'nosti*]'. A year after the 'Secret Speech', Khrushchev ordered the film out of distribution in an attempt to purge Soviet culture of the remnants of Stalinism. A seemingly innocuous Soviet musical comedy, Pyr'ev's film is about a man and a woman who find themselves in 'socialist competition' with each other as chairpersons of neighbouring collective farms on the southern steppe. But it was the imagery of abundance and almost overwhelming sense of happiness that bothered authorities and intellectuals alike about *Kuban Cossacks* during the Thaw. Pyr'ev belaboured the viewer with sounds and views of the land and people that inhabited his vision of the Kuban. The camera moves slowly across fields of wheat and village markets overflowing with objects. Pyr'ev allows fat peasants in embroidered vests and dresses to sing and speak at length about their happiness with such material abundance, which their collective labour has produced. Pyr'ev's heroes constantly reference the past, not as something to overcome, but as a moment to recapture. In such a conservative and nostalgic mode, Moscow and other urban spaces are visibly absent, and it is the space of the Soviet periphery that Pyr'ev explores.

As Taylor documents, the origins of the *kolkhoz* musical lie in Pyr'ev's experiences making films at Ukrainfil'm in Kyiv during the late 1930s with *The Wealthy Bride* (*Bogataia nevesta*, 1938) and *Tractor Drivers* (*Traktoristy*, 1939).[12] While working at Mosfilm on *Kuban Cossacks*, Pyr'ev continued to represent a definitively ethnic space in his mobilization of a Stalinist folkloric aesthetic. As a culmination of Pyr'ev's style, *Kuban Cossacks* reduces narrative to a bare minimum in order to emphasize the 'colourful' people and landscape that it explores. The speech of the Kuban, with its mix of Russian and Ukrainian, is frequently heard, and Pyr'ev himself later told the Union of Ukrainian Film Workers (SKU) that the film was intended as an homage to the Ukrainian national character.[13]

While such counter-realism was condemned as a lingering remnant of the 'cult of personality', Ukrainian cinema in the 1960s searched for a means of visualizing 'national character'. Film-makers now questioned whether folklore could transcend the backwardness trope and reveal something new for Ukrainian cinema. Much of the discussion about folklore's positive role in Ukrainian cinema centred on laying claim to Alexander Dovzhenko's legacy, which provided three key means for making Ukrainian cinema relevant again. First, the film-maker's relationship with folklore connected Ukrainian culture with cinematic modernism, and thus provided an alternative to the Stalinist conception of folklore, which supposedly had reduced Ukrainian cinema to stale allegory and stereotypical notions of the national character. Second, Dovzhenko located national representation within the genius of an *auteur*, a key concept for Thaw-era filmmaking. Third, Dovzhenko represented Ukraine as a fundamentally uniquely national space, especially in *Zvenyhora* (1929) and *Earth* (*Zemlia*, 1930). Restoring Dovzhenko's legacy in the 1960s became a way to combine a persistent interest in folklore with rejecting its Stalin-era distortions.

Recent historians have argued that the Thaw was not a unitary process and that the period encapsulated a diverse set of interests and values, some of which came into conflict with each other.[14] This chapter examines the ways in which Ukrainian film-makers and critics appropriated Thaw-era language about authenticity, realism and personal authorship, while affirming Ukrainian cinema's positive connection to folklore, which had potentially problematic associations with the tired clichés and stereotypes of Stalinist representations of non-Russians.

Narrative and Aesthetic Preoccupations of the Thaw

By the time Khrushchev articulated his rejection of the 'cult of personality' in February 1956, writers and critics had already voiced many of the General Secretary's concerns about the 'varnish of reality' in Stalinist literature and cinema. French critic André Bazin was perhaps the first to speak about the 'Stalin myth in Soviet cinema' in his 1950 article of the same title for the left-wing Paris journal, *L'Esprit*. In fact, Bazin suggested two years after the Secret Speech that his ideas in the article might have floated to Khrushchev himself because his statement that Stalin 'only knew the countryside and agriculture from film' seemed uncannily similar to the French critic's own argument.[15] Even if this particular claim is untrue, it is clear that Khrushchev took his cues from literary and art criticism. The label of the 'personality cult' that he popularized was drawn from a reference in Vladimir Pomerantsev's December 1953 *Novyi mir* (*New World*) article, 'On Sincerity in Literature (*Ob iskrennosti v literature*)', about the unbelievable and 'superhuman' qualities of Stalin-era literary heroes. Just as such literary heroes allegorically represented Stalin himself, Khrushchev was now using the critique of those literary heroes as a critique of Stalin.

The metaphor of the Thaw to represent the post-Stalin era was also a literary reference, from Ilia Ehrenburg's novella of the same title (*Ottepel'*), published in the May 1954 issue of the journal *Znamia* (*The Banner*). Ehrenburg's work was an indictment of the emotionally opaque and ethically compromised Stalinist subject, who had learnt 'how to say nothing' to serve their careerist ambitions and material comforts. The novella ends in the spring of 1953 (i.e., after Stalin's death), with the multiple psychological and emotional problems of the story suddenly resolved.[16] In Soviet film, Grigorii Chukhrai's *Clear Skies* (*Chistoe nebo*, 1961), among many other examples from 1956–8 and 1961–3, presents a similar immediate transformation from the frozen years of the post war Soviet Union to the freer atmosphere after Stalin's death, when people suddenly became more open, honest and friendly. Such discourse was ubiquitous during these years. First Secretary of the Ukrainian Cinematographers' Union, Tymofii Levchuk, stated during a March 1962 plenum, 'Let the elimination…of Stalin's cult of personality quickly teach [us to be] compassionate, considerate, and have a beneficial attitude towards one another'.[17]

Pomerantsev's article in *Novyi mir* first introduced readers to the major preoccupations of Thaw-era literary politics, calling on writers and artists to reject the 'stereotypical heroes, thematics, beginnings and endings' of Stalinist cultural production. Instead, it was believed that creative work should embody the ideas and express the personality of its author, rather than the narrow political principles of the day. Pomerantsev, of course, offered more substantive advice to the post-Stalin generation of creative workers, both in his definition of 'sincerity' as 'talent', and in identifying its antecedent in 'artifice [*delannost' veshchi*]' as a component of mimicry.[18] Fundamentally, he accused writers of not 'experiencing the village'.[19] He juxtaposed his principle of 'sincerity' with the 'varnishing of reality [*lakirovka deistvitel'nosti*]', which showed only the 'abundant banquet' and not the 'foul factory cafeteria'.[20] Pomerantsev concluded that writers needed to refocus their attention on 'the problem of bringing everyday life to light', to explore the diversity of human emotion and psychology.[21] Instead of the deeds of leaders and the 'things and objects' that adorned the fictional *kolkhoz* market, writers should concern themselves with 'ordinary' human experience.[22]

Film critics writing in *Iskusstvo kino* during 1954–5 demanded the same focus on the 'individual personality', 'simple people' and a 'struggle for the authentic' in Soviet cinema.[23] Later in the decade, Viktor Nekrasov explored transformations in Soviet cinema during the mid-1950s, positioning the new interest in human experience against the 'great events' of the Stalinist 'cinema of leaders'.[24] In 'Words, "Great" and Simple (*Slova, "velikie" i prostye*)', he distinguished a new 'prosaic' style found in Marlen Khutsiev's work from Iuliia Solntseva's *A Poem about the Sea* (*Poema o more*, 1959), a film initiated by the recently deceased Alexander Dovzhenko and based on his screenplay. While Khutsiev's early features were everyday stories about ordinary people, Dovzhenko's *Poem* addressed large issues of modernity and tradition with a narrative focused on the friendship between a general and a *kolkhoz* chairman set against the backdrop of the construction of the Kakhovka Hydroelectric Station on the lower Dnieper. Nekrasov wrote, 'I did not believe the film'. In associating Solntseva's film with a leftover Stalinist aesthetic, Nekrasov contrasted it with Khutsiev's *Spring on Zarechnaia Street* and *The Two Fedors*, which represented a return to 'the realism of everyday life'.

Nekrasov advocated a return to Stanislavskii's method in the precision of realistic details in acting. Solntseva's and Dovzhenko's film, he stated, 'is based on a highly conventional situation and means'.[25] Nekrasov identified a mode of speaking in film that was completely divorced from 'real life' in its lofty 'poetic' voice. As with

Kuban Cossacks, the association with a particular place is pervasive. The Dnieper, Kakhovka and the rootedness of the main characters all speak to the centrality of space within the film, even as these 'elements' foreground the 'stereotypical' theme of socialist construction. In contrast, Thaw-era works like Khutsiev's masterpieces and others like Mikhail Kalatozov's *The Cranes are Flying* (*Letiat' zhuravli*, 1957) and Chukhrai's *Ballad of a Soldier* (*Ballada o soldate*, 1959) are local only insofar as they focus on private human relations, which prefigure both landscape and event, the latter starkly subservient to ordinary human interactions. In these films, Nekrasov identified an entirely different manner of speech – 'a passionate, but not bombastic, truthful and not utilitarian, a speech, in which ordinary people speak, the same [people] who sometimes do great deeds'.[26]

Fundamentally, Pomerantsev and Nekrasov promoted a shift in thematic focus from event or setting to the human subject. Within this formulation, they promoted a de-spatialized image of character, a hero that would not be beholden to setting, someone who would exist independently of the spaces that they inhabited. On the contrary, in Stalinist representations of the Ukrainian, the human subject was placed within a particularistic landscape, one that was essential to their identity, and one which was in line with the location of the studio that claimed authority to produce such signature settings. Many Thaw-era Ukrainian critics, however, maintained that space remained fundamental to the exploration of character and psychology. The problem, as Nekrasov suggested, was that such thinking was implicated in Stalinist ways of thinking and making cinema.

Territorialized Socialist Realism and Stalinist Cinema's Folkloric Mode

Under a Stalinist mode of 'national' representation, the landscapes and peoples of the Soviet periphery achieved recognition as unique within a folkloric visual vocabulary, replete with costumes, dancing peasants and other evidence of 'national colour'. The figures, objects and landscapes, in addition to the plots and dialogue, that appeared in such films were rarely unfamiliar to audiences by the late 1930s, most of them conforming to what Katerina Clark called Socialist Realism's ritualistic mode. In *The Soviet Novel: History as Ritual*, she characterized Socialist Realist narrative as ritualistic in its reproduction of a 'master plot', the 'structuring force' of which consisted of Lenin's 'spontaneity / consciousness dialectic' from *What Is To Be Done?*[27]

In the canonical scenario, the hero is a 'modest' Communist, but lacks the discipline and leadership skills to accomplish the assigned task. In the end, he or she 'masters his [or her] wilful self... [and] attains an extrapersonal identity' of rational consciousness at the exclusive service of the collective.[28] Frequently, the hero achieves such consciousness with the help of someone more politically knowledgeable. In this respect, the model is the *Bildungsroman*. And yet, the hero's rationality and the realism of Socialist Realism also allowed for other means of expression. After all, nineteenth-century notions of realism were clearly not the only influence at work at the origins of Socialist Realism. As Gorky wrote, 'Reality does not let itself be seen... We must know a third reality – the reality of the future. We must somehow include this third reality now in our "everyday".'[29] Andrei Zhdanov clarified this more 'transcendent' definition of Socialist Realism in suggesting a union of 'proletarian realism' with 'revolutionary romanticism' at the root of Soviet cultural production. At the First Congress of Soviet Writers in 1934, Zhdanov characterized this combination as 'the most matter-of-fact, everyday reality with the most heroic prospects'.[30] Clark argues that '[i]n practice, the balance was actually tilted in favour of revolutionary romanticism, with its exaggeration and grand scale, and away from verisimilitude'.[31] From its beginnings as official policy for the arts, Socialist Realism was also an attempt to establish a cultured middle in the Soviet Union, which transcended both the elitist sensibilities of modernism and the supposed backwardness of unadulterated folk culture.

Ivan Pyr'ev's work was highly emblematic of the socialist realist 'master plot', along with its mixture of 'realism' with 'romanticism'. His films used folklore, but it was not emblematic of the narrative as a whole. His film *Tractor Drivers* provided one of the models for socialist realist narration, but also revealed how nationality could be read into Stalinist narrative. Klim Iarko, the hero, is a demobilized tank driver who had served on the Manchurian border. Returning to his native land in southern Ukraine, Klim becomes a tractor driver for the local *kolkhoz*. Klim hopes to meet Mar'iana Bazhan, a celebrated hero of labour, about whom he had read in an issue of *Pravda*. As the narrative develops, he must prove that he can rejoin the socialist community by shedding his military arrogance. Only after Klim subjugates his will to that of the collective does Mar'iana agree to marry him. In Pyr'ev's film, the consummation of the central relationship is determined, not by physical attraction, but through labour initiative and acceptance of social norms.

In focusing on plot repetition, the lack of individual conscious-ness and the hyperbolic elaboration of the heroic personality in Stalinist narration, Thaw-era critics such as Nekrasov followed the literary model of Pomerantsev, and generally ignored aspects of visual pleasure present in such films. While such critics identified the ritualistic mode of representing canonical events, settings and hero types, Stalinist cinema also contained visual codes in marking the non-Russian variations to the socialist realist 'master plot'. These variations indicate a parallel space of meaning production. In this vein, one could read Pyr'ev's film on a different level, one which fore-grounds the ethno-national elements of 'excess' as of equal impor-tance to its socialist realist 'master plot'. As Kristin Thompson writes, 'Excess is not only counternarrative; it is counterunity. To discuss it may be to invite the partial disintegration of a coherent reading'.[32] I tend not to accept that the visual elements of the Stalinist folkloric were 'counternarrative', but such folkloric play certainly affected a reading that worked in parallel with the narrative, and which occa-sionally presented moments of tension between style and narrative. I refer to this parallel space as the folkloric mode, which pervaded Stalin-era cinema from 1934 onward, yet its presence carried addi-tional meanings and connotations in the cinemas of the Union republics. With its folkloric imagery, Stalinist cinema domesticated national difference, while maintaining the spectacle of particular spaces and the peoples that inhabited them. With the use of folklore in Soviet cinema, we see two principles at work – the spectacle of dif-ference, and the narrative articulation of an undifferentiated Soviet people.

Just as many Soviet critics during the Thaw saw in Stalinist cin-ema's mobilization of folklore one of the clichés of the period – as one of the narrative components of promoting the false idea of abundance – scholars in the West have seen folklore at the root of modern culture more generally. Folklore's reproduction in popular art and political discourse has served to reify notions of tradition and authenticity, and to articulate the fiction of a culturally cohe-sive and socially egalitarian community. In *Language and Symbolic Power*, Pierre Bourdieu writes that the political use of folklore is to 'negate symbolically the hierarchy without disrupting it'.[33] While admitting that even democracies deploy folkloric imagery to blur hierarchies, other scholars have identified the use of folklore as a dominant source of cultural legitimacy in the totalitarian regimes of Nazi Germany, Fascist Italy, Ceauşescu's Romania and Stalin's USSR. In writing about Italian cinema under Mussolini, for example, Marcia Landy argues that cinematic folklore plays upon popular assumptions and images of national pasts, infusing them with a politically motivated teleology.[34] Frank J. Miller speaks of a 'cult of folklore' in the Soviet Union under Stalin, stating, 'Under the critical dogma of Socialist Realism, literature and indeed all art were supposed to manifest the folkloric'.[35] Folkloric imagery in Soviet cinema under Stalin was an attempt to make unique nationalities legible to the broader Soviet community by providing them with standardrized labels. The folkloric was also a means through which Soviet film-makers could articulate ethnic difference, albeit within the often genuinely popular confines of Socialist Realism.

Such a system sought a simultaneous modernization and historicization of nationalistic materials, ostensibly to purge them of their bourgeois elements, even as it spectacularized components of non-Russian cultural expression and historical material. While it fetishized unique spaces and bodies, the Stalinist folkloric was also a mobile form, in the sense that film-makers could easily transport its imagery from Ukraine to the Caucasus to Central Asia with only minor modifications. Emma Widdis argues that the Stalinist folkloric existed outside of geographic space, in an unidentified rural pastoral.[36] One participant at a 1967 Union of Cinematographers plenum, dedicated to the 'problems of the further development of national cinemas', parodied the cultural logic of Stalinism's representation of non-Russians: 'The Georgian is the one dancing the *lezghinka*; the Kazakh is the one singing about an apple grove; and the Ukrainian is the one relishing his *salo*'.[37] These cosmetic differences between nationalities, nonetheless, convey an Orientalist understanding of how to represent non-Russians in Soviet cinema: each variant of the Soviet ethnic communicates their difference indirectly through spectacular or poetic means, rather than directly through dialogue and narrative.

Pyr'ev's emblematic *Tractor Drivers* introduces its Ukrainian hero in a train compartment that he shares with a Georgian, identifiable with his thin moustache and dopey smile, and a Muscovite wearing ordinary workers' clothes and holding a written text in his hands. The three demobilized tank drivers are returning from the Manchurian border to their respective national spaces. While Klim plays the accordion, the three sing about their 'native land', the Soviet Union. After the song, however, each man in turn brags about his own particular native spaces – not so much communicating with each other as defining his subjective space of belonging. The Muscovite introduces an article about factory work in the capital and the sputtering, grinning Georgian talks about the wine and women of his republic, perhaps over-exuberant in his passionate gestures. We cut to a close-up of Klim, hugging his accordion with a romantic gleam in his eyes, as he talks about the Ukrainian steppe: 'You open the door, and the wind rushes in; you open the window and the scent of cherry blossoms catches you'. In Pyr'ev's vision of the Soviet ethnoscape, 'national' characters possess a quality of excess in their personalities, but one which does not obstruct the historicity of the present moment. The Georgian and the Ukrainian are each in love with a timeless quality of their native spaces, while the 'Russian' discusses the historically contingent 'space' of economic progress. Thus, the film's introduction presents a dichotomy between a political centre and an ethnic periphery associated with domesticity and safety, which is encoded onto human bodies in the form of national 'colour' (see Figure 1.1). The presence of non-Russians is not based on a principle of inclusion so much as

Figure 1.1   The 'Friendship of Peoples' in Ivan Pyr'ev's *Tractor Drivers* (1939)

it situates an extra-narrative and spectacular sentiment within the film's diegesis.

In transporting Socialist Realism to the Soviet periphery, the socialist realist plot was also called upon to unite the periphery with the centre. Nonetheless, *Tractor Drivers* accomplishes this while maintaining a firm dichotomy between both spaces. While the train united East and West, both geographically and nationally, the centre continued to function differently from the periphery. The peoples and landscapes of the Soviet periphery were fundamentally associated with domesticity, while world events characterized the centre; the periphery is associated with a timeless quality, while the centre becomes rooted in historical time. Pyr'ev places the objects of an ethnic material culture solely within the intimate site of the domestic realm. Mar'iana, for example, is adorned in an embroidered outfit within the space of the home, while wearing monochromatic workers' clothing in the field. Similarly, we view Bazhan's mother, a character who appears only in the home, dressed in a folk costume (see Figure 1.2).

Ihor Savchenko's historical epic, *Bohdan Khmel'nyts'kyi* (1941), offers another example of Stalinist cinema's folkloric mode. Savchenko's film evinces the interplay between historical time and folkloric time, the former represented through a narrative of uniting the Muscovite political centre with a colourful Ukrainian periphery, and the latter by the visual spectacle of 'national colour' itself. *Khmel'nyts'kyi*, based on Aleksandr Korneichuk's play of the same title (1939), concerns the Zaporozhian Cossack Hetman who first brought Left Bank Ukraine under Muscovite control during the mid-seventeenth century. Savchenko's film represented the culmination of the two parallel sites of meaning production in the Stalinist cinema of the periphery: first, *Khmel'nyts'kyi* is the quintessential Soviet historical-biographical film, a genre that was dominant from the late 1930s to the early 1950s. Evgenii Margolit writes that the genre was characterized by a theatrical and monumental style and a predominant focus on the leader as the principal agent of history. Within this genre, according to Margolit, the hero ceases to reside within a particular historical period and serves to justify the Soviet theory of government.[38]

Second, the elements in the film that identified a particularly Ukrainian ethnoscape came to dominate Soviet cinema at least until the late 1950s. In a dynamic common to the Stalinist historiography of early modern Ukraine, Savchenko's Cossack hero comes to *national* consciousness through his alignment with Muscovy, which

Figure 1.2 Domesticated nationality in Ivan Pyr'ev's *Tractor Drivers* (1939)

functions in this case as the agent of political and cultural modernization. The Muscovite state also performs the role of a counterpoint,
not only to an enemy nation – in this case, Poland – but also to the

spontaneity of Ukrainian 'colour', both seen as destructive forces. The narrative's job is not to destroy the elements of 'colour', however, but to bind them to the safe and domestic space of song, dance and material culture (Figure 1.3), and purge it of its spontaneous elements – violence and banditry. The film ends with Khmel'nyts'kyi, victorious over the Poles, signing the Pereiaslavl' Agreement with two Muscovite emissaries. While the agreement celebrates Muscovy's control over Left Bank Ukraine, the precise relationship between 'Russia' and 'Ukraine' is complicated by Savchenko's framing. After signing the agreement, the Hetman is clearly elevated in relation to the Muscovite emissaries, demonstrating that, as a sovereign, Khmel'nyts'kyi held a higher rank than the vassals of Tsar Alexei I present during the meeting (Figure 1.4). The image shows two nations signing a treaty as equals, rather than the Russian state with a subordinate people. In this way, the arena of visual representation occasionally overshadowed the strictures of the narrative's historical teleology.

Savchenko's film remains heralded as a high water mark for national cinema in Ukraine under Stalin. The film-maker and now historian of Ukrainian cinema, Vasyl' Illiashenko, wrote that *Bohdan Khmel'nyts'kyi* was a 'grandiose elegy on the struggle of the Ukrainian people for their liberation and self-determination'.[39] With Pyr'ev's *Tractor Drivers* and especially with Savchenko's *Khmel'nyts'kyi*, socialist realism became territorialized, and came to embody Soviet particularistic conceptions of national cinema. During the Thaw, however, critics writing in *Iskusstvo kino* tended to view these filmmakers and the style that their films embodied as outdated, or worse, as relics of the period of the 'cult of personality'. The monumentalism of *Khmel'nyts'kyi*'s hero in particular clashed with the democratized image of the hero (Pomerantsev's 'little man'), which many critics and film-makers promoted during the Thaw. This later period foregrounded storytelling – in Russian, *povestvovanie* – over visual spectacle and the romanticism of Stalin-era socialist realism. Thus, the very project of making national cinema at the beginning of the 1960s seemed besides the point to all but a few Thaw-era critics and prominent film-makers working in Moscow. Consequently, those wishing to assert the relevance of Ukrainian cinema as *national* cinema had to discover new models and influences, not only learning how to speak the critical language of the Thaw, but also discovering a pre-Stalinist origin for it.

Figure 1.3   The Stalinist folkloric in Ihor Savchenko's *Bohdan Khmel'nyts'kyi* (1941)

Figure 1.4   The Hetman wilfully signs the Pereiaslav Treaty with the Russians in *Bohdan Khmel'nyts'kyi.*

Alexander Dovzhenko and the Construction of Ukrainian National Cinema

The meanings of national cinema, however, were never fixed and tended to fluctuate between qualitative definitions, and ones which foregrounded other contexts. According to Tymofii Levchuk in 1968, 'Ukrainian national cinema' was born at the same moment as Soviet cinema itself, when Lenin made the nationalization decree in August 1919. Although seemingly arbitrary, considering that films had been produced in Ukraine for a decade prior to this date, Levchuk justified his dating of the fiftieth anniversary of Ukrainian national cinema on two grounds: first, as he explained to Sviatoslav Ivanov, the head of Ukrainian Goskino (Derzhkino), that although film production in Ukraine existed before Lenin's decree, Ukraine had only become a nation during that year with the formation of the Bolshevik government in Kharkiv, whereas earlier film production had occurred within a Russian colony. Second, because foreign capital financed such pre-revolutionary production, it was not 'Ukrainian in character'.[40] Levchuk's justification, circular though it may have been, nonetheless affirmed the USSR's nation-building project, along with the continued meaning that republican authorities placed on the dual origins of nation (Ukraine) and state (the Soviet Union). Yet he also brings to bear questions of representation: without a certain 'character', a film's national specificity and identity was suspect.

Levchuk was not offering his reader a new way of thinking about the origins of Ukrainian cinema. Rather, he merely repeated two elements that constituted the established meaning of national cinema in the Soviet Union since the 1930s, if not before. Around this time, we begin to see the ethno-territorial claim of Kyiv Studio to certain thematic material, rooted in a folkloric conception of national difference and present in visual and aural spectacle. Pyr'ev, a Russian filmmaker, came to Kyiv to make films about Ukraine, before returning to Moscow to make generically Soviet productions. While ethnically Ukrainian, Savchenko too worked in Moscow before returning to Ukraine to make Ukrainian-themed films. Thus, within this system of non-Russian film production, national identity was tied to institutions and territories, rather than individuals. This was also the logic of the Soviet Union's federal structure. At the same time, personal identity and character sometimes emerged at the forefront of discussions of national cinema.

With this alignment of folkloric theme and production space, we begin to see the origins of the national film. When critics began writing histories of Soviet cinema after the World War II, it was within the context of this alignment between character and territory that they identified national cinema, rather than as constituting the totality of production on the Soviet national 'periphery'. In Nikolai Lebedev's *Outline History of Cinema in the USSR* from 1947, the prominent critic privileges questions of character in his definition of Ukrainian national cinema. He writes, 'Despite a quantitatively large film production, Soviet Ukrainian cinema during the first years of its existence was Ukrainian only in a territorial sense [...] But it did not become Ukrainian national cinema in spirit and style'.[41] Ukrainian film critic Borys Buriak concurred, writing much later that before Alexander Dovzhenko, there was no Ukrainian national cinema, only directors who came to work in Ukraine.[42]

While Lebedev and Buriak admitted that Ukrainian cinema came into existence contemporaneously with the Ukrainian SSR, they privileged the system of representation – indeed, a formal and thematic specificity – over a geo-political explanation of national cinema. Because the economic fact of film production alone could not inject suitable meaning into such a term, Lebedev had to look elsewhere for a point of origin, which he found almost a decade after Lenin's decree in Dovzhenko's film, *Zvenyhora* (1927). While narratively and stylistically eclectic and highly modernist, which would later stand at odds with Socialist Realism and Stalinist culture as a whole, the film introduced spectators to a canonical Ukrainian ethnoscape that came to visual and political 'maturity' in the films of Savchenko and Pyr'ev. Moreover, *Zvenyhora* and Dovzhenko's *Earth* (*Zemlia*, 1930) became historical reference points, from which most 1960s film-makers asserted a positive claim to Ukrainian national cinema.

As the first of two efforts explicitly located in Ukraine during the revolution, *Zvenyhora* introduces a number of stylistic and narrative elements that remained consistent throughout Dovzhenko's body of work. The main character in *Zvenyhora*, known only as 'old man' (*did*), becomes a symbol of continuity and tradition, and a 'generalized national image of the Ukrainian peasant', according to critic Rostislav Iurenev,[43] while the Cossack character represents a historical point of origin for the Ukrainian nation, simultaneously and trans-historically characterizing the particular nature of the contemporary Ukrainian revolutionary. In this case, this trans-historical Cossack can be either a Ukrainian Bolshevik (the hero, Timosh) or a nationalist (his brother Pavlo). The film constantly moves between these two models of national character, the former embodying Lenin's notion of building socialist nations, and the other a parody of false consciousness and 'bourgeois nationalism'. Finally, *Zvenyhora* introduces the landscape as an important visual / narrative component, which, through stylized tableaux-like imagery, invites the spectator to contemplate its meaning-producing quality. The Ukrainian land also serves to unite the episodic quality of the film, which jumps from the revolution to the Cossack Hetmanate of the seventeenth century, to the Norman invasion of the ninth century and back to post-revolutionary Soviet Ukraine.

The film is modernist in its narrative and stylistic eclecticism, mixing rapid montage in the scenes of revolutionary change with paced shots of peasant communities in Ukraine; slapstick comedy exists alongside the histrionics of melodrama and the action of a war film. Margolit points out that Dovzhenko's *Zvenyhora* was one of the first Soviet films that borrowed freely from folkloric motifs, seeing in Dovzhenko's film the 'organic union of fairy-tales, legends, songs, and the *lubok*'.[44] The film's central character, the old man, functions as a catalyst for relating the national epic, and he himself becomes the preserver of that tradition through his appearance in each of the episodes. Life in contemporary Ukraine is connected allegorically to folkloric narratives set against the backdrop of the unchanging Ukrainian space of Zvenyhora. Historical/revolutionary time constantly abuts with a de-historicized mythological time, which is in essence cyclical, due to the presence of the static images of Zvenyhora and the old man. This is an anti-materialist perspective, where humans, in their stability over time, function as objects in nature. The nationalistic value of this perspective is in the perceived dominance of the stability of place over the mutability of history, and the revolutionary process represented in the film is only legible as positive insofar as it conforms to the film's allegorical constructs.

Bohdan Nebesio writes that while ostensibly anti-nationalist, the mythical/historical narrative of *Zvenyhora* promotes the idea of Ukrainian history as separate from Russian history, and that the grandfather's stories, and thus 'tradition', 'can be reconciled with...the new socialist state'.[45] *Zvenyhora* is a pre-socialist realist text because it resists the linear narrative from spontaneity to consciousness, instead presenting the audience with an eclectic mix of legend and recent political history. Moreover, this film, along with *Earth*, foregrounds Ukrainian folklore and a nationalist mythology that would have been unfamiliar to most Soviet citizens outside the republic. Dovzhenko's image of Ukrainian space is uncanny because it does not fit itself neatly within the Soviet Union as a whole.[46] In contrast to Dovzhenko's work, we see in prominent examples from the work of Pyr'ev and Savchenko that the organization of space becomes a method of simultaneously defining difference, but within the political space of union or sameness. Pyr'ev and Savchenko domesticate folkloric material for the purpose of creating a familiar and popular image of the Soviet ethnic periphery. But in formulating the familiar, domestic space of 'national colour' in the service of Socialist Realism, the implicit spectator is a contemporary Soviet citizen, invited to gaze at the antics of 'backward' Ukrainians, without any assumed identification.

Film-makers at Kyiv Studio in the 1960s constantly sought to rest on Dovzhenko's laurels. The Dovzhenko cult during the Thaw constituted a search for consensus among film-makers of different generations and political and aesthetic visions, as much as it was a demand for recognition in Moscow by weaving together the history of Ukrainian cinema and the Soviet *avant-garde*. Through Dovzhenko, the *shestidesiatniki* (Sixties generation) could find common ground with film-makers at the studio who came to creative

maturity under Stalin, while justifying modernist experimentation. After all, Lebedev, the epitome of a Stalin-era critic, called the
definitively *avant-garde Zvenyhora* 'the first genuinely Ukrainian work
of cinema', due not only to its Ukrainian theme, but also because
Dovzhenko was 'organically connected to Ukrainian culture'.[47]
Ukrainian cinema boosterism of the 1960s viewed Dovzhenko's
style within a continuum of the film-maker's biography, his personal
expression and national representation. As the seventieth anniversary of Dovzhenko's birth drew near in 1964, everyone at the studio
had some claim to the film-maker's legacy, whether that was a direct
pedagogical relationship, a chance encounter, or simply an aesthetic
affinity. Dovzhenko became the pre-eminent pre-war film-maker,
the embittered victim of the 'personality cult', a writer who carried
on the traditions of Taras Shevchenko and Ivan Franko, a member
of Soviet cinema's holy trinity alongside Eisenstein and Pudovkin,
and the 'inventor', according to Ukrainian poet and screenwriter
Dmytro Pavlychko, of 'poetic cinema'.[48] While 'poetic cinema' functioned more broadly in Soviet critical debates about the re-examina-
tion of Modernism and the early-twentieth century *avant-garde*, its
association with Dovzhenko imparted a clear nationalistic value to
the term in Ukraine.

At the same time, Dovzhenko himself made the transition from
the *avant-garde* to Socialist Realism, as his later work came increasingly to be identified with a Stalinist aesthetic by Thaw-era critics
of the late 1950s. By the early 1960s, however, Dovzhenko's position
in Soviet and Ukrainian culture had been redeemed entirely, and
critics praised his work like never before. While critics and filmmakers interested in Dovzhenko's Ukrainian-flavoured modernism heralded films like *Zvenyhora* and *Earth*, the director's Civil War epic
Shchors (1939), about a Bolshevik commander who died fighting
Petliura's nationalists in 1919, held particular weight in 1960s discussions of Dovzhenko as the bridge between the Soviet *avant-garde* and
Socialist Realism. Film critic Semën Ginzberg stated that *Shchors* was
the only film of its time that completely escaped from the 'cult of
personality'.[49] Although Stalin himself commisioned Dovzhenko to
make the film, suggesting to him that it should be the 'Ukrainian
Chapaev', the result bore little similarity to the Vasil'ev Brothers'
1934 blockbuster. With its mix of the Eisensteinian monumentalism
of *Alexander Nevsky* and *Ivan the Terrible* and the Stalinist folkloric
of Savchenko's historical films, *Shchors* comes to exemplify Katerina
Clark's notion of Socialist Realism's 'modal schizophrenia', with 'its

proclivity for making sudden, unmotivated transitions from realistic discourse to the mythic or utopian'.[50] The most powerful figure in the film was not the leader, however, as in Savchenko's epic, but a fictional character, an old Ukrainian peasant named Vasyl' Bozhenko who joins the Red partisans, and imparts a degree of 'folk wisdom' to Shchors's strategy. While such characters were ubiquitous in the historical-biographical genre, nowhere do they dominate the narrative and imagery to such an extent as in Dovzhenko's film.

In the critical language of the 1960s, *Shchors* was the film in which Dovzhenko most successfully combined Socialist Realism with his own brand of 'cinema poetry'. It was in this realm of the 'poetic' – the space that Bozhenko inhabited in the film – that the folkloric elements were contained. In this sense, Dovzhenko's 'poetics' referred to his use of extra-narrative elements of national spectacle. In referring to Dovzhenko as the 'poet of cinema',[51] however, critics privileged these elements of folkloric excess, which suggested a fundamental difference in his aesthetic outlook from others who employed folkloric representations during Stalinism. According to several critics, Dovzhenko's films were 'plotless [*bezfabul'nyi*]', and his use of the folkloric image threatened to inhibit the structure of the narrative, and thus they skirted the boundaries of formalism. Yet, according to a 1964 conference dedicated to strengthening 'Dovzhenko studies [*dovzhenkovedenie*]' in film criticism, it was this very 'plotlessness' that made the director so necessary for early Soviet cinema.[52] Clearly, Nekrasov's counterpositioning of the Thaw-era problematic of 'sincere' realism and Dovzhenko's Stalinist aesthetic was no longer relevant to Soviet critics by the mid-1960s.

Nonetheless, Ukrainian cinema's use of folklore still demanded justification during the Thaw in order to position it between the two extremes of formalism and the 'cult of personality'. Once again, the problem of folklore was one of 'realism' and 'authenticity'. Could folkloric representations transcend the political uses to which they had been put – ratifying and justifying the mythical 'Friendship of Peoples' – and instead reveal something new in Soviet cinema? Ukrainian filmmakers during this decade had the daunting task of making folklore relevant for a new generation of spectators, and film critics in the republic found themselves trying to justify what they saw as a distinctly Ukrainian cinematic tradition.

The fact that Kyiv Studio continued to mobilize a folkloric imagery as an affirmative mode of national representation into the 1960s indicates that we need to consider the form of Stalinist representation more seriously than did Thaw-era detractors. Ukrainian film-makers were embroiled in a controversy regarding the importance of folklore for Ukrainian cinema's particularity. In this debate about the 'original form of Ukrainian film art', visuality rather than narrative took centre stage as supporters and detractors of this style explored the relationship between Ukrainian theatre, folklore and the cinema. This debate made evident to many film-makers that an image of Ukrainian difference required the continued existence of folklore as a particular quality, even if cinema's implementation of it could transcend Stalin-era falsifications.

Despite such a complicated relationship between what was defined as the essence of Ukrainian cinema's 'national form' and folklore, Moscow critic Igor' Rachuk essentially closed off the debate in his official biography of Dovzhenko, published in 1964. Therein, he wrote that, as a 'son of the Ukrainian land, [Dovzhenko...] hated all who came out of a national, *khutorians'kyi* white-wash with the external prettyness of folkloric elements'.[53] The implication was that, if Kyiv Studio now laid claim to Dovzhenko's name, its film-makers had to follow the critical consensus on their patriarch's creative work. In approaching Thaw-era aesthetic discourse within a Dovzhenkoist idiom, however, Ukrainian film-makers insisted upon the maintenance of the human subject's organic connection with the Ukrainian landscape. In fact, within the ethnographic orientation of the 1960s, Ukrainian film-makers made an even stronger claim for the determining influence of landscape on human consciousness.

The visual representation of Ukrainians under Stalinism was fundamentally *not* about knowledge; rather, the folkloric mode was a means to recreate the Soviet periphery as a familiar ethnoscape, where 'national colour' was domesticated and existed in the realm of the expected. We cannot believe that Stalin in fact learnt about the state of agriculture from watching Pyr'ev's *Kuban Cossacks*, as Khrushchev suggested during his 'Secret Speech'. After all, archival documents reveal Stalin's incessant concern with the everyday affairs of grain production and collection.[54] The problem for Khrushchev was that film not only has an obligation to reveal the truth, but also to build and maintain the expectation that spectators will see the truth. Instead, Pyr'ev's films, for example, were creative attempts to reflect a familiar image of the Russian/Ukrainian periphery, but made no pretence to authenticity. Within such a system of representation, politics and subjecthood itself were reoriented towards the centre, and Ukrainian nationalism diffused within the safe realm of folklore.

Visualizing a Profitable, but 'Authentic' Image of Ukraine

Terry Martin argues that the 'nationality question' had been resolved with the 'Friendship of Peoples' mythology of the late 1930s, articulated and accomplished through the ordered circulation of cultural products like books, films and performers, rather than through political negotiation between the various nations of the Soviet Union. The specificity and formal dimensions of cultural texts come into play, however, when we consider how post-Stalinist cultural products drew upon an earlier mode of display. When the examination of national character reappeared in Ukrainian cinema during the 1960s, it was built upon the visual, if not ideological, foundations of the Stalinist folkloric. But the cultural context for giving visual meaning to nationality had shifted in this later period, with Thaw-era discourse on 'sincerity' and 'authenticity' providing the basis for a new understanding of Ukrainian character and folklore.

Pyr'ev's and Savchenko's films were genuinely successful, attracting unprecedented numbers of spectators. This was the predictable outcome for a film industry that had sharply limited domestic film production, and dispensed with foreign imports. Film spectators had little else to watch at the time.[55] But, in being emblematic socialist realist texts, these films were formally coded for mass consumption. Their iconography of the Soviet periphery and narrative of union contained tropes that were all too familiar, and neither their folksy humour nor nostalgic worldview intended to challenge the viewer. Beginning in 1952, however, both production and consumption of films rose exponentially from the low of 1951 to the pivotal year of 1968.[56] In many ways, this explosion of film culture that occurred during the Thaw seemed to affirm the Stalinist precept of 'art for the masses'. The emphasis under Stalin was on penetrating mass consciousness, rather than on tapping new consumer markets. Film-makers, like writers and artists, had a responsibility to speak in a language understandable to the masses, but the message was uniformly oriented towards socialist modernization and Soviet unity.

Soviet authorities never denied this responsibility, but cinema became accountable to other demands after Stalin. Film-makers and studios were to develop their own 'brands' in the industry, paving the way for greater emphasis on differentiation over and above ideological and industrial cohesion. As I show in the following chapter, the language of differentiation empowered republican studios to represent 'their own' nationalities, and to make films for 'their own' spectators. While the Stalinist cinema of the periphery presented national difference only to, finally, deny it a political space, post-Stalinist cinema sought to exploit such difference. The next chapter explores changes in the Soviet studio system that took place in the late 1950s and early 1960s, which placed new emphasis on national studios, and the development of national cinema. Dovzhenko Studio adopted this definition of national cinema because it understood one of its goals as speaking to and for a Ukrainian audience. In staking a claim to a section of the 'differentiated' public and its own thematic material, Ukrainian film-makers and the Dovzhenko Studio leadership articulated its own principle of film authorship that attempted to tie personal expression, a more general principle of the Thaw, to national belonging. Dovzhenko Studio's principal task by the early 1960s, however, lay not only in establishing the ideological basis for autonomous cultural production in Ukraine, but in seeking recognition from Moscow of the very relevance of Ukrainian cinema itself.

Chapter 2

REBUILDING A NATIONAL STUDIO DURING THE EARLY 1960S

At the beginning of the 1960s, Dovzhenko Studio was beneath the radar of the Soviet cultural establishment. While a few minor blockbusters emerged from Kyiv during the late 1950s, most authorities and spectators alike mocked Ukrainian cinema if they thought about it at all. The Twenty-Second Party Congress in October 1961 provided a simple discursive response to this problem: Ukrainian cinema had yet to recover from the effects of the 'cult of personality'. According to many voices in Kyiv at the turn of the decade, Stalinism had reduced Ukrainian cinema to stale allegory and stereotypical notions of the Ukrainian folk character. Whereas Mosfilm had successfully established modern production facilities, had their pick of the best of VGIK graduates and profited from the extensive growth of distribution networks and mechanisms for film criticism and promotion, the Kyiv Studio found itself in the same position as it was on the eve of the war. From 1936 to 1956, the state refused to publish a single work of film criticism in Ukrainian or on Ukrainian cinema. During the same year, film-making institutes were closed in both Odessa and Kyiv.[1] Neither of these decisions, enacted based on a conception that such institutions were hotbeds of bourgeois nationalism, were reversed during the 1950s. Even the most slavish supporters of the Communist Party confidently criticized this 'legacy of the cult'. While Kyiv Studio was rebuilt structurally after the war, a sharp curtailment of production in the late 1940s depleted its personnel, who were forced to look elsewhere for employment. Ivan Korniienko, the first of a new generation of Ukrainian film critics in the mid-1950s, argued that the cult 'shackled the development of Ukrainian film art, film scholarship, and film criticism'.[2]

By 1960, however, Ukraine had made some progress, with the publication of the illustrated magazine *Novyny kinoekrana* (*Screen News*) and the establishment of academic departments for screen acting, film direction and cinematography at the Kyiv Institute of Theatrical Arts (KITM). Nonetheless, Dovzhenko Studio still found itself at a stark disadvantage compared to central studios, especially as the mid-1950s' emphasis on rebuilding the Soviet film industry increasingly came to mean the channelling of human and financial resources towards Mosfilm, Gorky Studio and Lenfilm. Throughout the 1950s, the national cinemas of the Union republics remained in a decisively peripheral position in relation to the central studios. During the next decade, however, several ideas for overcoming this divide between Moscow and the Union republics, and for building industrially and aesthetically modernized national studios emerged, particularly in Ukraine.

At the same time, real problems remained. The new leadership that took control of the Ukrainian film industry in 1962 remained divided on the issues of native cadre development, language policy and the thematic and aesthetic foci of Ukrainian national cinema. They did, however, share a desire for Ukrainian cinema to participate in the cultural Thaw, but wanted it to do so in a uniquely Ukrainian manner. Soviet cinema's growing commercialization during the 1960s also forced them to contend with questions of Ukrainian cinema's profitability. This chapter chronicles Dovzhenko Studio's growth from an insignificant provincial studio in the late 1950s and early 1960s to one of the principal institutions of national cinema in the Soviet Union. Republican studios had a difficult time making films on a par with those produced at central studios, largely because the Soviet film industry did not attribute much importance to them, either as profit-making enterprises or as politically and artistically necessary. The combination of demands for industry restructuring and cadre deployment along national lines, nonetheless, set the stage for transforming the ways that studios and individual filmmakers conceptualized national representation and the consumption of national films.

The Industrial Demands of 'National Cinema'

According to Ukrainian film industry authorities, the first problem of developing a viable national cinema was of a financial nature: how to address the sharply unequal distribution of capital between Mosfilm and the republican studios. While Central Asian, Caucasus and Baltic studios had more modest goals, Ukrainian authorities continually demanded throughout the late 1950s and early 1960s a share of industry production equal to that of the central studios. In 1963, Mosfilm planned to make 25 films, and in turn Tymofii Levchuk demanded that Kyiv produce 20–25 during his speech at the First Congress of the Ukrainian Cinematographers' Union the same year.[3] Unless it was willing to slash budgets for their productions even further, however, Goskino would continue to set production plans at ten to 15 features per year in Kyiv. When the Nineteenth Party Congress in 1952 resolved to increase film production, republican studios understood this to be an all-Union affair, a project for extensive infrastructure development, both in Moscow, and in the republics. Moreover, with the elimination of the centralized Ministry of Cinematography, which occurred two weeks after Stalin's death in March 1953,[4] industry power shifted to the Ministries of Culture in each of the Union republics. With this partial devolution to republican ministries, authorities within the separate administrations for feature film production had considerably more power over the creation of production and thematic plans. After 1953, production increased most notably in Kyiv, Odessa, Moscow, Leningrad and Tbilisi, although, because budgets were still determined within the All-Union Ministry of Culture, Mosfilm and Gorky benefited disproportionately.

Moreover, despite the devolution to republican organizations, the Administration for Feature Film Production in Moscow still insisted on approving screenplays prior to production and completed footage for all-Union distribution. A January 1962 circular from the Ministry of Culture in Moscow, for example, complained that republican studios had been illegally approving screenplays for production before central organs had given them permission to do so.[5] This suggests that the central Ministry of Culture still preferred to conduct business directly with individual studios, without the input of republican-level organizations. Teresa Rakowska-Harmstone argues more generally about the 1960s-70s that, while devolution re-established the idea of power-sharing between Moscow and the Union republics, the former did not invest the republics with any meaning-ful share.[6] Nonetheless, there were possibilities for change afloat in the early 1960s.

Very early in his role as First Secretary of the CPU, Petro Shelest defended the maintenance and advancement of Ukrainian institutions for artistic education and cultural production, seeing in them not only a validation of the republic's unique position within the USSR, but also as economically necessary for Ukraine's independent cultural development, its *'samostoiatel'nost'*.[7] Thus, the new leaders of Ukraine's film industry saw in Shelest a potential ally.

The other possibility for changing the vertical distribution of power between the central organs and republican film-making organizations lay in the formation of the Union of Cinematographers. During its first plenary meeting in February 1962, the new creative union set as one of its goals the development of republican studios. First Secretary Ivan Pyr'ev gave voice to these concerns in his opening speech, mentioning the necessity of developing professional 'national cadres' in the republics. He spoke of 'new forms of interrelations and mutual aid', and in Kyiv later that year, he rejected the practice of importing directors from central studios to work in the republics. 'You have a lot of your own people,' he emphasized, 'so why [should we] come [to you]?'[8] Although Ukraine still had practical problems in attracting their 'own people', Pyr'ev's statements were understood as a policy of native cadre development, which Sviatoslav Ivanov and company could implement, presumably with Shelest's assistance.

Delegates at the February 1962 plenum in Moscow and the January 1964 plenum of the Ukrainian Cinematographers' Union articulated several problems of centre/periphery relations, with the unequal distribution of capital occupying much of the discussion. Typical of speeches from republican delegates, Armenian director Stepan Kevorkov spoke about the 'much more difficult work' that republican studios had to do in comparison to central studios. He complained that the national studios routinely received less money for productions, due to the industry's rating system.[9] Under this policy, studios were rated on a scale of one to five, with level one studios like Mosfilm, Lenfilm and Gorky receiving the most generous funding, thanks in large part to Pyr'ev's own role in resurrecting Mosfilm. Armenfilm, along with most of the republican feature film studios, were rated 'threes', while Dovzhenko Studio and Gruziafilm (in Tbilisi) maintained a middle ground with level 'two' ratings. In a catch-22, films produced at republican studios were generally of inferior technical quality due to funding limitations, thus justifying the continued practice of underfunding productions. According to a 14 November 1964 Council of Ministers order, the payment of studio management, in addition to creative and technical personnel, was based on the studio's rating, which in turn was determined by the number of full-length films released each year by the studio. Along with this quantitative determinant, those rated level one included film studios that 'ha[d] a particularly important meaning for the development of Soviet feature film-making'.[10] Kevorkov argued that this inequality, based as it was on a subjective notion of 'importance', should be at the basis of any discussion of the 'development of national cinemas'.[11]

Even the quantitative aspect to this assignment of 'pay categories' contained a degree of inequality, as the question of 'importance' also constituted the method of determining the very means of production, and thus, the level of production. In the mid-1950s, many republican studios were selected for significant expansion, also in answer to party demands for increased overall production. While the industry still worked towards increasing production in the early 1960s, the idealism of the previous decade had faded with a concern that spectatorship for domestic productions had reached its peak.[12] Further increases would occur almost exclusively at the most profitable studios, Mosfilm, Lenfilm, Gorky and, to a lesser extent, Odessa. Meanwhile, the reconstruction projects begun in the 1950s at republican studios, under the banner of 'developing national cinemas', remained unfinished into the 1970s.[13] Thus, republican studios faltered, both under the system of centralization, and under the new conditions of the industry's profit-mindedness.

Apart from the studios themselves, authorities in the Ministry of Culture (and later in Goskino) also assigned films a 'pay category' from one to five, which determined the level of pay the cast and crew received in addition to their modest salaries.[14] Authorities determined these categories in the early 1960s mainly through subjective means – whether a film was politically and/or artistically 'significant'. Later assessments tended to include box office results, but this was only on a quasi-official basis until Filipp Ermash took control of Goskino in 1972. Studios and republican-level organizations could only recommend ratings that would then go to Moscow for approval, which effectively established a third layer of bureaucracy between the film and distribution. While Mosfilm productions required approval in Moscow alone, Kyiv productions required approval in Moscow and in Kyiv.[15] Thus, in many cases, the devolution of authority to republican-level organizations only served to further the careerist ambitions of the quasi-authorities placed in these organizations.

Inequalities between centre and periphery were as much a creative and administrative problem as a concern about quality of life. During a January 1962 meeting in Kyiv to discuss the programme for the February plenum, directors Sigismund Navrotskii and Oleksii Shvachko complained of low pay for workers in the Ukrainian industry, especially in comparison to those working in Moscow.[16] At the First Congress of the SKU the following January, film critic and Chairman of Feature Film-making in the Ministry of Culture, Vladimir Baskakov, told the assembled Ukrainian delegates that they needed to think less about money and more about their jobs, a statement that did not garner much applause in such an atmosphere of tension between the central industry organizations and republican studios.[17] Thus, Shelest and Ivanov, among many other advocates of national cinema in Ukraine, were working against powerful industry interests vested in the continued dominance of Mosfilm and the industry's overall profitability. Many officials in the Ministry of Culture and later in Goskino perceived republican studios as simply a drain on state finances which served no one's interests.[18]

In the early 1960s, the Soviet Union began a second round of film industry reconstruction, which attempted to address some of these inequalities. First, industry authorities determined that the ministries of culture had become overextended through managing an expanded domestic film industry. The decisions of the February plenum highlighted the drafting of 'a proposal on an organizational reconstruction of feature film-making'.[19] This proposal resulted in the establishment of the State Committee on Cinematography under the Council of Ministers (Goskino) in early 1963, which divorced both the Administration of Cinematography and the Administration of Infrastructure and Distribution from the control of the ministries of culture.[20] The Council of Ministers appointed journalist and former Deputy Chairman of the Central Committee's Department of Propaganda and Agitation Aleksei Romanov to head the new Goskino. As someone who was politically orthodox but wanted to see the industry function smoothly, Romanov shared concerns about the inequalities in salaries and bonuses identified by many film-makers in the republics. In September 1963, he wrote to the Chairman of the State Committee on Labour and Salaries A. P. Volkov and the Soviet Minister of Finances V. F. Garbuzov, asking them to amend the pay scale for workers in the Ukrainian film industry, which was set 10 per cent lower than the rate for workers in the RSFSR. In support of his request, Romanov mentioned that Ukraine was 'one of the most important Union republics', and that the ministry needed to raise salaries so that its film industry could compete with central institutions.[21] The Soviet salary reform that went into effect on 1 May 1965 officially mandated the standardization of labour compensation throughout the entire country, which solved this most overt form of inequality among workers in the film industry, but maintained unofficial practices that favoured central studios, such as the distribution of bonuses based on pay scales.[22]

Ideas began circulating in the early 1960s, initially within the Union of Cinematographers, to amend the protocols for calculating and distributing bonuses, the most popular of which was a plan for profit-sharing. In a 1961 project entitled 'Conditions and Measures for the Further Development of Soviet Cinematography', the Union Presidium suggested that 'a part of a [film's] profit go towards the incentive of good work at studios and for the introduction of new technology'.[23] In April 1962, Ukrainian film-makers Navrotskii and Oleksandr Pankrat'ev submitted their own 'Measures for the Further Development of Soviet Cinematography' on behalf of the Ukrainian Union, in which they derided the current system by which studios sold their films 'as products' to the organs of distribution in order to pay off loans to Gosbank. They stated that such practices did not ensure that studios were 'interested [in the] results of advancing a film in distribution, or with its success with spectators'. The authors proposed a new system of financing, whereby studios distributed films themselves through the organs of distribution. This would produce real results in making studios care about a film's profitability, and would correlate overall profits with the amount the studio would receive for its budget and future investment. In addition, such a reform would allow republican studios to market their films to local audiences more directly.

Deputy Minister of Culture in Ukraine Svitlana Kyrylova followed suit in a proposal to her counterpart in Moscow, N. N. Danilov, 'On Measures for the Further Improvement of the Organization of Production of Feature Films', in which she suggested 'establish[ing] honorariums [i.e., bonuses] in relation to the amount of box office returns calculated from the sale of tickets at theatres, instead of the award' currently in use.[24] Both plans, their authors asserted, would eliminate the 'subjectivism' inherent in decision-making. The plans made direct reference to profit-sharing with members of the studio collective for films that achieved an above-average attendance, thus further ensuring a profitable product.[25]

The idealism contained in these proposals is notable in their engagement with Thaw-era concerns about public opinion.[26] The proposal for a system of profit-sharing assumed that audience interest was necessarily of greater value than the so-called objective standards determined by industry assessments, which were in fact quite arbitrary and based on prejudices against republican studios. By claiming that republican studios were better qualified than central organs to assess what audiences would or would not like, the proposals asserted a principle of both professional knowledge and local experience. In the form of the proposals, republican studios asserted a greater claim to speak for 'their own' spectators more than central organizations could. While none of these proposals became official Goskino policy, they constituted the discourse of the early 1960s, and determined the types of claims that film-makers and Communist Party and industry officials in Ukraine made to market the particularity of their products.

Selling Ukraine as a Comedic Space

At the same time, organs of distribution in Ukraine were increasingly weary of promoting 'their own' pictures. During a republic-wide meeting of rural projectionists in Kyiv on 4–6 April 1962, one participant stated that he hated showing Ukrainian films because the audience would leave the theatre before the end. This statement received several nods from his colleagues in the audience.[27] This projectionist's complaint pointed to the long-standing negative reputation of Dovzhenko Studio. More seriously for Ukrainian filmmakers and authorities in charge of republican film production, however, such criticism indicated that Dovzhenko Studio's 'product' did not correlate to a 'national' audience in the sense of being in tune with what that audience wanted to see. Valentyn Fomenko wrote in *Pravda Ukrainy* that theatre managers needed to cover the name of Dovzhenko Studio on film posters to avoid showing a film that no one would see.[28] In a 24 July 1960 article printed in *Radians'ka kul'tura*, critic Valentyn Rybak-Akymov reported that during the screenings for a festival of Ukrainian literature and art in Moscow, only 20 people showed up at the theatre. He complained that the same screenplays with the same situations and the same characters appeared repeatedly.[29] Ukrainian writer Oleksandr Mykhalovych said during a 1963 union meeting that Dovzhenko Studio was a 'disgrace' at which 'millions of spectators' laughed.[30]

While the central press in particular lambasted Dovzhenko Studio's work, continually claiming that its productions were not popular with Soviet audiences, a number of films did attract sizeable crowds in the early 1960s, such as Volodymyr Denysenko's *Soldatka*, which sold 24 million tickets in 1960. Other box office performers included Makarenko's *Human Blood is Not Water* (*Krov liuds'ka – ne vodytsia*, 1961), which sold over 21 million. Moreover, Sergei Paradjanov's *Ukrainian Rhapsody* (*Ukrains'ka rapsodiia*, 1961) sold 20 million, and Viktor Ivchenko's *Ivanna* (1961) sold over 30 million.[31] With the average domestic production attracting 13 million spectators, these films were box office successes. Moreover, each of them dealt with Ukrainian subject matter. Due to the standards in place within the industry however, they were not deemed 'important' by the central organizations, and the people who made them received little credit. Thus, we should approach criticism of Dovzhenko Studio with caution, especially when we consider that the studio found itself with far fewer 'leaders in distribution' during its heyday in the later 1960s and early 1970s. And yet, nearly all the letters sent to Ukrainian newspapers and the studio itself from the early 1960s dealt with films that were at least mildly successful, but aesthetically unsophisticated genre productions, which did not carry cultural value, and were condemned for their rejection of 'contemporary' methods and aesthetic concerns.

Comedy constituted one of the most prolific and successful genres at Dovzhenko Studio in the early 1960s. It is here that stereotypes of Ukrainian peasant life reflected and produced a type of national kitsch and, while the genre was a money maker for Ukrainian cinema, it also provided a reason for Ukrainian cinema's poor reputation in the first place. Nonetheless, Soviet comedies are among the films most remembered today, and were screened constantly on television and in theatres. Moreover, comedy appeared in the Dovzhenko Studio repertoire almost twice as frequently as in Soviet cinema as a whole during the period 1958–62. While these films tended to be the most popular in the late 1950s and early 1960s, they were also the most maligned.

In her 1966 monograph *The Film Comedy: Conflict, Character, Genre*, Svitlana Zinych wrote that, despite the powerful presence of comedy and satire in Ukrainian folklore, Ukrainian films had not developed the genre past its theatricalized clichés of embroidered vests, baggy trousers and silly old men. 'In the majority of our movies,' she wrote, 'the everyday details are only a hollow shell (*pasyvne tlo*), a choice of accessories, which in no way helps to reveal the Ukrainian national character.' Comedies did not demonstrate psychological complexity in their representations of national subject matter. Zinych argued that the character of the old man (*did*) in particular, 'who initially represented the national wisdom of the Ukrainian people in the works of Dovzhenko and Savchenko', now presented an offensive stereotype that was only intended to make the public laugh. Her complaints were even sharper about those comedies that 'remained nationally indifferent', where the 'sphere of the national is confined to the Ukrainian names of the heroes'.[32] Like many critics working within the framework of the goals for national studios after Stalin, Zinych resisted a narrowly folkloric definition of national character, while remaining committed to the overarching principle of national representation above and beyond newer, Thaw-era concerns with the individual's psychology. Two Ukrainian comedies from 1963 – Oleksii Mishurin's *The Gas Station Queen* (*Koroleva benzakolonki*) and Artur Voitets'kyi's *Path-Shmath* (*Stezhki-dorozhki*) – particularly irked Zinych for these reasons, of excess on the one hand, and ignorance on the other.

Mishurin's *Gas Station Queen* was, beyond question, the most successful Ukrainian comedy of the early 1960s. Selling more than 35 million tickets in the year of its release, the film continued to play in Kyiv theatres throughout the 1960s and 1970s. Mishurin's film is about a young woman Liudmyla (played by the rising star, Nadia Rumiantseva), who wants to become a soloist in the Kyiv-based travelling ensemble, 'Ballet on the Ice'. After failing the trials, she applies for a job as a tour guide in Yalta. Liudmyla roller-skates from Kyiv to the Crimean coast, but only finds work at a truck stop on the outskirts of town as a gas station attendant. In her own move from spontaneity to consciousness, Liudmyla goes from being unhappy with the cards fate has dealt her, to a realization of her task in raising the cultural level of the abrasive characters that pass through her station. Thus, Mishurin's plot was situated between Stalinist and Thaw-era concerns with its reconciliation of the dichotomy between individual happiness and the needs of the collective. At the same time, the characters she meets on the way include a rude truck driver whose persistent shout of the Ukrainian '*UVAHA!* [attention!]' signals his demand for quick service, an unkempt rural film projectionist, whose mobile projection facility constantly screens out-of-date films, and the Ukrainian folk costume-wearing manager of the station, who needs to learn the value of Liudmyla's creativity. In the end, she helps each of them overcome their backwardness. Moreover, she refuses to take a position of authority in the *obkom* Department of Education, resolving instead to continue her job as a gas station attendant and consequently her cultural mission.

Despite the box office success of *Gas Station Queen*, S. P. Ivanov commented during a union plenum in 1965 that it was typical for Ukrainian films in that the film crew threw together a bunch of stereotypes with some 'petty plot', which told the audience nothing about contemporary life in the republic. Screenwriter Petro Lubens'kyi recalled the rabid criticism of the film when he and Mishurin took it to the Ministry of Culture in Moscow for approval.[33] Despite this, authorities saw the potential for profit and approved the film for release. Critics continued to pan the film in the republican and central press. And indeed, the film demonstrates many of the problems that Zinych would identify in her 1966 monograph: the gaudy folk costumes, the characters' naive relationship to modernity, superstitious religious beliefs and the Ukrainian language itself relegated to loud and impertinent speech. The film's narratively-motivated dialogue, on the other hand, occurs in Russian, and Liudmyla's role functions as a sort of Russification, as the frequent patrons of the station gradually lose their 'Ukrainianisms' by the end of the film. This shift even becomes self-referential, as Taras the projectionist begins the film with a small *kinoperedvizhka* (mobile projection facility) labelled with the Ukrainian letters 'КІНО', and graduates to a vehicle that plays wide-screen films, which is labelled in Russian, 'КИНО' (Figure 2.1).

The film's teleology is somewhat surprising, given that the 1962 thematic plan called for a fuller description of Liudmyla's past, including her move from Poltava to Kyiv to pursue her dreams. The studio – and Lubens'kyi, according to his rich description of his inspiration[34] – intended the film to 'widely employ Ukrainian folk humour and satire', and Liudmyla's own language was initially supposed to be Ukrainian. Like many attempts to make Ukrainian-language films in the early 1960s however, a Ukrainian *Gas Station Queen* was not feasible because few actors knew how to speak 'correctly'. Moreover, the name recognition of Russian star Rumiantseva in the leading role allowed audiences to ignore the studio that made it. From these circumstances, we might read the theme of Russification in the plot as a movement away from lowbrow *surzhyk* to a literate

Figure 2.1   Taras, the unkempt Ukrainian projectionist in Oleksii Mishurin's
The Gas Station Queen (1963)

tongue.[35] Initially, the studio intended Mishurin to shoot the film in
Ukrainian, but as no popular actors who spoke it were available, they
chose Russian to accomplish this purpose instead. As Borys Buriak
stated in 1964, quoting Alexander Dovzhenko: 'It is better to speak
perfect Russian than poor Ukrainian.'[36]

Recent VGIK graduate Artur Voitets'kyi's coming-of-age *kolkhoz*
comedy *Path-Shmath* appeared the same year. After Mechyslava
Maievs'ka quit the production owing to disagreements with lead
actor Ihor' Borysov, Voitets'kyi transformed the production from a
Soviet comedy of manners similar to *Gas Station Queen* to a much
subtler situation comedy, which omitted any mention of or identification – linguistic or otherwise – with Ukraine. While sharing the
narrative scheme of Mishurin's film, with its focus on a creative but
self-serving individual who must make an occupational sacrifice,
Voitets'kyi's film validates the Thaw-era theme of personal satisfaction, even at the expense of the functioning of the *kolkhoz*. After
graduating from his course in accounting, Roman receives a post on
the *kolkhoz* where his uncle is the chairman. Although happy about

his nephew's arrival at first, his uncle is soon informed that he has no real interest in accounting, and that he was sent on official orders. He dreams, instead, of becoming a mechanical engineer. The chairman is not receptive to his fickle nephew and forces him to stay at the *kolkhoz*, despite Roman's incompetence at his new job. Eventually the young man begins to value his life on the *kolkhoz*, especially after he falls in love with Oksana. At this point, however, his uncle chooses him to act as liaison to the Ministry of Agriculture in matters related to the development of corn. Eventually retired accountant Kalistrat Kalistratych – who had befriended Roman early during his stay on the farm – convinces the chairman to allow his nephew to stay due to his skills in mathematics. The film ends as Roman feels the desire to leave once again, this time to pursue a graduate degree in accounting.

Screenwriter Mykola Zarudnyi criticized the film for its lack of 'Ukrainian atmosphere'. Screenplay editor S. Fomina complained that, while Mikhail Belikov's camera work was done nicely, there were no 'Ukrainian landscapes' in the film.[37] To many at the studio, Zarudnyi's screenplay had fallen too much under the influence of its cosmopolitan director, Artur Voitets'kyi, a VGIK graduate (albeit from Vinnytsia) whom the studio collective considered nationally unaware.[38] At the same time, Voitets'kyi's intention was to present a more sophisticated comedy that did not essentialize Ukraine and Ukrainians in the manner of such films as *The Gas Station Queen*. As Fomina suggested, the landscape is reduced to a generic rural background that does not suggest either particularity or any essential quality. It exists, in fact, as a counterpoint to the mobile hero. Voitets'kyi transformed Zarudnyi's conflict between place and individual to one between personal satisfaction and official responsibilities. Moreover, in Zarudnyi's screenplay, Roman wanted to be a tractor driver, very different from his desire in the film to work in the urban profession of engineering. In the process of Voitets'kyi's transformation and modernization of Zarudnyi's screenplay, the rural landscape suggests nothing apart from its association with the occupation that the state has imposed upon the hero, a type of generically-determined backwater. Of course, the hero learns to value the simple people that inhabit such a place, but neither the plot nor the image facilitates identification between the hero and the land. Zinych criticized the film for ruining Zarudnyi's ethnographically informed screenplay with a non-nationally informed narrative and hero. The studio and Ukrainian Goskino recommended a category

four rating for the film, essentially limiting the film in distribution
to second-run suburban theatres and rural *kinoperedvizhniki* in the
republic.[39] In the places that *Path-Shmath* screened, however, it was
successful, and Tsvirkunov successfully appealed the rating on that
basis in November 1964.[40]

While comedies like *The Gas Station Queen* were indeed the most
profitable genre within Dovzhenko Studio's repertoire in the late
1950s and early 1960s, Ukrainian film-makers considered the form
to be a primitive holdover from the 'cult of personality' in its dated
and condescending representation of Ukrainians. Kyiv film critic
Mykola Berezhnyi warned Dovzhenko Studio filmmakers in January
1964, 'When you give them [the audience] films like this to laugh at,
they are laughing at the land itself'.[41] Thus, market success within
the genre carried a degree of guilt for the studio, even though
reform proposals emerging from the Ukrainian Cinematographers'
Union and Ukrainian Goskino advocated a profit-sharing principle, whereby the industry would correlate pay categories (and thus
bonuses) to box office success. At the same time, as we saw with
Ukrainian Goskino's and the studio's reception of Voitets'kyi's *Path-
Shmath*, film-makers and industry authorities in the republic were
unwilling to sacrifice the particular mode of national representation – grounded in the production of a Ukrainian ethnoscape –
that made Dovzhenko Studio a unique cultural institution. Thus,
Kyiv filmmakers felt three simultaneously interlocking pressures: to
make films that rejected Stalinist clichés and engaged with Thaw-era
concerns; to make films that sold tickets; and to remain committed
to the production of a specifically Ukrainian culture. As the new
administration soon realized, however, they could hardly accomplish
any of these tasks with the current group of creative personnel at
Dovzhenko Studio, recruited from either pre-war assistant directors
and cinematographers, or more likely, from the Ukrainian theatre.

Narratives of Return

As *Path-Shmath* moved from pre-production to production and
reception, we see a project at the confluence of old and new concerns at the studio – between a Stalinist mode of folkloric representation and Thaw-era concerns about the primacy of individual
personality. Voitets'kyi's film positioned the conflict between personal satisfaction and obligation to the state as grounded in a spatial politics, one which informed many other films from the early
1960s. During this time, *kolkhozy* were having trouble convincing

young people to stay, and it was especially difficult to compel them to return after receiving advanced degrees in cities. Moreover, the 'Virgin Lands' campaign initiated in the mid-1950s was now running out of steam, and educated young people no longer wished to spend their lives so far away from Soviet cultural and political centres. The 'return narrative' constituted a veritable cycle in literature and cinema throughout the post-Stalin era. From the returning soldier in the 1950s to the worker returning from the Virgin Lands in the 1960s and the returning émigré in the 1970s, this narrative cycle dealt with problems of reincorporation into the social fabric of everyday life in the Soviet Union. In the Ukrainian films in this cycle, they also presented an ambivalent dichotomy between attachment to the local (family, landscape and ethnic or regional identification) and responsibility to country and humanity more broadly. Dovzhenko Studio itself was engaged in a spatial politics of its own in its attempt to attract Ukrainian VGIK students to return. The new leadership of the studio and Ukrainian Goskino positioned the return to Ukraine for students born and raised in the republic as a national obligation, while indicating that a decision to stay in Moscow might be grounded in personal satisfaction and material comfort.

Although Voitets'kyi attained employment at Dovzhenko Studio, principally because of his place of birth in the republic, his VGIK education subjected him to contemporary cultural politics in the capital. Voitets'kyi, as one of the film-maker returnees to Ukraine, while interested in the same aesthetic problems as his VGIK colleagues who ended up at Mosfilm and other studios around the USSR, was expected to make films in the 'spirit of Dovzhenko', with all the baggage that came with such a mission in the late 1950s and early 1960s. The studio realized that it had to find a middle ground to satisfy both the needs of an artistically 'modernized' studio engaged with Thaw-era concerns, and its more traditional national representational goals. The biggest obstacle to the former goal was in attracting directors and other creative personnel to the studio. Navrotskii stated during the June 1962 union plenum that the 'problem of cadres' was the 'Rome, to which all roads led'.[42] He identified the problem of Ukrainian students leaving the republic for a VGIK education in Moscow, only to then refuse employment in Kyiv after graduation. When they returned to Ukraine, Navrotskii complained, they stayed long enough for one or two projects, and then went back to their new families and larger apartments in the capital.

Consequently, Kyiv Studio in 1960 was left with virtually the same staff they had a decade earlier.[43] After the war, Kyiv brought its personnel from either outside the republic or from the theatre. Among the studio's pre-war film-makers, only five remained after the war. Writer Oleksandr Levada became the Ukrainian deputy to the Minister of Cinematography in 1950, and chose to invite directors in the theatre to work at Kyiv Studio, reasoning that general experience was preferable to the relative inexperience of a recent VGIK graduate. The same year, Savchenko returned to Ukraine to make his final picture, *Taras Shevchenko*, bringing his VGIK students Alexander Alov, Marlen Khutsiev, Vladimir Naumov and Sergei Paradjanov with him as assistants. His senior students Alov and Naumov completed the film, with Paradjanov staying on as Assistant Director, after Savchenko died of a heart attack. The three of them all stayed at Kyiv Studio after graduation, while Khutsiev went to Odessa. Nonetheless, after the success of Alov and Naumov on *The Restless Youth* (*Trivozhnaia molodost'*, 1954) and *Pavel Korchagin* (1956), they left Ukraine for employment at Mosfilm. Paradjanov stayed, largely because he did not garner similar recognition with his rather unremarkable Ukrainian comedies. Other directors from the 1950s continued as temporary workers, coming to Kyiv to shoot one or two films before returning to more lucrative projects in Moscow.[44] By 1960, there was considerable discussion in the press about why Dovzhenko Studio had not yet replaced these rising stars, who had left for greener pastures in the north-east.

While Navrotskii was correct in identifying the greater financial and material benefits to working in Moscow, he ignored Kyiv Studio's complicity in warding off young directors. Critic Kostiantyn Teplyts'kyi reported on the March 1962 plenum in *Radians'ka kul'tura*, suggesting that a key reason for Dovzhenko Studio's backwardness was its lack of respect for younger cadres, which limited their career progression and reduced their creative potential to a seemingly endless cycle of assistant positions on film crews. He argued that the studio needed to give young people the chance to express themselves honestly and independently. In this respect, he offered more serious criticism, writing, 'There is not that essential creative atmosphere at the studio, [there is] no activity, no cooperation, no precision, no courageousness, and moreover, no innovation'.[45] In May 1962, the Soviet Union presidium sent a letter to the central committee of the CPU, focusing their attention on the 'problem of cadres'. The message from Ukrainian filmmakers suggested that times were indeed changing in its complaint that Ukrainian cinema was lagging behind 'the Russian masters'. They quoted film director Mykola Mashchenko at the plenum, who stated that youth at the studio were in a far more uncomfortable position in Kyiv than they would be in Moscow, where they 'meet with sensitive treatment'. Mashchenko stated that none of the great films from Mosfilm could have been made in Kyiv due to the 'provincialist' and 'localist' attitudes of the leadership. Here, too, the focus was on catching up to the centre, over and above reproducing the same comedies and melodramas touching upon Ukrainian themes that characterized production in the late 1950s and early 1960s.

In suggesting that creative sterility resulted from the 'problem of cadres', studio authorities referenced a more general issue that arose in the mid-1950s with the decision to increase cinema production. Studios discovered that they needed not only material resources but human resources as well to make the 150 films per year that the central committee demanded. VGIK in the 1950s was not equipped to train enough personnel for an industry of this scale. Republican studios needed to pull directors and actors from the theatre to make up for the lack of creative personnel, which became an inefficient and bureaucratically troublesome practice by the 1960s. The central studios collaborated on the establishment of a film actors' theatre in central Moscow, in order to avoid the necessity of employing theatrical personnel. Another means of solving the 'problem of cadres' came with the establishment of the higher courses on directing and screenwriting at Mosfilm, intended as a more practice-oriented approach to film education than VGIK, which would predominantly admit postgraduate students working in other fields. As a result, young people were recruited into the field on a level unseen since the 1920s.[46] In many ways, this influx of young film-makers paralleled the structural transformations of Western European film industries in the late 1950s and early 1960s, which in part established the groundwork for such film movements as the French New Wave and Young German Cinema. In both the Soviet Union and France during the late 1940s and early 1950s, the film industry was composed of skilled tradesmen. The change in the late 1950s was part of a general reorientation of cinema that privileged the role of the director-intellectual, or *auteur*, over the skilled professional.

While Mosfilm and a few other studios benefited from this influx of young talent, Dovzhenko Studio – and even, to a larger degree, other republican studios – suffered a definitive lack of educated personnel. The most pressing issue concerned the financial burden of maintaining a studio with increased output. In May 1962, the Union presidium reported to the central committee of the CPU that a delegation sent to VGIK discovered that none of the Ukrainian students studying there wished to return to Kyiv due to the 'unfriendly manner' at the studio.[47] During the March 1962 Union plenum, director Leopol'd Bezkodarnyi was clearly resentful at being forced to work at Dovzhenko Studio on the basis of his nationality.[48] By 1962, the dual practice of importing Moscow directors to Kyiv and Ukrainian theatre directors to cinema no longer appeared as a viable response to the 'problem of cadres'. With the exponential expansion of the industry, along with the creative advances of the Thaw, these options were both logistically untenable and aesthetically unwarranted. The most viable option in 1962 for solving the 'problem of cadres' was to create a space to which budding Ukrainian film-makers wanted to return.

The decisive step in promoting 'native cadres' came from the appointment of Vasyl' Tsvirkunov to the position of Dovzhenko Studio managing director in April 1962.[49] Ukrainian Minister of Culture Rostislav Babiichuk removed Pavlo Nebera as studio head ostensibly for his failure to take steps to establish and maintain a local base of native cadres. The decision, however, originated from people in the centre. During the May plenum of the SKU, Pyr'ev arrived in Kyiv seemingly with the sole motive of 'encouraging' the ministry to remove the inexperienced and disliked Nebera from his position.[50] Tsvirkunov assumed the directorship with the promise to improve planning mechanisms, work towards solving the 'problem of cadres' and move the studio towards the aesthetic principles and box office successes of the central studios.[51]

At the same time, Tsvirkunov was well connected to young Ukrainian writers in the early 1960s and was conversant with, and in many cases, supportive of, demands to revive Ukrainian language and culture. He also possessed impeccable 'national' and party credentials: Tsvirkunov was born to a peasant family in 1917 in the village of Novoukraina in Zaporiz'ka oblast' in south-east Ukraine. He graduated from the Voroshilovs'kyi Pedagogical Institute in present-day Luhans'k in 1938 with a degree in Ukrainian literature, and taught in a rural middle school in Luhans'ka oblast' before the war started in June 1941. He joined the party in early 1942 and became the head of the political section of a partisan brigade on the Vokhovskii Front in Central Ukraine. In 1953, the Luhans'k party committee nominated him as Chairman, but he entered graduate school two years later at the central committee's Academy of Social Sciences in Moscow, graduating in 1959 with a job as art and literature editor for the Russian-language CPU journal of Marxist theory *Kommunist Ukrainy*, later becoming Senior Editor for *Radians'ka Ukraina*. After taking his position at Dovzhenko Studio after the first congress of the Ukrainian Cinematographers' Union in January 1963, he travelled to VGIK, where he convinced several Ukrainian graduates of their national obligations to return to work in Ukraine, with the additional promise that Dovzhenko Studio would be a space where youth 'experimentation' would be met with sympathy.[52]

* * *

Mykola Mashchenko made *Stories from the Red House* (*Novely krasnoho domu*) in 1963 as an allegory of return, which read the studio's 'problem of cadres' into a *kolkhoz* drama about the conflict between an authoritarian chairman and a bright young agronomist. Written by Vasyl' Zemliak, and produced on the cusp of Tsvirkunov's trip to VGIK, the film's allegorical message of recovering from the 'cult of personality' seemed especially appropriate. Mashchenko's film tells the story of a Ukrainian village after World War II. The conflict between Chairman Stokolos and agronomist Maksym is set up as one between a Stalin-era careerist and an honest specialist. Through flashbacks, we learn that the hero was a partisan in the war, and occupied an old red house on the *kolkhoz* as the Fascists retreated. More recently, the red house provided the setting for Maksym's romance with Dusia. Due to his conflict with Stokolos, however, he leaves to work at a brick factory in Moscow, where he writes numerous letters to Dusia but never receives a response. He imagines she has forgotten about him and married someone else. After hearing of Stokolos's death, however, Maksym returns to the *kolkhoz* where he meets Dusia once again, and discovers that he is the father of her child. He notices the changes that have occurred after the death of Stokolos and his cult of personality, and stays at the kolkhoz to work the rest of his life in peace.

Officials in Ukrainian Goskino and the new studio leadership were well aware of the film's allegorical message and its teleological treatment of the personality cult from Zemliak's short story. Tsvirkunov, S. P. Ivanov and Zemliak acknowledged that the studio's prior leadership had driven many capable film-makers away from Kyiv, but suggested that Ukrainian VGIK graduates had an obligation to return to the republic. Due to ideological problems with central Goskino, Mashchenko's film, completed by summer 1963, was not released until May 1965, which made its theme particularly dated.[53] Nonetheless, Mashchenko's *Stories from the Red House* managed to do what the new studio leadership demanded: incorporate Thaw-era concerns into a framework of national representation. Moreover, its allegory promoted the obligation of Ukrainian filmmakers to return.

The problem remained, however, as to whether these young VGIK returnees were knowledgeable of or willing to approach a national representational mode in their work at Dovzhenko Studio. Artur Voitets'kyi, for example, would continually resist working in such a mode, opting to adapt Gorky and Chekhov instead of Oles' Honchar and Oleksandr Korniichuk.[54] Other returnees like Iurii Illienko and Leonid Osyka came to accept the Ukrainian theme as fundamental to their work, but first went through a process of personal 'Ukrainianization'. Since the development of 'native cadres' became the principle upon which the studio had decided to base its solution to the personnel problem, Ukrainian VGIK graduates could supply only a fraction of its needs, especially as such returnees came to Kyiv in the early 1960s as unknowledgeable and, as dissident Ivan Dziuba would argue, 'de-nationalized' Ukrainians, unprepared to engage with nationality politics.

'Ukrainianizing' Creative Cadres, Writing and Embodying an Image of the Nation

In privileging 'native cadres' in the creative professions, the studio leadership went beyond economic attempts to catch up to the central studios. Herein, they were addressing difficult questions about local cultural knowledge, and suggested that some film-makers had a greater ability to embody particular concerns of national importance. Although Navrotskii's and Pankrat'ev's 'Measure for the Further Development of Soviet Cinematography' did not generate fundamental changes that were not already forthcoming, perhaps the most important question that emerged out of their 'measures' concerned the practice of educating native cadres within Ukraine. After all, VGIK graduates presented their own problems for the studio, even if the studio leadership was now firmly committed to accepting them. At the same time, educating cadres in Kyiv presented even greater logistical problems, above the need for qualified young director-*auteurs*.

Many film critics and film-makers in the republic believed instead that the key to building Ukrainian national cinema was the development of professional screenwriters and actors. Several directors readily admitted that the top Ukrainian writers of the war generation – Honchar, Mykhailo Stel'makh, Ivan Le – did not translate well to the screen.[55] Rybak-Akymov wrote in a 1960 editorial that the only way to solve the problem was to educate 'our own national cadres of film dramatists'.[56] Navrotskii argued for a deliberate strategy of developing professional cadres of screenwriters who would be tied by a labour contract to Dovzhenko Studio.[57] As he stated in a March 1962 newspaper editorial, professional 'screenwriters [should] write screenplays', not writers who were not trained to do so.[58] To this practical and pedagogical end, 1961 saw the establishment of a film school at the Karpenko-Karyi Theatre Institute in Kyiv (KITM), with undergraduate programmes in film directing, acting for the cinema and cinematography (but not screenwriting). By the 1970s, several prominent film-makers and screen actors had received their education there, but in 1961 the film school at KITM carried all the baggage of Dovzhenko Studio itself: that it was provincial, and thus perceived as inferior to similar institutions in Moscow. If the studio employed only personnel trained at home, some argued, it could never recover its poor reputation among industry authorities and spectators. Levchuk and the Ukrainian Union attempted to support both methods, at least until KITM developed its curriculum further.

In many ways, the 'actor problem' was similar to, but also more intense than other aspects of the 'problem of cadres', simply due to the nature of the profession. In desiring to move away from the discouraged practice of employing theatrical actors for the screen, the studio leadership did not have many 'native' professional screen actors to take their place, and frequently had to fill roles with those from Moscow. Moreover, the screen actors that had a contractual agreement with Dovzhenko Studio were frequently unknown to a broader audience, and their employment in major roles would not help the film at the box office. On the rare instance that a Kyiv screen actor became known, he or she would likely find their talents wasted by staying in Ukraine. To give only the most prominent example, Sergei Bondarchuk played the title roles in Dovzhenko's final film *Michurin* (1948), Savchenko's *Taras Shevchenko* (1951) and Levchuk's *Ivan Franko* (1955), before moving to Mosfilm to direct and star in his celebrated *Fate of a Man* (*Sud'ba cheloveka*, 1959). Despite official discouragement of Ukrainian actors leaving Kyiv for Moscow in a August 1962 Ministry of Culture order, popular Ukrainian actors found little holding them back from a better career in the capital.[59] Thus, due to distribution concerns, most Ukrainian directors continued to favour theatrical actors or those from Moscow over 'native' screen actors, the latter of which were employed for minor roles in the majority of cases.[60] This practice incurred the continual enmity of Kyiv-based screen actors, and they developed a reputation for depression, alcoholism and a lack of skill. B. Mykolaienko wrote in October 1962 that staff actors at Dovzhenko Studio 'remain in the condition of...illegitimate children'.[61]

During the February plenum in Moscow, Navrotskii addressed the 'actors' problem' in a language that central authorities might have better understood: Kyiv needed a Film Actors' Theatre because Ukrainian actors would work for less money than their Muscovite colleagues.[62] This at first seems to contradict his statement in the 'Measures for the Further Development of Soviet Cinematography' that Ukrainian cadres should be paid the same as those in Moscow, but Navrotskii's interest in this earlier document was on increasing the prestige of Kyiv directors and screenwriters. The problem of actors, by comparison, was predominantly one of fiscal responsibility and administrative efficiency. In other words, it simply cost too much time and money to move actors between Moscow and Kyiv. In his unceasing efforts to solve the 'problem of cadres' in the early 1960s, we get no indication that Navrotskii's concerns were 'nationally' motivated. A self-described Polish old Bolshevik who emigrated after the formation of the Polish Republic, he first worked in Leningrad at Belgoskino and Lenfilm, then came to Kyiv Studio directly after the war to help rebuild the studio. His ideas about the studio's 'independence' from Moscow had little to do with cultural nationalism, and instead Navrotskii worked towards building a stable base of personnel and developing technological infrastructure. For the same reason, he argued against such nation-building projects as the construction of a history of Ukrainian cinema museum, a separate Ukrainian cinema archive and a new Kyiv Film Institute on the basis that they would merely become financial burdens for the studio and the union. Moreover, they were politically unnecessary, according to Navrotskii, and in fact carried an element of 'nationalist narrow-mindedness'.[63]

Pavlo Nechesa, the head of the actors' studio established in December 1962, had for a very different understanding of the necessity of promoting Ukrainian actors over those from Moscow. Nechesa had been the first managing director of Kyiv Studio, appointed to the position in 1929, and came out of retirement to take control of the actors' studio in 1962. Like other Ukrainians of his generation who fondly remembered the Ukrainianization policies of the 1920s, Nechesa became a strong advocate for Ukrainian actors. His orientation and intentions were different from those of Navrotskii, as he was clearly interested in the particular qualities that Ukrainian actors had to offer. Chief among these qualities was the ability to speak good literary Ukrainian. Nechesa's reasons were clear: Ukrainian national cinema demanded films in the vernacular. Opposing him in this project were not only individuals like Navrotskii, who had never learnt the language and placed no importance on Soviet nationalities policy, but also the Ukrainian organs of distribution. During the Ukrainian union's first congress in January 1963, Nechesa claimed that the head of Ukrainian distribution, L. Ia. Zahorodniuk, once stated that only 'banderists'[64] wanted films in Ukrainian. The rest of the Ukrainian people prefered Russian-language films. Nechesa countered with the assertion that 'distribution continues to ignore the national form of cinema art', and dismissed the statements of Zahorodniuk and those like him on the basis that they 'incorrectly understand policy on the nationalities question'.[65] Nechesa was committed not only to promoting Ukrainian actors, but also to making sure that they knew the language of the republic, frequently demanding that actors who did not speak 'correctly' take night courses on the Ukrainian language.[66] S. P. Ivanov gave tacit support to Nechesa's platform later in the year when he stated during a studio meeting: 'When the actors are not Ukrainian, and the language is not Ukrainian, and even the author of the screenplay is not Ukrainian, to speak about the national form of Ukrainian cinematography remains mere words [*rozmova*], and we can't reconcile [ourselves] with this.'[67]

But the actor problem went far beyond questions of language acquisition. In his evaluation of Ukrainian cinema in 1963, Oleh Babyshkin identified the chief aesthetic problems in Ukrainian cinema as a preponderance of 'sociological schemas' and the 'dominance of stereotypes' in the representation of Ukrainians on screen.[68] During the March plenum of the union, Levchuk stated that all of Dovzhenko Studio's productions the following year were

in the language of backwards clichés about a tedious and bland people, and not less about their tedious and bland passions... Instead of
the diverse and living *kolkhoznik*... a half-witted old man looks at us
from our screen with drunken eyes. He resembles our *kolkhoznik* like
a piece of driftwood [resembles] a tree...

Developing native cadres was a means of satisfying these concerns with authenticity, while infusing new talent into the studio
that was not exclusively reliant on the goodwill of central studios.
Nechesa's concern with employing Ukrainian actors in many ways
echoed debates about language politics in 1960s Ukraine more
generally. As Babyshkin and many others complained, 1962 saw
only one film produced entirely in Ukrainian (Ivan Kavaleridze's
Poviia). Although concerns about producing films in Ukrainian
had emerged as early as the mid-1950s,[69] little was accomplished
in this area until a decade later. An 8 January 1962 studio meeting
on the actor problem determined the necessity for more training
in the Ukrainian language, organized through the dubbing section of the studio, along with the establishment of a large actors'
theatre with 150–200 individuals to meet the demands of all three
Ukrainian feature-film studios (Dovzhenko Studio, in addition to
Odessa and Yalta).[70]

While film-makers at Dovzhenko did not find Pidhornyi interested in the 'problem of cadres', and even less so with the cultural
concerns that sometimes accompanied this problem, S. P. Ivanov
reported in October 1963 that Shelest was indeed concerned about
such a state of affairs when he took power that year.[71] Later in 1963,
Ivanov wrote to the studio leadership about the lack of Ukrainian-
language films, and henceforth demanded express permission from
Ukrainian Goskino to complete a film in Russian.[72] The studio
director responded during a studio meeting in October 1964, in
which he promised to solve the problem, in part through encouraging directors to employ Ukrainian actors who knew the language
adequately.[73]

Locating the National Self between the Folkloric and the Thaw: Volodymyr Denysenko's *A Dream*

In late 1963, Volodymyr Denysenko began working on *A Dream* (*Son*),
a film significant for addressing and offering solutions to so many
early 1960s concerns at Dovzhenko Studio. Denysenko was also a
native returnee, who first studied theatrical directing at KITM in the

late 1940s, during which he was accused of a nationalist conspiracy and sent to Kolyma. After the amnesty of 1953, he applied to VGIK, and studied under Dovzhenko, but returned to Kyiv the following year to complete his KITM studies. In 1962, he collaborated with Ukrainian poet Dmytro Pavlychko (also a rehabilitated national-ist)[74] on a screenplay about the young Taras Shevchenko, and began shooting the Ukrainian-language film with a cast of KITM acting students, including Ivan Mykolaichuk in the leading role. *A Dream* was both nationally aware and conversant with Thaw-era stylistic concerns.

Whereas Savchenko's 1951 *Taras Shevchenko* follows the Ukrainian national poet's adult years, which he spent as an imperial conscript and in Central Asian exile, *A Dream* deals with a period of the poet and painter's life that he spent in serfdom. While employing the poem of the same title contained in Shevchenko's major poetic work, *Kobzar*, as its source material, *A Dream* was generically a historical biography. Yet, unlike Savchenko's film, which closely follows the trajectory of a folkloric representation of a leader's *vita* and his con-nection to his native land, Denysenko's film is more in line with the 'portrait of the artist'. Denysenko's *A Dream* prefigures such films as Tarkovskii's *Andrei Rublev* (1966) in its representation of the self-sufficient hero-artist. Denysenko's first major work was intended to explicate the events that led to Shevchenko writing the title poem. The narrative, however, refused to rely on a strict chronology of events in Shevchenko's life; instead, a number of associations and metaphors are maintained throughout the film. The manner of the production is distinguished from Savchenko's earlier film on Shevchenko due to the poetic and occasionally non-realist style of the later work, with its emphasis on imagery rather than characters and events. Here the metaphor of the dream works throughout the film's narrative and drives the plot.

A Dream begins in the Peter and Paul fortress as an older Shevchenko, bald with his recognizable drooping moustache, is led up a staircase by two guards. After an interrogation, Lieutenant General Dubel't charges the poet with spreading revolutionary propaganda through his political associations and through his lit-erary and artistic work. The interrogation takes place entirely in Ukrainian. There is no attempt to maintain the linguistic authentic-ity of the interaction, which of course would have been in Russian. As Dubel't reads Shevchenko's sentence, a voice-over of the title poem is interjected into the foreground. The rest of the story occurs in flashbacks, and sometimes flashbacks within flashbacks. Shevchenko is a boy, abused by the village priest, but soon discovers his interest in painting. He visits a local artist, who convinces him to approach his master, Count Engel'gardt. The latter promises to make him a court artist, but the young Shevchenko instead becomes his house serf. They travel to Riga together, and then to St. Petersburg. There, Engel'gardt discovers that he can make money from Taras's talents, and sends him to study at the Petersburg Institute of the Arts where Shevchenko meets the Russian painter Karl Briulov and poet and tutor to the future Alexander II, Vasilii Zhukovsky, who arrange to buy his freedom.

For perhaps the first time in Soviet cinema, flashbacks continually interrupt the narrative, but not to provide backstory in the manner of Mashchenko's *Stories from the Red House*. Here, flashbacks function as moments of self-consciously 'subjective narration', to use Maureen Turim's phrase, which constitute a break in the narration. As such, these flashbacks operate as 'psychoanalytic confessions' read into historical time.[75] Instead of a folkloric-materialist progression of time, whereby the narrative of Ukrainian-Russian unity is read into the natural fabric of history, and where such a historical end-point determines the basis of a mature national consciousness, the flashbacks in *A Dream* call into question such a notion of historical time. History itself becomes highly subjective as it is read through Taras Shevchenko's own memories. In this way, flashbacks serve to connect the subjective and personal with the political and social history of the nation and the hero's memories trigger the movement through time.

The young Taras constantly imagines himself in two places at once, in the actual space of Riga or St. Petersburg, and in the mythological space of the Ukrainian village. He simultaneously inhabits both the ideological space of an idealized pastoral and a modern political consciousness of class and national oppression. While viewing himself within the cultural context of the imperial metropole, he seeks identification with his Ukrainian childhood. This is understated within the narrative itself, and works solely on a visual level. At the same time, *A Dream* follows many Soviet conventions for historical films, such as the operatic rendering of folk songs, rather than the naturalistic rendering of them in later works of Ukrainian poetic cinema.

Critics in the republic warmly received Denysenko's film, as they saw in it a 'highly artistic' use of 'native cadres' and a representation of Ukraine that resisted common stereotypes. Even the image of Shevchenko in *A Dream* was updated from a dour-looking middle-aged man with a droopy moustache and wool Cossack hat to the finely-dressed and wide-eyed youth that Mykolaichuk played, a role that he had long dreamt of.[76] During an initial screening of the film, one member of the Dovzhenko Studio Artistic Council stated that *A Dream* visually articulated the meaning of 'line four' in his passport.[77] Nonetheless, the film did little for Dovzhenko Studio's reputation, despite a number of positive reviews. Its significance was entirely local, despite its visual sophistication along with its ability to translate Thaw-era discourses about authorship and personal expression to the republican screen. Poet Dmytro Pavlychko, cinematographer Mykola Chornyi and actor Ivan Mykolaichuk all received distinction from the Verkhovna Rada (the Ukrainian legislature) for their work on the film, and Denysenko won the title 'Honoured Artist of Ukraine' for his direction.

Perhaps we may attribute the indifference non-Ukrainians displayed towards *A Dream* to a general apathy of audiences towards nationalities projects, associated as they were with the formulaic tone of the Soviet press in recognizing such anniversary events. The Shevchenko Sesquicentennial, celebrated throughout the Soviet Union during the spring and summer of 1964, bore the mark of an official gala, but one whose object was little known outside of Ukraine apart from information conveyed during the major anniversary years. *A Dream* did little to 'inform' audiences about the life of Shevchenko because, in its simultaneous engagement with the historical-biographical genre while appearing chronologically fragmented, audiences unfamiliar with the hero probably left the theatre no wiser as to who he was, apart from the 'great figure of national importance to the Ukrainian people', as the Soviet press had already informed them. In March 1964, First Secretary of the Union of Ukrainian Writers Oles' Honchar delivered a major speech about 'Shevchenko and the Contemporary' in Moscow's Great Theatre, which set the tone for the sesquicentennial. He opened the speech with the words:

> The Taras Shevchenko Anniversary has become a celebration of our brotherhood, a hallowed celebration of multi-national socialist culture. [...] It is precisely this [Leninist] Friendship [of Peoples] that has brought us all together as one with a feeling of honour and love towards the genius son of the Ukrainian people, towards the great poet-revolutionary.[78]

Honchar listed Shevchenko among other 'national' poets in the Friendship of Peoples canon from the rest of the Union republics, who 'alongside Pushkin, Dostoevsky, Tolstoy, Chekhov and Gorky represent our native artistic culture before the world, and become ornaments of a universal culture'. Thus, Honchar reduced Shevchenko's personal significance to a mobile and ahistorical mythology of 'all-Union cultural history'.

What emerged of the Shevchenko image in the realm of popular culture constituted an element of Ukrainian national kitsch. An image published in *Novyny kinoekrana* displays a Taras Shevchenko icon surrounded by embroidered fabrics (*rushnyky*), and presiding over a garishly decorated room with embroidered wall hangings, ceramic objects, bucolic landscapes and a woman in full national costume inspecting a female headpiece. What in the 1920s might have been identified as nationalist was now located within the safe, domestic space of Stalinist folklore.

Despite Honchar's predictable speech on the continued significance of the poet, and the continued predominance of such domesticated Ukrainian national imagery, the inclusion of Denysenko's *A Dream* as a component of the 1964 anniversary served to complicate Shevchenko's image in the republic, which paved the way for his use by young intellectuals and dissidents. Ivan Dziuba recalled hearing someone ask in the movie theatre after watching *A Dream*: 'Have you seen how the Banderists come in gangs to this movie?...'[79] indicating that such a complicated and modernist treatment of the poet, and one which continually affirmed his Ukrainian identity in opposition to imperial Russia, was already implicated in nationalist discourse. During and after the sesquicentennial, there were periodic unofficial gatherings of Kyiv's young people and intellectuals at the statue of the poet in Shevchenko Park (across the street from Shevchenko University). After one such gathering in May 1966, Kyiv intellectuals asserted that they were trying to 're-claim the great *Kobzar*' from Russia'. CPU Cultural Affairs Department chair Iurii Kondufor demanded that security organs pay attention to such 'anti-social' gatherings.[80] Just as future dissidents Ivan Svitlychnyi and Dziuba had articulated their dissent over Soviet cultural infrastructure, Denysenko presented an image of Shevchenko that resisted characterization within a folkloric teleology, which was nonetheless produced upon the representational material and within the production context of a Stalinist mode.

Disposing of 'Those Notorious Attributes': Toward an Ethnographic Politics of Representation

While no one at Dovzhenko Studio, within the Union or Ukrainian Goskino admitted as much, the 'problem of cadres' appeared to be solved by 1965, and people stopped talking about it. The studio hired several young Ukrainian directors – most of them VGIK graduates rather than from the theatre or Moscow imports – while Tsvirkunov also helped establish actors' and screenwriters' studios in Kyiv, all of which brought Ukrainian cinema out of the immediate personnel crisis of the early part of the decade. Moreover, budgets for Dovzhenko Studio productions began to increase noticeably along with central Goskino's acknowledgement that Ukrainian cinema had improved. Whereas only two films had been awarded with a pay category of one or two in 1963, four had received the first pay group and six more the second in 1965.[81] Of course, Ukrainian film production remained on a smaller scale than the Ukrainian Cinematographers' Union desired, but with the immediate administrative crisis resolved, studio politics shifted from the various concerns over personnel and catching up to the central studios to more directly confront issues of artistic representation.

As I have shown in this chapter, and will continue to demonstrate, both of these areas of concern were part of the same continuum. The nationalities of the directors, screenwriters, actors and other members of film crews in Ukraine were considered determining factors in how films themselves were positioned within the politics of national representation at the studio. Members of the studio collective banked their reputations on their abilities to participate in the cultural Thaw, which not only implied engagement with such discursive abstractions as 'sincerity' and 'authenticity', but through this, an effort to transform the popular image of Ukraine and Ukrainians more generally. Ukrainian screenwriter Mykola Zahrebel'nyi acknowledged Denysenko's *A Dream* as the 'first film at Dovzhenko Studio, which I'm not ashamed to say that this is a film from Dovzhenko Studio, where our people are shown [*pokazanyi*]'. In this sense, 'shown' implied more than mere presence, as the writer then counterposed *A Dream* to 'those notorious attributes' which continued to plague Ukrainian cinema: 'There's the Zaporozhians, there's the Haidamaky, there's the Dnieper.' He called for a rejection of the domesticated image of Ukrainians in Soviet cinema:

'To show' them, as he stated, 'not to simply pose them, not to simply display them in the background'.[82] As Zahrebel'nyi indicated,
films produced at Dovzhenko Studio during the early 1960s visited
the canonical sites of national importance, and looked in on the
canonical people that inhabited these spaces. Films such as *The
Gas Station Queen* presented spectators with particular spaces in
the republic, but did so within an all too familiar mode of national
branding, which appeared out of touch with Thaw-era concerns
with 'authenticity'.

Other than commercial success, or rather, in addition to commercial success, film-makers and the new leadership at Dovzhenko
Studio sought recognition from Moscow of Ukrainian cinema as
a legitimate art, one which did not require self-parody. In rejecting 'those notorious attributes', Ukrainian cinema asserted a new
claim to national originality, but one in dialogue with Thaw-era
concerns with 'sincerity' and 'authenticity'. Ukrainian cinema was
engaged in seeking recognition during the early 1960s. In this way,
Ukrainian cinema's reputation was intimately tied to a broader
image of Ukraine and Ukrainians in the Soviet Union. If Ukraine
continued to be an image of rural backwardness, Ukrainian cinema too would have such a reputation, largely because it was
considered responsible for producing such meaning. While the figure of Taras Shevchenko was associated in popular culture with
Ukrainian kitsch, Denysenko attempted to update the image of
the national poet to signify not only national awareness, but also
youth, a contemporary sensibility and intelligence. While members
of the studio collective and the Ukrainian intelligentsia generally
approved of Denysenko's picture, it failed to garner much recognition for Ukrainian cinema more broadly within the Soviet Union.
It did not dispel 'those notorious attributes', largely because *A
Dream* remained tied to the generic system of non-Russian cultural
production under Stalin, despite significant stylistic and narrative
innovations contained therein.

In the following chapter, I examine Sergei Paradjanov's *Shadows
of Forgotten Ancestors*, the first film that brought international
fame to Ukrainian cinema since Alexander Dovzhenko's *Earth*
(*Zemlia*, 1930). The elements of its fame had as much to do with
the eccentricities of the director and his personal style as it did
with the unusual material upon which the film was constructed.
Paradjanov's film and the drama that surrounded its production
marked a new means of national representation in the cinema,

based not on the familiar sites of Ukrainian folk spectacle present in such films as *Tractor Drivers*, *The Gas Station Queen* and even *A Dream*, but on the principle of ethnic self-discovery, necessitating a journey to unfamiliar territory and thus a different means of rendering national space itself. *Shadows* worked with a conception of, and relationship between, space and its inhabitants that was specific to its particular site of exploration, rather than constituting a generic site of all-Union importance within the 'Friendship of Peoples' mythology.

Chapter 3

SERGEI PARADJANOV'S CARPATHIAN JOURNEY

In the July 1965 issue of the Ukrainian illustrated monthly *Ranok* (*Morning*), readers might have seen a poem by Hanna Shaburiak extolling the beauty of Hutsulshchyna, the 'Land of the Hutsuls'.

> I am quite sure and I simply don't believe
> That I will find something more my own in life,
> Than the colourful Hutsul land.
> They say the ornamental designs of Kosmach,
> Like a tunic of earthly beads, -
> Is the germ of great Ukraine.[1]

The poem at once takes possession of 'Hutsul land' by calling it 'my own', while the term 'colourful' pointed towards its domestication within a folkloric mode. Shaburiak, moreover, assumed her readers' familiarity with the material culture of the region in her reference to the 'ornamental designs of Kosmach', the latter a village with several health spas, camping resorts and a folk arts (*kraevedcheskii*) museum nearby. The next line, 'Like a tunic of earthly beads', connects these multiple meanings for the tourist observer, associating Hutsul-made objects with the landscape itself, interweaving nature and culture. The final line places a particular nationalistic value on Hutsulshchyna: this is the primordial space, which gave rise to the modern nation.

The Hutsuls are, trans-historically and metonymically, the pre-modern 'us' in the present. Yet in claiming Hutsulshchyna as one's own – perhaps because of this claim to possession – Ukrainians would have had to admit the exceptionality of such a space. While they probably had never met one of these iconic sheep-herding mountain-eers called 'Hutsuls', living predominantly in the sparsely populated Chernivets and Ivano-Frankivsk provinces, readers were inevitably familiar with Hutsulshchyna as a site of national importance to the republic. Magazines like *Ranok*, and other newspapers and travel guidebooks, had recently been promoting the new 'Hutsulshchyna' camping lodge near Kosmach, where Ukrainian tourists could enjoy hiking in the Carpathians, relaxing in health spas, and watching real Hutsuls make their favourite kind of sheep's milk cheese, *brynza*, on the nearby collective farm 'Radians'ka Verkhovyna'. Hutsulshchyna, and the Hutsul herself, straddled several contiguous sites of mean-ing production, at once a 'colourful' oddity on display for poets and tourists alike and as a scene of national belonging for various gen-erations of Ukrainian artists and intellectuals.

Sergei Paradjanov's *Shadows of Forgotten Ancestors* (*Tini zabutykh pred-kiv*), released in Kyiv theatres shortly after Shaburiak's poem, was one of the most amazing expressions of this aesthetic unity of possession and difference, and it charted new territory for Ukrainian cinema. Supporters and critics of the film both understood the originality of the film and the watershed that it in fact became for Dovzhenko Studio. True to the 1911 novella by Mykhailo Kotsiubyns'kyi's of the same title, the plot of the film could not be simpler: a Hutsul boy named Ivanko falls in love with a girl named Marichka from a rival family. As a young man, he has to take work as a shepherd high up in the mountains and leaves Marichka alone, pregnant, in the village below. Ivanko returns at the end of the grazing season to find that his love has fallen into the Cheremosh River and died. After a prolonged period of mourning, he marries another woman, Palanha, whom he never loves, and refuses her the children she desires. Eventually his wife has an affair with another man, and the film ends with a fight between the two men, after which Ivanko dies from his wounds.

The simplicity and linearity of the plot, however, contrasts with the chaos of the camera work and the Orientalizing beauty of the Carpathian ethnoscape. In their standard textbook, *Film History: An Introduction*, David Bordwell and Kristin Thompson call *Shadows* 'a flurry of hysterically modernist techniques'.[2] The film's eclecticism is evident in the frequent shifts between literary, theatrical and uniquely cinematic visual motifs. *Shadows* is divided into 'chapters', indicated by a red intertitle, which not only pays homage to the literary source of the story, but also to a broader literary tradition that treated Hutsulshchyna as a site of national significance. Beyond the literary narrative, however, Hutsul performance and the spectacle of ritual and everyday life lie at the centre of the film. Cinematographer Iuri Illienko frames Hutsul dancers in tableaux, standing in a perfect line, as if performing onstage for an implicitly visible audience. At other times, he aligns the spectator's view with a participant in the action, but fluidly moves between subjective and objective perspective without cutting, which evinces the intimate connection between difference and possession present also in Shaburiak's poem about Hutsulshchyna cited at the beginning of this chapter. Breaking from classical film form, the makers of *Shadows* eschewed the establishing shot and frequent close-ups, demonstrating their principle interest in community and human interaction with the landscape over and above the mountain vista and the individual. Finally, *Shadows* is experimental in its use of sound, with an eclectic mix of symphonic and diegetic music and dialogue, the latter seemingly found on location. In employing these visual, narrative and aural motifs, taken from the cinema, theatre and literature, the filmmakers hoped to place the fictional story of Ivanko and Marichka within an authentic site of folkloric reality.

At the time, no one would have called such a film an ordinary example of Dovzhenko Studio's repertoire or, for that matter, that of any of the film capitals of the 1960s. *Shadows*, nonetheless, became a popular phenomenon in the USSR that stretched far beyond the film festival circuit. Part of the reason for this popular reception of such a 'hysterically modernist' film was because *Shadows* was in dialogue with a long tradition of Carpathophilia in Eastern Europe. Hutsulshchyna and the Carpathians were exploited by Soviet cinema as early as 1939, when western Ukraine was first incorporated into the USSR. Under Stalin, the agents of history were not the Carpathian highlanders, but the modernizing state. By comparison, *Shadows* emphasized ethnographic authenticity, which relocated Hutsulshchyna as an implicit counterpoint to the modernizing state. In stressing 'authenticity', 1960s-era engagement with the Carpathians denied the applicability of the modernization narrative. The discourse of authenticity in and about *Shadows* functioned both to question Stalin-era aesthetic principles, a common element of the cultural Thaw, while establishing a new means of Ukrainian representation.

Long before Paradjanov's film appeared on the big screen in late 1965, Dovzhenko Studio began promoting it within the republic as a cultural object of national importance. A press release from early 1964 stated that 'Hutsuls [themselves] were making this film', which produced an 'astonishing' effect of 'authenticity' in the production. It went on to stress the leading actor's personal connection to Hutsulshchyna: 'Ivan Mykolaichuk was born in those very same Carpathian lands[...] He does not perform, but lives in this image.'[3] Whereas Shaburiak's 'Sonata of Hutsulshchyna' demonstrated how objects of a material culture become nationally possessed, the press release showed how the human image itself embodied such a site of national importance. In both the poem and film, humans become not mere inhabitants of the land, but in fact part of the land.

In conflating land and people, such representations helped establish a new ethnographic mode of representing Ukrainians in Soviet visual culture. The poem and the film, moreover, addressed a reader/spectator who was positioned as a participant/observer, called on to decode the nationalistic value of their visual qualities. Like the folkloric, the ethnographic mode identifies a particular relationship between visual style and how non-Russians are written into film narration. The folkloric mode, associated with Stalinist cinema, introduced the spectacle of 'national colour' within a classical organization of filmic space and narration. The Stalinist narrative teleology indicated that, while non-Russian subjects were primordially located in particular spaces, the 'national' hero nonetheless stands above them. By contrast, the ethnographic mode highlighted visual style and circular narration, and the human subject exists within the landscape, unable to stand apart from it. Whereas earlier Ukrainian films that dealt with national subject-matter imagined porous national boundaries – either through the return narrative or within the political union of Ukraine and Russia – *Shadows of Forgotten Ancestors* suggests an entirely enclosed and ahistorical space, penetrated only by the filmmakers and, indirectly, the spectator. Paradjanov's film certainly contained a cohesive narrative structure, but its intended ethnic texture is conveyed, not through narrative, or not through narrative alone, but through its observational camerawork, at times even documentary-like, which alternately serves to alienate and attract the spectator. This attraction/alienation principle that the camera establishes parallels Shaburiak's construction of ethnoscape through a possession/difference dialectic. To make sense of the poem's and the film's nationalistic value, the reader/

spectator had to first possess such difference within themselves, and convergently, understand Hutsulshchyna as the 'germ of great Ukraine'.

In earlier chapters, I used the term 'folkloric', in contrast to 'ethnographic', to refer to Stalinist cinema's mobilization of folklore to justify a political programme of patriotic unity. The folkloric mode sought to represent a simultaneous modernization and historicization of particular non-Russian national traditions. In Chapter 1, I examined Ihor Savchenko's 1941 historical-biographical film, *Bohdan Khmel'nyts'kyi*, to show how plot and iconography became uniform in the Stalinist cinema of the periphery, even as they continually brought attention to particularistic concerns of individual nations within the Soviet Union. In this chapter, I address how and why this shift from the folkloric to the ethnographic took place in representations of the Ukrainian Carpathians. As I argued in Chapter 2, this emphasis on representing difference over unity, and style over narrative, fits into larger cultural processes related to Thaw-era aesthetic problems, indigenization policies at republican studios and political imperatives that favoured limited devolution of authority. This chapter looks closely at the cinematic results of those processes, in one of the most unusual films released in the Soviet Union during the 1960s.

Paradjanov's *Shadows of Forgotten Ancestors* functioned on many levels – at once affirming a domesticated and generically driven notion of the folkloric for Ukrainian Transcarpathia, while remaining a highly experimental film appearing at the height of the cultural Thaw. By winning a number of awards at international film festivals – most notably in Mar del Plata, Argentina, Rome, New York and Sydney – *Shadows* became the first film that Western critics would identify as 'Ukrainian' rather than generally 'Soviet' or 'Russian'.[4]

As Dovzhenko Studio's press release determined, the guiding principle of media hype was the film's supposed ethnographic authenticity, located in the actuality and spontaneity of Hutsul performance on screen. In promoting Paradjanov's film, the language of authenticity took on a signification that, while building upon Thaw-era concerns with representational honesty, pointed towards a style that transcended realism. In this way, the promotional language for *Shadows* approached a type of jargon, in the sense that 'authenticity' took on, as Theodor Adorno suggested in *The Jargon of Authenticity*, a quality of 'mystification'. With such 'magical' properties contained within the concept of 'authenticity', its idealized content appears to exist simply in mobilizing its discourse. Authenticity, thus, conflates reflection on a philosophical problem with the actual objects of that reflection,[5] in this case those objects which provided the film with its ethnic 'texture'. In positioning Hutsuls and Hutsulshchyna as authenticated objects, they are meant to transcend both their contemporary and historical existence.

Important here, also, is the specificity of the claim to authenticity – that is, the historical context in which it arose – in addition to the formal practices that were intended to render cinematic objects authentically. Even when the press attempted to subvert the studio's claim to a transcendent ethnographic authenticity, it approached the film according to its own visual and conceptual logic, rather than *vis-à-vis* the film's ideology or realist verisimilitude. Whereas these latter concerns were related principally to the aesthetic principles at work within the film, the problem of authenticity touched on the very processes of production, which were also on display and constituted a key source of Paradjanov's film's final meaning. One satirical drawing, which appeared in the 19 November 1964 issue of *Radians'ka kul'tura*, depicted the director, flanked by his cinematographer Iurii Illienko and set designer Hryhorii Iakutovych (Figure 3.1). All three are engulfed in an enormous *keptar'*, an iconic sheepskin vest worn by the Carpathian highlanders, with their ordinary clothes underneath. We see Paradjanov and Illienko in contemporary clothing – the director seemingly in a three-piece suit, and Illienko in a more casual shirt with rolled-up sleeves – while Iakutovych is outfitted in a second embroidered shirt, along with the characteristic feathered hat of a Carpathian highlander. Even as Illienko holds a camera to identify his profession, the visual metaphor of the shadows behind them indicates that the lights – and ostensibly the camera too – had been turned on them. While in the film, and in Kotsiubyns'kyi's novella from which it was adapted, the 'shadows' are cast ostensibly by the lost culture of the Hutsuls, who now lurk only in the distant and secluded corners of time and space, the cartoonist associated these shadows with the celebrity status of the film's production almost a year before any common reader of the newspaper had actually seen it on the screen. The cartoonist made the film-makers into actors within a second drama about the production of the film, in which the spectator too is invited to participate in the film's discourse of authenticity.[6]

The problem of authenticity in *Shadows of Forgotten Ancestors* demonstrates how the film became a matter of popular interest, associating

Авторам фільму «Тіні забутих предків» С. Параджано-
ву. Ю. Ільєнку, Ю. Якутовичу

Дружній шарж художника М. Маловського.

Забутих предків тіні нам
з екрану
Вони в цілому показали
непогано.
Важаємо ж їм створювати
нині
Уже не предків,

І тим більш не тіні —
Так само переконливо
й любовно
Сучасників портрети
повнокровні.

Юрій БОБОШКО.

Figure 3.1 'To the authors of *Shadows of Forgotten Ancestors*', drawing from 19 November 1964 in *Radians'ka kul'tura*

questions of cinematic authorship with film style and popular reception. In positioning such a self-consciously strange film in relation to notions of 'the authentic', moreover, its authors and studio representatives, as well as the press, implied a conceptual distance from the Stalinist folkloric with the assertion that Ukraine might still be unfamiliar territory. The principle of authenticity thus determined the production context as well as the film's aesthetic means.

*   *   *

As a student of Ihor Savchenko (dir., *Bohdan Khmel'nyts'kyi*), Paradjanov first came to Ukraine while working as an assistant director on his teacher's *The Third Blow* (*Tretii udar*) and *Taras Shevchenko* in 1948–50. After Savchenko's untimely death in the midst of filming the latter, Paradjanov returned to the film institute in Moscow to complete his studies under Alexander Dovzhenko, who helped him procure a permanent position at Kyiv Studio in 1952. There, he made his first film, *Andriesh* (1952), a fairytale that expanded upon his thesis project from a year earlier. A non-event in Soviet cinema at the time, in hindsight *Andriesh* looks vaguely familiar, and introduces several themes that preoccupied the director in *Shadows* and later films: the animacy of nature, material culture and an interest in folklore.

Many of the film director's biographers attribute this interest in the ethnic exotic to Paradjanov's cosmopolitan upbringing.[7] He was born to a Russified, middle-class, Armenian family in Tbilisi in 1924, a period during which many Armenians were leaving Georgia for Armenia, due to the ethnic conflict that emerged during Menshevik control of the city (1917–18). The Parajanians, who remained successful businesspeople during NEP, opted to stay.[8] Sergei first attended a technical school for rail workers during the war, having avoided military service after failing the health exam. A year later, he decided on a career in singing, graduating from the Tbilisi Opera Academy in 1945. After another change in career plans, he ended up in Moscow at VGIK studying film directing. Paradjanov returned to Kyiv to serve as assistant director on Vladimir Braun's *Maksimka* (1952), where he met and married Svitlana Sherbatiuk, the daughter of the Ukrainian ambassador to Canada. Ivan Dziuba recalled the first time he heard the name 'Paradjanov': the future Ukrainian dissident was attending a performance of the Kyiv Philharmonic in 1959, and caught sight of Svitlana, whom he defined as the most beautiful woman at the concert. He asked his friend who she was, to which the reply was, 'Don't bother, some Armenian has already abducted [*zaharbav*] her', alluding to a common stereotype of the Caucasus kidnapper.[9]

Paradjanov was equally derogatory in his first recollection of the people he met in Ukraine. During a December 1964 meeting in Moscow to honour Paradjanov's success with the film, he decried the 'provincialism [*khutorianstvo*] and little-Russian mentality [*malorossiishchina*]' that prevailed at the studio, alluding to the safe and static folkloric imagery that characterized Ukrainian cinema particularly during the 1950s.[10] And yet, apart from *Andriesh*, the films that he made before *Shadows* were largely part of this system of Stalinist folklorics: from the *kolkhoz* comedy *The Top Guy*, a musical, *Ukrainian Rhapsody* and a social drama about resistance to a religious cult in the Donbass called *Flower on the Stone* (*Kvitka na kameni*, 1962), there was little indication of what Paradjanov had to offer Ukrainian cinema. He intentionally detached himself from studio politics and, consequently, we have few documents that reveal much about his early career in Ukraine.

We receive some sense of the director's future concerns at a meeting of Dovzhenko Studio's directorial board in June 1962 regarding *Flower on the Stone*, during which Paradjanov complained of his failure to reveal the 'authentic Donbass atmosphere'. He blamed this shortcoming on the screenwriter's refusal to allow the actors to speak in 'contemporary Ukrainian'.[11] These concerns with linguistic authenticity, which would take centre stage in the production of his next film, might seem strange coming from such a determined monoglot, but for Paradjanov, performance of ethnicity was of key importance in his aesthetic outlook. In essence, the director was more concerned with the sound of the Donbas dialect (*surzhyk*) than with what the characters were saying. In this respect, he had little interest in Ukrainian language politics of the early 1960s, with its emphasis on promoting a standardized, literary Ukrainian in the cinema. Vadym Sobko, the screenwriter that Paradjanov blamed for the lack of linguistic authenticity in *Flower on the Stone*, for example, stated during the First Congress of the Ukrainian Filmmakers' Union, 'If we continue to speak such *surzhyk* in films, we will beat ourselves with our own most important weapon'.[12]

In Volodymyr Denysenko's *A Dream*, moreover, one complaint about the film was Mykolaichuk's vaguely western Ukrainian-inflected speech. Tymofii Levchuk suggested that another actor – one who spoke standard Ukrainian – overdub Mykolaichuk's lines due to the gravity of Shevchenko's representation.[13] Thus, many at the studio, especially among the older generation who used Ukrainian in their daily lives, viewed the respectability of a literary language as an escape from folkloric representations, with its frequent mobilizations of *surzhyk* or Ukrainian-accented Russian as components of aural spectacle in Ukrainian cinema. Shevchenko, Ukraine's first modern cultural figure, could not in good conscience speak in the 'language of backward clichés'.[14] Paradjanov, in highlighting the 'authentic', however, viewed national difference as an aesthetic, rather than political, problem. Difference had to be discovered, experienced and revealed, and in this project, the outsider's lack of knowledge might contribute more than those who commanded cultural authority, associated as they were with a compromised position *vis-à-vis* a discredited Stalinist aesthetic. In other words, even if Ukrainian characters stopped speaking Russian, neither authenticity nor realism would necessarily be the result. In fact, the flawless Ukrainian speech of historical figures like Briullov or Zhukovsky in *A Dream* seemed anything but authentic, and rather highlighted the explicitly political project at the root of Denysenko's work.

Despite his penchant for linguistic spectacle and rejection of mainstream language politics in Ukraine, Paradjanov in no way offered a return to the Stalinist folkloric. In fact, he wrote extensively about his early 'failures' in 'Eternal Motion', his first and only work of film theory, published in *Iskusstvo kino* four years later as he was coasting on the success and fame garnered from *Shadows*. Therein, he emphasized his journey to discover the 'authentic' Ukraine while collecting materials for production:

> When I began work on the film *The Top Guy*, I exposed myself to the Ukrainian village for the first time. And I was exposed to the staggering beauty of its texture, and its poetry. And I tried to express its charm on the screen. But from the blows of the plot – and this, in essence, was an unimportant humouresque – the entire task was shattered. Not with what proved to be landscapes, stone-like peasant women, storks, tractors, and straw wreaths. The material on which the films *Flower on the Stone* and *A Notion* were made is deeply memorable to me. The folk thread, sewing, the imprint. Ancient songs of Ukraine. I wanted to convey the world of these songs in all their protogenic charm. I wanted to convey the folk 'vision' without museum make-up; to return all of this staggering embroidery, reliefs, and tiles to their creative source, to merge them into a united spiritual act.[15]

Here, Paradjanov tells us that his inspiration came from travel and observation. He positioned himself as an amateur ethnographer in his active discovery of Ukraine's 'protogenic charm'. Paradjanov tried to distance himself from a Stalinist folkloric, represented by the 'landscapes, stone-like peasant women, storks, tractors, and straw wreaths', and later with 'museum make-up'. In the articulation of his aesthetic principles, Paradjanov demanded his ethnic subject carry elements of folkloric colour, but asserted that authenticity warranted such exotic human images. Moreover, landscapes could not exist independent of culture, as generic spaces in nature. Paradjanov believed that space not only determined human culture, but that humans were part of the landscape itself. As 'Eternal Motion' argued, his journeys took him to the Carpathians, where he discovered the ideal and transcendent space for a more expressive national representation, a space both familiar from his earlier travels and yet 'savage', strange and unfamiliar.[16] In encountering the Ukrainian periphery, Paradjanov had discovered a space seemingly untouched by Soviet modernity, and it was such a space that invited an extensive and inclusive discussion in the Republic on the authenticity of the 'Ukrainian national character'.

Carpathophilia in Context

In 1962, Paradjanov and his cast and crew began their ascent into the mountains, which would transform the thematic focus of Ukrainian cinema for the next 15 years. The national spectacle of the Ukrainian Carpathians represented in Paradjanov's film, however, has a much longer history, first emerging in Polish literature with Józef Korzeniowski's 1840 romantic play *The Carpathian Highlanders*,[17] then as the subject of Lviv ethnographer Volodymyr Shukhevych's four-volume work, *Hutsulshchyna* (1899–1909), and later alongside Ukrainian modernism with the work of artists Ivan Trush (1869–1941) and Olena Kul'chyts'ka (1877–1967) and writers Ivan Franko (1856–1916), Mykhailo Kotsiubyns'kyi (1864–1913), Ol'ha Kobylians'ka (1863–1942) and Vasyl' Stefanyk (1871–1936). After World War II, the Carpathians provided not only an ideological component of Ukraine's 'reunification' but more importantly, it became an exotic space of self-knowledge for Kyiv artists and intellectuals, a space they could identify as essentially different from the Russified East.

The imagery of the Carpathians in Ukraine emerged in tandem with a broader visual discourse on mountains, enlisted primarily towards promoting the growing potential for tourism in the Caucasus and Crimea. As Anne Gorsuch and Diane Koenker argue, 'For eastern Europeans inside multinational empires, tourism became one mechanism to help to define self and Other, and it contributed to reifying nation-building projects'.[18] As Paradjanov's film finally hit theatres in fall 1965, *Ranok* published a photo montage that complimented *Shadows*. The magazine highlighted a group of men and women dressed in traditional highlander costumes preparing a horse for tilling the fields alongside a group of backpackers leaving a large tourist centre. While Caucasus tours were far more extensive and prevalent in the tourist literature, the Carpathian tours were unique in the Soviet Union in that the organization of tourism centred on experiencing the region's inhabitants, rather than solely on nature activities and relaxation.[19] With the increasing popularity of tourism, Kyivans and other eastern Ukrainians were invited to visit the mountains, and to associate it with their own national space as the 'germ of great Ukraine', waiting to be discovered and personally possessed.

Viktor Ivanov's *Oleksa Dovbush*, a minor hit for Dovzhenko Studio in 1959, attempted to establish the national importance of the Carpathians, but did so within a conventional generic and stylistic framework of Stalinist cinema. As a popular historical epic, the film located a primordial struggle between Ukrainians and Poles among the Carpathian Hutsuls. Dovbush, the legendary eighteenth-century bandit-turned-rebel leader of the highlanders, defends the Hutsuls against the arbitrary will of the Polish *szlachta*. After swearing a blood oath to a dying revolutionary to avenge his comrades' deaths at the hand of the local Polish lord, Pan Jablonski, Dovbush leaves his life of petty crime to gather a group of Hutsul rebels. Typical of the socialist realist 'master plot', the titular hero moves from the spontaneity of local banditry to the social consciousness and responsibility of a revolutionary leader. Moreover, the film answered the demand in Ukrainian cinema to locate a historic – and, indeed, somewhat familial – connection between east and west Ukraine. Although 'Russians' are absent in the film, the presence of the Cossack Mykhailov in Dovbush's group as a representative 'from Ukraine' narratively associates the two liberation struggles of the *haidamaky* and the *opryshky*, and writes the impetus for 'unification' of the two parts of Ukraine into the eighteenth century. Most importantly for rendering the film as Socialist Realism, this agent of Ukraine's anger is an iconic 'positive hero', at once extraordinary in his combat abilities and flawlessly virtuous in his moral outlook. The camera constantly hovers on Dovbush's face in close-up, his eyes revealing compassion and beauty, while his thick moustache emphasizes his paternal sternness and absolute commitment to the revolutionary cause.

While over 23 million people saw *Oleksa Dovbush* in 1959, critics were dismissive of its 'traditional dramaturgy', perhaps pointing towards its Stalinist mode of narration. Nina Ignat'eva wrote in the January 1961 issue of *Iskusstvo kino* that while 'a striving for poetic elevation ... is in general associated with works of Ukrainian cinema, this sometimes emerges as "sugary" and falsely "touching little pictures [*kartynky*]" '. This is precisely what happened with Ivanov's film, she argued, with its sappy love story and endless shots of cliff faces and men on horseback chasing each other. The plot, Ignat'eva wrote, was 'traditional' in the 'stupidest meaning of the word'.[20] Nonetheless, what the critic found appealing about the film was the 'colourfulness of Hutsul everyday life and the originality of Carpathian nature'. Here we find the critic more willing to accept the film's ethnographic texture, while the director's intention seems to be closer to the folkloric message of trans-historicity and a narrative of unity through diversity. Critics, however, noticed the film's representation of the Hutsul's exotic world, transposing it in the process onto the chaos of Carpathian nature. Here, despite the fairly democratic historical teleology (eastern and western Ukrainians uniting to eliminate Polish aristocratic injustice) of a chapter leading towards Ukrainian unification, critics largely picked up on the film's ability (or lack thereof) to represent these human objects accurately and authentically. As Ignat'eva suggests, it is the film-maker's gaze – like that of the tourist above – which catalogues and defines such authenticities.

Paradjanov also weighed in on the debate about *Oleksa Dovbush*, but from a distance of seven years. In 'Eternal Motion', the director caustically wrote,

> They [the film crew] came to the Carpathians cinematically educated. More importantly, they drew it with exotic and decorative motifs, but we did not recognise any Hutsuls in the film. We did not see their gait, did not hear their charming speech, and the movement of thought.[21]

Paradjanov counterposed his conception of ethnographic authenticity with film-makers' specialized knowledge of cinematic technique and generic conventions. As Ignat'eva and Paradjanov implied, film-makers would judge a film's realism not only according to narrative convention, but also according to the visual quality of the human object. Paradjanov wrote in his article that aesthetic 'power is [located] in the authentic object',[22] and here it seems he could alternately be speaking about the 'ornamental designs' or the Hutsul itself.

As he did with his own film *Flowers on the Stone*, Paradjanov took offence to the 'inauthentic' language of *Oleksa Dovbush*. Like the Donbass miner, Hutsuls should not speak either perfect Russian or Ukrainian, despite the problem of comprehension that dialect presented.[23] Paradjanov's claim to authenticity in *Shadows of Forgotten Ancestors* was associated with a process of de-familiarizing the ethnic texture of the film, and with a rejection of direct translation. In this way, he imagined the ethnographic concept of 'national colour' as a particular form of untranslatability in his film. Whereas *Oleksa Dovbush* employs the sounds of the *trembita*, *floiar* and *drymba* – the traditional instruments of the Hutsuls – it does so with the accompaniment of a symphonic score. While Ivanov's film occasionally uses dialectal terms and phrases, especially to characterize Uniate priests and older Hutsuls, the bulk of the dialogue is spoken in flawless literary Russian. Paradjanov would later break with both of these normalizing conventions in crafting the unusual soundtrack in *Shadows*. The elements of soundtrack include untranslated voices and non-verbal music, which function to immerse the spectator in the ethnoscape of Hutsulshchyna, rather than perform a mediating role with the cinematic conventions of musical composition and dubbing-over with literary voices. As Paradjanov certainly believed after reading Kotsiubyns'kyi's novella in 1961, this interest in de-familiarizing the aural dimensions of ethnic texture also informed the writer's own use of language.

When production on *Shadows* began, the studio intended that the adaptation of Kotsiubyns'kyi's 1911 novella would contribute to the celebration planned for the writer's centenary in 1964. The novella's plot is structured around Ivanko's three journeys into the mountains. The first time is as a child, when he hears a Pan-like creature play the flute. His second journey concerns his time spent as a shepherd, where he first encounters the Marichka nymph, and the third time occurs after Iura beats Ivanko, during which the Marichka nymph lures him to his death. In a manner typical of literary impressionism, Kotsiubyns'kyi blurs the boundaries between objective and subjective narration. The reader is never confident whether the supernatural elements of the story are really occuring, or if Kotsiubyns'kyi is offering us an interpretation of events already filtered through Hutsul demonology: his text is littered with references to 'sad mountains', 'sleeping walls', 'breathing fire' and the Cheremosh 'relating its dreams'. Through such metaphors, inanimate objects and natural processes are imbued with anthropomorphic agency. The Hutsuls interact and communicate with these objects and 'dark forces' as they would with other human beings. These visual cues point towards Kotsiubyns'kyi's explicit interest in creating a 'painterly' text. He consistently referred to his 'exotic' stories about Hutsuls, Tatars and peasants from Moldavia and Capri as 'sketches' and 'pictures', demonstrating his concern with modernist literature's intertextual relationship to the visual arts. Here, 'colour' is not only an ethnographic trope, as in Shaburiak's poem, but also an important textual component, which serves as the iconographic bridge from the object of nature to the human subject and its material culture.

Paradjanov brought these painterly concerns with ethnographic colour to the cinema in his adaptation. In the writer's language, 'colour' is embedded in his excessive use of metaphor, which frequently functions intertextually by reference to visual forms: 'The entire world was like a fairy-tale', Kotsiubyns'kyi writes at the beginning of the novella, more likely an allusion to the contemporaneous Symbolist renderings of fairy-tales than to the oral or written texts themselves.[24] As Paradjanov would be in his adaptation, Kotsiubyns'kyi was concerned with the verbal and aural ethnoscape of the Carpathians. The language of the narration furthermore conveys the confusion of narrative voice. When the writer travelled to the Carpathians for his fieldwork, he experienced a different form of Ukrainian than the one he grew up with, and wanted to convey these differences with the hybridized language that he employed in the text. For example, Kotsiubyns'kyi used the term '*bovhar*' instead of the standard Ukrainian '*pastukh*' for cowherd, and '*buryshka*' for '*kartoplia*', meaning potato. In this way, Kotsiubyns'kyi's language functioned on the level of 'colour', in that it sought to convey a spectacle beyond the direct capabilities of a literary text.

Not surprisingly, such an impressionistic text, initially published in Hapsburg Lemberg (now Lviv) in 1912 to avoid Russian imperial censorship of Ukrainian-language literature, also fell outside of the commonly acknowledged Soviet canon of Kotsiubyns'kyi's work. A 1929 Kyiv edition of the story, however, attempted to highlight a realist *Shadows* by including a series of illustrations drawn by Olena

Kul'chyts'ka. Her images functioned to normalize the strangeness of Hutsulshchyna and its culture. The illustration of Ivanko beginning his ascent into the mountains presents a clear and almost clichéd narrative line. This juxtaposition of realist illustrations with the writer's impressionistic language further affected the novella's generically hybridized quality. Stalin-era criticism of *Shadows*, what little there was of it, emphasized Kotsiubyns'kyi's 'sociological' concerns. For example, P. Zlatoustov wrote during the same year as the publication of the Kul'chyts'ka-illustrated version that the writer was largely interested in the 'demoralization' of poverty, which expressed itself in the Hutsul culture of vendettas, superstitions and 'savage customs'.[25]

Although Zlatousov's interpretation remained dominant into the 1960s, and critics of Paradjanov would draw on him and his protégés to disparage the film's lack of verisimilitude to Kotsiubyns'kyi's original, a critical divergence also emerged in the years leading up to the writer's centenary. Olena Kravets's work of criticism, *M.M. Kotsiubyn'skyi on the Everyday Life of the People* (1963), for example, advanced the writer's work as an example of fictional ethnography, which was moreover a defence of the development of national culture, literature and art in Ukraine.[26] The promotion of Kotsiubyns'kyi as a nationalistic icon was certainly different from the proto-socialist realist author and intimate friend of Gorky that Stalin-era scholars had identified. Alongside this re-evaluation of Kotsiubyns'kyi, Paradjanov was given a greater degree of artistic freedom to interpret this most eccentric work of Ukrainian modernism.

Performing the Authentic Object in *Shadows of Forgotten Ancestors*

In adapting a work of such importance to the history of Ukrainian literature, Paradjanov was strangely uninterested in hiring Ukrainian actors for the leading roles. Illienko convinced him to hire his wife, Sovremennik Theatre actress Larisa Kadochnikova, as Marichka. For the role of Ivanko, Paradjanov found MKhAT actor Gennadii Iukhtin perfect for the job.[27] Thus, we find the director particularly uninvolved in the cultural politics of Dovzhenko Studio at the time, wishing instead to appeal to the leading actor's fame over an ability to speak Ukrainian. As assistant director Volodymyr Luhovs'kyi recalls, Ukrainian Goskino was at first supportive of Iukhtin for his ability to bring in audiences, which might be impossible with an unknown Ukrainian actor. Clearly, Goskino hoped for another hit along the lines of *Oleksa Dovbush*.

When the Film Dean of the Kyiv Theatrical Institute Viktor Ivchenko asked Paradjanov to consider his acting student Ivan Mykolaichuk for the role of Ivanko, the director was less than excited. Due to Ivchenko's seniority at the studio, however, Paradjanov was compelled to send a telegram to the Carpathian village of Chortoryia where Ivan lived, requesting that the acting student come to Kyiv for a script reading. The director had no intention, however, of casting Mykolaichuk in the role, and even refused to watch him read for the part. During his audition, Luhovs'kyi recalls that if the cinematographer had not been there, he would have mistaken the performer for an actual Hutsul.[28] While Paradjanov and Illienko continued to insist upon Iukhtin, the Dovzhenko Studio Artistic Council viewed Mykolaichuk's reading and voted overwhelmingly for him, thus prioritizing authentic performance over marketing possibilities.

After finalizing the details of production, Paradjanov and the cast and crew travelled to Verkhovyna, the largest town in Hutsulshchyna, where they began work on the film. Ukrainian graphic artist Hryhorii Iakutovych was hired as a set designer and 'guide' through the Carpathians.[29] Iakutovych, a respected young graphic artist and specialist in Carpathian studies, was illustrating a newer edition of Kotsiubyns'kyi's novella. His images were strikingly different from Kul'chyts'ka's 1929 drawings, the former reflecting interest in the *avant-garde* during the Thaw. The expressions of the figures are crudely drawn, and space itself is flattened and de-contextualized. Human figures fade into the background. The randomly-placed symbols in this visual environment lack both the depth of natural space and the psychological investigation of Kul'chyts'ka's earlier illustrations.

Paradjanov also hired Uzhhorod painter Fedir Manailo (1911–78) as an 'artistic consultant' on the film, to whom screenwriter Ivan Chendei introduced the director earlier in 1963. While Manailo worked in a number of styles and genres during his long career – from Socialist Realism to romantic mountain vistas – his images of Hutsuls from the 1930s, which interested Paradjanov, were strictly in a neo-primitivist vein. Texture, colour and pattern are the important formal elements in these paintings. Faces are crudely rendered and do not reveal the subject, as they are subsumed under the objects and symbols of everyday life and material culture. We also notice the characteristic neo-primitivist flattening of space in Manailo's Hutsul images, which heightened their collage-like feel. In Paradjanov's decision to include these artists within the film crew, he associated himself with a revived appreciation for Ukrainian modernists, whose interest in the Carpathians implicitly connected them with the independence and autonomist movements from the turn of the century through the 1920s.

Yet claims about the film's authenticity were grounded in a notion of ethnographic realism which valued the particular visual quality of the human object and its organic relationship to the natural world over representations grounded in generic or Stalinist conventions. Paradjanov's decision to film almost exclusively on location in Hutsulshchyna represented the convergence of Ukrainian modernism with the unique Thaw-era realist discourse. For the director, Hutsulshchyna was a space which was both mediated through such modernist representations and a real site of ethnographic knowledge. In promotional material about the film, press releases constantly emphasized that the film crew spent extensive time in the Verkhovyna region, investigating the sounds and colours emanating from the 'strange' land of the Hutsuls. It furthermore stressed that Paradjanov was shooting the film not far from the leading actor's native village. As the cast and crew completed filming in late summer of 1964, features on the production of the film gradually appeared in the Republican press, particularly on the actor himself. Iurii Bohdashevs'kyi's article in the June 1964 issue of the Ukrainian-language film monthly *Novyny kinoekrana* emphasized the specificity of his upbringing, mentioning by name his uncle Petro and aunt Varka. The film was being shot 'not far from the village where the boy was born'. Mykolaichuk's activity while on location for *Shadows* blurred the line between his role and his performative self. Bohdashevs'kyi explained,

> Ivan met with the Hutsuls, listened to their songs, their leisurely stories. People liked this affable boy, and called him 'our Ivan'... And in fact, he was 'their own'. His house [*khata*], where he grew up among a rambunctious crowd of brothers and sisters, was not far away.[30]

Two months later, as the film was in post-production, the magazine featured an interview with Paradjanov, who also affirmed the crew's 'intimate' familiarity with the exotica of Hutsul material and spiritual culture. Critic Oleksii Miroshnychenko's accompanying article brought out the authentic character of Mykolaichuk, whom we can look in the eye and see his resemblance to the Ivanko that Kotsiubyns'kyi himself had found in the Carpathians. In a repetition of Luhovs'kyi's audition story, Miroshnychenko reported that Ivan's performance of *koliadky* (Christmas carols) so affected Paradjanov that the director was scared to halt the action after Illienko completed the shot, for fear that the crew would disturb the event itself. At another point, Mykolaichuk purportedly invited the crew to his home in Chortoryi so they could experience 'genuine Hutsul customs'.[31] In December, L. Korobchak featured an article solely on the actor, quoting Mykolaichuk about his role in *Shadows*: Ivanko 'is my *zemliak* [fellow countryman]. He is close to me, and I can sense him.' The author continued:

> The 23-year old actor found himself in the fairly-tale Carpathian region – dear to his soul – both legs on Hutsul land with the cries of the shepherds, sounds of the *trembita* and little girls singing. Mykolaichuk worked with delight, the character came out easily and freely, and [he] improvised well.[32]

In describing Mykolaichuk's authentic character, however, critics objectified him not as an ideal Ukrainian, but as a feature of the Carpathian ethnoscape. Poet and Dovzhenko Studio screenwriter Ivan Drach reviewed the film for *Literaturna Ukraina*, writing that the actor 'naturally' perceived the world 'as a Hutsul' from the time he was born. He concluded by asking the spectator to 'rush to sip from [the film's] pure Carpathian spring'.[33]

Mykolaichuk was a willing participant in this everyday performance as both a Hutsul and as a Soviet citizen conscious and proud of his Ukrainian nationality. When applying for membership to the Ukrainian Union of Cinematographers in March 1966, the actor answered each of the questions on the Russian-language application in Ukrainian. He listed his social position as 'peasant [*selianyn*]' (rather than 'civil servant [*sluzhashchii*]', which was more common for a film industry worker) and crossed out the Russian letter 'g' (for '*god*'), writing in a Ukrainian 'r' (for '*rik*') in the line for date of birth.[34] When reporting in *Mystetstvo* (*Art*) magazine on his trip to Argentina for the Mar del Plata film festival, Mykolaichuk indicated that he, as a Ukrainian from the western oblasts, rather than the film itself, was the attraction for the many émigrés in the audience. He reported that he brought his audience copies of Shevchenko's *Kobzar* and a birch branch as 'women and men' cried in memory of their native land.[35] Mykolaichuk promoted himself as the embodiment of the Carpathian land, which, metonymically, stood for Ukraine as a whole. The actor was able to perform the cultural work of moving the unfamiliar periphery of the Carpathians to the centre of Ukrainian identity. In his description of the Mar del Plata event, he worked to merge the image of Shevchenko (whom he had played in Volodymyr Denysenko's *A Dream*) – existing dually within the 'Friendship of Peoples' mythology and Ukrainian nationalist discourse – with that of the Hutsul, the ethnographic oddity.

*   *   *

With the first screening at Dovzhenko Studio, the film brought credibility to Paradjanov as the film's author, but also contributed to an evaluation of what it meant to be Ukrainian among the many members of the Kyiv intelligentsia invited to the event. Director Iurii Lysenko told the studio Artistic Council that this was a film that taught him a lot about his own people that he had not previously known.[36] Critics and film-makers openly distinguished between a Stalinist-derived folkloric mode that relied on melodramatic or comedic performance, and a modernist abnegation of space and psychology, which simultaneously functioned to de-familiarize and authenticate the Carpathians as essentially and ethno-nationally Ukrainian.

We should not, however, fail to see that Paradjanov's adaptation, which stressed de-familiarization over legibility, was itself, and for those reasons, a form of ethnographic spectacle. The Hutsuls were both possessed in the sense that the film crew captured them on camera for popular consumption, and fundamentally strange in their non-standard Ukrainian speech and folk culture. Hutsul folk culture was both on display and transformed into a collage of colour, which at times emulates impressionistic painting (Figure 3.2). Thus, with its emphasis on visual and aural texture, the authenticated Hutsul ethnoscape transcends notions of Thaw-era realism entirely. Yet much of the claim to authenticity remained located within a discursive play between text and context, inside and outside – between the Carpathian native, represented on screen through Mykolaichuk and other 'real' Hutsuls, and the recorder/ viewer, represented dually by the film-maker who journeys to Hutsulshchyna and the virtual tourist who views the native in a reconstructed and ahistorical Carpathian ethnoscape.[37] The studio promotional material implied that the film-makers themselves had penetrated such a 'distant' region, heretofore unknown to modern audiences. These Hutsuls were in fact '*playing*' themselves,

Figure 3.2   Camera movement emulates impressionistic painting in *Shadows of Forgotten Ancestors*

similar to Mykolaichuk. Yet Mykolaichuk was above all an *approachable* Hutsul – an individual who had journeyed from the unknown (Hutsulshchyna) to the known (Kyiv) – while the Hutsul extra was still an ethnographic found object that Paradjanov had discovered for the audience.

The central press first took notice of *Shadows* after Paradjanov screened it before a general meeting of the Union of Cinematographers on 24 December 1964. In providing a Russian context for the screening, participants in the discussion afterwards were considerably more apt to discuss its importance to Ukrainian culture. Evgenii Pomeshchikov, screenwriter on Ivan Pyr'ev's *Tractor Drivers*, spoke first, informing those present that his identity as a Ukrainian qualified him to evaluate and translate the film. He told the others,

> This is a simple people who preserve to this day what is dear and national... Paradjanov is not Ukrainian, but having resided in this Verkhovyna, he was so deeply penetrated with its spirit, with its powerful national tradition, that I can't find another word for this picture [other] than authenticity, and this authenticity is extraordinarily decorative.[38]

Pomeshchikov indicated the importance of clothing and other objects of material culture in articulating this notion of authenticity, the revelation of which required a special kind of journey to Hutsulshchyna. In her review of the film for *Sovetskaia kul'tura* in August, Elena Bauman assured readers that the film would present the kind of ethnographic material endemic to the 'ethnographic museum' due to its essential 'decorativeness.[39]

Paradjanov told readers in his article 'Eternal Motion' that he 'fell in love' with the exotic space of Hutsulshchyna, regardless of the fact that he could not understand the language of its inhabitants.[40] The studio and press continually celebrated the crew's desire to film on location, within the pristine alpine nature and among actual Hutsuls. Paradjanov, in his many statements about the film, made it clear that the journey to view and then to define artistically the Carpathians was an essential aspect of authenticating the space itself.

The particular space that Paradjanov 'offered up to visitors', however, was not (simply) a familiar bucolic landscape. The film-maker lacked interest in recreating the iconic mountain vista, or employing the static close-ups that Ivanov featured in *Oleksa Dovbush*, as he associated them with a tired Stalinist mode. In fact, most of *Shadows* is conducted in medium shots, which avoids both psychological exploration of the heroes and villains, while also giving the feeling of disorientation due to the absence of clear establishing shots. The rare long shot in Paradjanov's film eliminates the horizon that characterizes the mountain vista, and effectively flattens the landscape to a palette of colours and textures (Figure 3.3). Rather than a strategy of intercutting to show simultaneous action in different spaces – a hallmark of classical narrative style – a mobile camera explores space, follows the course of a single action, or remains completely static with a long lens, rendering certain scenes into an exotic tableau of human activity. These latter scenes of stasis are highly theatrical, frequently with Hutsuls performing folk dances and songs directly for the camera, while the mobile camera suggests recent developments in documentary techniques rising out of hand-held camera technology and the aesthetic influence of Sergei Urusevskii, the cinematographer behind such famous Thaw-era films as *The Cranes are Flying* (1957) and *I am Cuba* (1962).

Through the processes of visual and aural de-familiarization, nature is subsumed within an artistic, musical and literary metaphor. The film does not invite identification with the protagonists, nor is the spectator positioned to gain rational knowledge about

Figure 3.3   Flattening of space in Sergei Paradjanov's *Shadows of Forgotten Ancestors* (1965)

the Carpathians, something the Soviet tourist might expect from Hutsulshchyna. The 'mystery' of the Hutsuls is not revealed in *Shadows of Forgotten Ancestors*. They are essentially unknowable beneath the realm of their own demonology and the colourful objects that they appear as. It is style and form, therefore, along with how the industry, the film-makers and critics positioned and marketed the film, which invites the spectator and offers him or her knowledge.

And yet, the drama within the film and the drama of production are linked within the aesthetic decisions that the film-makers made. Illienko's use of point-of-view shots provides a suggestive example of how the film's authors became present in *Shadows*. As the film opens with Ivanko's brother's death, we inhabit a tree's perspective as it comes crashing down on the young man's body, suggesting the continued theme of nature's agency in the lives of the Hutsuls. In the scene that follows, a jerky camera surveys a procession of women playing jew's harps as a man's voice chants a funeral dirge. The POV-style shot does not, however, reveal a diegetic origin, as Ivanko himself steps into the shot, excluding him as the most obvious subject.

Later, we see another example of this movement from an authorial POV to a subjective POV. The extended scene of a fight between Ivanko's and Marichka's fathers occurs in one continuous shot. Initially, the camera follows Ivanko's father with a jerky movement to the right, which reveals Marichka's father with axe in hand. With the camera still moving to the right, the latter raises his axe. The camera tilts jerkily, still further to the right, framing Hutentiuk (Marichka's father) in the bottom right of the frame. At this moment, we notice that the camera has *become* Paliichuk's (Ivanko's father) line of sight as the axe comes down over the lens and blood fills the screen (Figure 3.4).

This seamless movement from objective to subjective POV serves to place the authors within the film by associating them directly with a diegetic origin. The camera, by drawing attention to itself, imparts itself into the narrative. The film, through its visual style and acting style, prohibits identification with any of the characters. But the presence of such a subjective and self-reflexive camera, together with the production drama, makes it available for identification with the filmmakers. If the idea and the process of the journey to the

Figure 3.4 Subjective violence in Sergei Paradjanov's *Shadows of Forgotten Ancestors* (1965)

Carpathians, then, is essentially transformative for the creators of the film, and validated by such non-conformist figures like Dziuba and Drach, along with establishment figures like Pomeshchikov and studio and union authorities alike, the *experience* of the film becomes transformative for the spectator. This actual and virtual journey connects urban sites of Ukrainian self-consciousness with the Carpathians, and metaphorically 'opens' or 'reveals' what was lost to modern cosmopolitan sensibilities.

*   *   *

The Carpathian exotic was both textually canonized and naturalized in Ukrainian art and literature, with the promotion of 'traditional' Carpathian song and dance, and more recently in images of tourism and in films like Viktor Ivanov's *Oleksa Dovbush*. Paradjanov did not break from the convention of a folksy and anti-modern image of the Hutsuls; in fact, the film intensified the sense of the Hutsuls' isolation from the geo-political and historical space that surrounded them. Like Dovzhenko's *Earth*, the surface of Paradjanov's film reveals an overly simplistic story – classical, in its allusion to *Romeo and Juliet* – but one which is subordinated to method and aspects of stylistic excess. The camera's proclivity for erratic movement and subjective positioning is the most obvious sign of modernist technique, but the foregrounding of symbols from Hutsul mythology, with which the film assumes the spectator's familiarity, and the elaboration of the aural and material culture of a civilisation clearly distant from the features of modern life, also contributes to the cinematic experience of de-familiarization. Hutsuls appear as strange. But they also have a history of appearing in a particular generic mode, which Paradjanov intentionally disrupts. Thus, de-familiarization is possible due to a process begun in the later nineteenth century of the literary incorporation of Hutsulshchyna. Moreover, the project of Stalinist national cinema was to make non-Russians knowable within a particular mode of domesticating the Soviet periphery. Paradjanov's project was to transform these knowable curiosities back into strange beings.

Yet Paradjanov's goal was of a dual nature: he aimed not only at de-familiarization but also assimilation or possession of Hutsulshchyna through the process of the journey, either real or transposed through the filmic medium. The recurring POV shot, like the one from the beginning of the film, is neither first-person nor third-person narration. It is, in fact, a hybrid of the two forms. But in producing such a hybrid of subjective and objective narration, Paradjanov has substituted the world of the Hutsul with his own aesthetic principles and interests in the exotic. Illienko contributed to this substitution in his technique of, as Italian film-maker Pier Paolo Pasolini put it, 'making the camera felt'.[41] As Pasolini defined a style of 'poetic cinema', there is no identification with the protagonist; rather, there is identification with the filmmakers and their worldview expressed through a manipulation of images. The immediacy of Paradjanov's and Illienko's images establishes their very presence.

The spectator is made to be aware, not only of the camera, but also of a meaning, which originates from an author; an author who demands to be unhindered in his or her 'quest'. Three separate 'authors' emerged from *Shadows of Forgotten Ancestors*, Paradjanov, Illienko and Mykolaichuk. Each of these new authors stood in for a particular kind of claim to authenticity: Paradjanov was the outsider who travelled to the Carpathians to gain intimate knowledge of the Hutsuls; Illienko, whose camera the spectator 'senses' (we see the camera move in step with his, and even perceive its shadow at times) in almost every scene, moves fluidly from objective to subjective narration, without so much as a cut; and Mykolaichuk, whose presence as a 'local' could be generalized beyond the confines of the Carpathians through his representation, both behind and in front of the camera.

* * *

During his opening speech at the Ukrainian Filmmakers' Union plenum on 1 March 1965, Tymofii Levchuk introduced *Shadows of Forgotten Ancestors* as a 'turning point' in Ukrainian cinema, and explicitly tied it to a national phenomenon. He stated that despite their horrible oppression at the hands of imperialists and capitalists, 'A fragment of our Ukrainian people – the Hutsuls – were able to keep their native language, their colourful folklore, their manners and customs, and their songs!'[42] A Marxist might well ask the First Secretary of the Union why he appeared to be celebrating feudal backwardness. Clearly, Levchuk was uninterested in presenting a proper materialist interpretation of Hutsul history. Instead, he mentioned Paradjanov's attention to an 'actual' representation of everyday life. Its ethnographic details provide the film with its 'national form', and Paradjanov 'revealed the depths of the life processes of the Ukrainian people' in *Shadows of Forgotten Ancestors*, the difficulty of which had not been 'mastered' until then. Earlier he even stated that the ethnographic elements found at the basis of *Shadows* 'will be one of our prerequisites for the moulding of our product'.[43] In foregrounding authenticity (over and above realism), *Shadows of Forgotten Ancestors* had established a new context for discussing Ukrainian cinema, and ultimately, 'national cinema' in the Soviet Union as a whole. Instead of literary concerns with film narrative, Paradjanov demonstrated that national meaning might be located exclusively within a film's imagery and soundtrack. The visual and aural qualities in *Shadows* marked off a site of Ukrainian difference, a site located outside of a rights-based agenda focused on language use. Paradjanov had revealed an undiscovered country in Hutsulshchyna, but Levchuk, along with other promoters of the film, transposed its meaning to the whole of Ukraine. In the process, Ukraine itself became the undiscovered country, newly and authentically revealed through *Shadows of Forgotten Ancestors*.

Ukrainian cinema had established a certain imagery of authenticity, located not only within Hutsulshchyna, but also within the authenticating potential of the individual artist. Despite such statements on the 'authenticity' of national representation and the embodiment of the national spirit that the film seemed to invite everywhere that people saw it, there was also a campaign launched against the film. Perhaps out of jealousy, or perhaps out of a genuine dislike for Paradjanov and his film, some at the studio later found it fruitful to call attention to the film's lack of a Carpathian audience, thus essentially using the film-makers' and critics' own language of authenticity against it.[44]

The following two chapters take up the theme of 'national authorship' as the establishment of a new type or 'genre' of cinema production – Ukrainian poetic cinema – which asserted a specifically Ukrainian claim to Thaw-era aesthetic problems, while intersecting with nationalist politics, on the one hand, and with real audiences, on the other.

Chapter 4

PARADJANOV AND THE PROBLEM OF FILM AUTHORSHIP

When Sergei Paradjanov first journeyed to Hutsulshchyna in 1963, no one expected much from him. The April 1962 thematic plan for Dovzhenko Studio had the director slotted to make *Iurka, the One-Kid Team* (*Iurka, besstannaia komanda*), another *kolkhoz* comedy along the lines of his previous work in *The Top Guy* (*Pershyi khlopets'*) and *Ukrainian Rhapsody* (*Ukrains'ka rapsodiia*).[1] *Flower on the Stone* was released with little fanfare, and maintained Paradjanov's mediocre reputation. Tymofii Levchuk listed the latter film as one of the 'dull' productions of the previous year during the First Congress of the Ukrainian Filmmakers' Union in January 1963.[2] Nonetheless, he was a reliable director who volunteered to take on projects that no one else wanted.[3] Instead of *Iurka*, the studio put him in charge of a film commemorating the Kotsiubyns'kyi centennial, an event significantly overshadowed by the Shevchenko sesquicentennial. From this perspective, the success of *Shadows* after his return to Kyiv in 1964 seemed all the more significant. Upon their initial viewing of the film, the studio and the union (not to mention Paradjanov himself), immediately recognized that it was the most significant Ukrainian film since Dovzhenko's time.[4] Moreover, they viewed the director as an altogether different kind of individual from what he had been to them before going to Hutsulshchyna, one who was not merely 'talented', but set apart from the studio collective, and possessing genius.[5]

Perhaps more pertinent to cinema in the 1960s, however, Paradjanov had become a Soviet *auteur*. In 1954, French critic and director François Truffaut wrote in *Cahiers du cinéma* of two kinds of film directors – those that simply 'set up the scenario (*metteur-en-scène*)', and the '*auteur*', the director-author. Truffaut called on film-makers to reject their beholdenness to screenwriters with their penchant for 'psychological realism' and, as film authors, to invent their own visual and narrative style. Truffaut associated cinematic meaning with the 'mark' of such a director-author, and less so with the qualities that were already present in a literary screenplay.[6] This director-author would be someone performing the simultaneous roles of intellectual, artist and craftsman. While such a context is difficult to transpose to the post war Soviet Union, we might note that the cultural Thaw was grounded in a similar notion of the artist's 'personal expression' above the political demands of the party and state.

And while we should not assume he had read *Cahiers du cinéma*, Alexander Dovzhenko wrote in a similar vein as Truffaut the following year in *Iskusstvo kino*. In addressing the static quality of Soviet literary adaptations, the only living member of Soviet cinema's 1920s *avant-garde* called on directors to use a visual vocabulary that was not beholden to literary modes of narration. Thus, the screenplay should be left to the interpretive powers of the director.[7] During the early 1960s, others writing in *Iskusstvo kino* also identified the necessity for a specifically 'cinematic' treatment of literature, the interpretation of which should be left to directors rather than screenwriters.[8] In its notion of the individual artist as the producer of cultural meaning, a Thaw-era *auteur* theory developed in the Soviet Union, which rejected the Stalinist 'cinema of leaders' in favour of a cinema of great directors. While Thaw-era literary and film critics were careful not to position their ideals of personal expression in opposition to the socialist community or politics, the intellectual culture of the 1960s introduced a greater focus on the transcendent value of art and the autonomy of the author. As the venerable film director Sergei Gerasimov noted in 1960, 'Young [directors] understood [the glorious future] with a particular resonance, and directly connected [it] ... with *their own* conceptions'.[9] His tone was only partially in support of such 'youthful' narcissism, as he expressed a certain ambivalence towards the apolitical character of Thaw-era productions like *The Cranes are Flying* (*Letiat zhuravli*, 1957) and Alexander Alov and Vladimir Naumov's *Pavel Korchagin* (1956), the latter an idiosyncratic adaptation of Nikolai Ostrovskii's classic socialist realist novel, *How the Steel was Tempered* (*Kak zakaialas' stal'*, 1934).[10] Especially after the Pushkin Square protest on Soviet Constitution Day in December 1965, authorities were concerned with the political power that the 'creative youth' attempted to wield in defence of personal expression.[11]

As an emergent Soviet *auteur* after making *Shadows of Forgotten Ancestors*, Sergei Paradjanov both alarmed and intrigued authorities in the film industry and within the Communist Party. Paradjanov's film came to the attention of the highest authorities in the CPU, with even Shelest taking note of the film-maker's accomplishment.[12] In the aftermath of *Shadows*, many of the young returnees to Kyiv Studio became committed Paradjanovites in their aesthetic outlook and interest in a Ukrainian ethnoscape. Moreover, studio authorities participated in the construction of a Ukrainian *auteur*, seeing in Paradjanov and his followers the possibility of disrupting ingrained modes of national representation and to 'return to Dovzhenko', the original Ukrainian *auteur*. Nonetheless, the cultivation of 'personal expression' at the root of both *auteur* theory and Thaw-era cultural expression constantly intersected with a new Ukrainian nationalist movement, precisely because the intellectuals who comprised the latter were interested in many of the same problems of identity that emerged during the cultural Thaw as the film-makers themselves. During the 1960s, Ukrainian nationalism in Kyiv took on new dimensions that were more in dialogue with the 'Thaw generation' than with the independence movements during the Revolution and during and after World War II. Thaw-era Ukrainian nationalism, moreover, constituted a dissident message geared towards a particular audience; in many ways, the same audience that Paradjanov and his followers intended for their supposedly apolitical films.

While the 'Ukrainian west' remained an important source of cultural inspiration for the Ukrainian dissident movement, the political and cultural spaces of Kyiv, with its historic mix of Russian and Ukrainian-speaking publics and the hybridized nature of the political system centred in the Ukrainian capital, defined its nature.[13] Moreover, the dominant Ukrainian cultural and educational institutions – not only Dovzhenko Studio, but also the republican Writers' Union, Ukrainian-language publishing houses and Shevchenko University – were all located in Kyiv, and most of the dissident nationalists emerged from a working relationship with and within them.

In essence, the Soviet political system, along with the cultural institutions that it created, provided the groundwork for real debate on language, history and national identity. Of equal importance was the simultaneously cosmopolitan and provincialized nature of Kyiv as a political and cultural centre. The leaders of republican cultural institutions, along with non-conformists and dissidents alike, felt the pressure to prove that they were as good as Moscow, and struggled to achieve recognition as such. The discourse of national authorship – that individual artists/writers/film-makers could embody the national genius – sought not only to differentiate Ukrainian culture from mainstream Soviet culture, but also to promote an elitist agenda of high cultural sophistication that placed Ukrainian art and literature in the same league as that of Russia and Europe as a whole.

Ivan Dziuba and other Ukrainian dissidents divided the nation into intellectuals and the 'de-nationalized' masses, indicating clear allegiance with the former, while the latter represented the hopeless cause of Ukrainian autonomy rooted in any kind of mass movement. Similarly, Paradjanov stated in December 1971 before an audience of 'creative youth' in Minsk that the mass 'audience should apologise' to him for not understanding his films.[14] We must assume that he was not referring to his present supporters who came to listen. Thus, a Ukrainian *politique des auteurs* not only emerged as a socio-aesthetic phenomenon and as a successful means to differentiate Dovzhenko Studio's product from that of other studios, but also within the realm of film industry and audience politics.

The intersections between audience politics and dissident politics became public on 4 September 1965, during the official premiere of *Shadows of Forgotten Ancestors*. Expectations were high for the crowd that gathered at the Ukraina Theatre in central Kyiv that Saturday evening, the majority of whom had procured tickets through connections to people who worked on the film, at Dovzhenko Studio, or from other state or party institutions.[15] Others demanded entry, and when the box office closed, rushed the doors. Ukraina director Fedir Brainchenko alerted the *militsiia* to the problem, but allowed Paradjanov to introduce the film, in the hope that he could help calm the situation. Instead, the film director launched into an embellished monologue about the conflict with industry authorities over dubbing the film into Russian. The confident Paradjanov asserted that 'blacks, the French, and Argentines' understood it, but 'the organs [of power] aren't allowing the film to be released, on the grounds that our people won't understand it'.[16] Paradjanov suggested that Goskino's insistence on a Russian dub was based on the principle of pragmatic comprehension and on the equally mundane problem of violating industry policy.[17]

In directing this statement to his intended audience, Paradjanov elicited sympathy for a principle of personal expression, which was divorced from the specific qualities of the on-screen language. Linguistic comprehension, in Paradjanov's view, would actually disrupt a broader understanding of the author's intentions. Dziuba, along with Shevchenko scholar Mykhailyna Kotsiubyns'ka (Mykhailo Kotsiubyns'kyi's niece), journalist Viacheslav Chornovil, poet Vasyl' Stus and literary critic Iurii Badz'o viewed the occasion of Paradjanov's premiere as the perfect opportunity to draw attention to the government's recent arrest of several Lviv writers and intellectuals, not only because of the film's focus on western Ukraine and implicit questions of Ukrainian identity, but also because of the high-culture prestige that accompanied *Shadows* wherever its producers and handlers took it. In line with his own conception of authorship, expressed most succinctly in an article for *Radians'ke literaturoznavstvo* earlier that year, Dziuba saw in the film an expression of the director's 'self'.[18]

Brainchenko initially watched in silence as his intentions to maintain order during the premiere were thwarted further. After Paradjanov's contentious introduction, Dziuba and Kotsiubyns'ka approached the stage to present the film director and costume designer with flowers. Dziuba took the microphone from Paradjanov to proclaim that the 'reaction of 1937' had returned.[19] As the secretary of the theatre Partkom scrambled for the PA system to drown out Dziuba's speech, the latter quickly informed the audience of arrests during the previous two weeks of 19 Ukrainian intellectuals accused of a 'nationalist conspiracy'.[20] Dziuba was forcibly escorted off stage, but Chornovil shouted above the commotion: 'Rise up against the return of Stalinism!'[21] As the *militsiia* entered the theatre, Brainchenko grabbed the microphone from Dziuba's hand. The projectionist started the film as chaos erupted between the police and the ticketless spectators. Ivan Mykolaichuk, who was also present for the premiere, recalled with horror the violence of the *militsiia* that accompanied the event. 4 September marked a watershed in Ukrainian cultural politics, in that Dziuba's act transformed an official gathering into what amounted to a street riot. Dziuba and his friends had brought post-Stalin 'literary politics' into a public space. To indicate the magnitude of this event, in September 2010, Ukrainians marked its forty-fifth anniversary with a re-enactment at the Ukraina movie theatre.[22]

Like many of the film-makers, writers and intellectuals associated with Ukrainian dissident politics during the 1960s and 1970s, Dziuba was born into an eastern Ukrainian peasant family, educated in Russian-language institutions and came to consciousness as a Ukrainian through a diversity of intellectual pursuits that encompassed literature, history and law. Until late 1962, he was a senior editor for the Ukrainian Writers' Union journal, *Vitchyzna* (*Homeland*), and was responsible for publishing non-conformist writers like Ivan Drach, Dmytro Pavlychko, Lina Kostenko and Oleksandr Syzonenko. When Dziuba resolved to act on 4 September 1965, he was in the midst of writing his major political tract, *Internationalism or Russification?* Therein, he complained of a 'de-nationalization' of the Ukrainian people, owing to Soviet population resettlement policies and a conscious effort in Moscow to 'provincialize' Ukrainian culture, which had the effect of 'pushing Ukrainian language into the background'.[23] Each of these problems emerged from a 'violation in Leninist nationalities policy', according to Dziuba.[24] In essence, the purpose of the book, according to the author, is to justify the principle of criticizing the uneven implementation of a continually affirmed Soviet policy.

As recent work on Soviet dissidence suggests, the defence of the principle of 'socialist legality' constantly butted heads with the messianic principle of the intelligentsia's role in Russian/Soviet society.[25] In affirming both a natural and legal connection between cultural production and nationality, Dziuba was trying to reconcile this division, while opportunistically maintaining a properly Leninist position. Dziuba remembers telling poet and screenwriter Ivan Drach that *Shadows* was 'an anti-Soviet film', but that he should keep that fact secret.[26] Specifically, Dziuba pointed out in his tract that films from Ukrainian studios were dubbed into Russian, even in Ukraine, thus promoting the second-class status of the vernacular.[27] In refusing a Russian dub for *Shadows*, Paradjanov thus resisted this process (at least, from Dziuba's perspective) of 'killing' the Ukrainian people.[28] The film pointed towards a more general significance for Ukrainian cultural activism, as Dziuba's very concept of 'de-nationalization' when applied to individuals and social groups made explicit the cultural labour involved in maintaining a meaningful category of national identity. If Ukrainians could lose a sense of themselves as 'Ukrainians' in Siberia, Karelia, Slovakia, Canada, *Ukraine*, etc., Dziuba showed that instruction in Ukrainian language, history, literature and film was absolutely necessary, indeed a civil right, wherever Ukrainians lived. Thus, the journey towards ethnic self-knowledge implicit in *Shadows* was also a principle upon which Dziuba attached hope for a newly nationalized Ukrainian people.

Yet, what kind of public was it that went to see *Shadows* that night, to which Dziuba and others addressed their protest? The literary critic had several choices for a venue that evening, including Denysenko's *A Dream*, playing at the Leningrad an hour earlier, and the premiere of the long-anticipated military comedy, *Keys from Heaven* (*Kliuchi vid neba*), directed by the ever-popular Viktor Ivanov (*Oleksa Dovbush* and *After Two Hares*), which was playing at the Sputnyk at the same time.[29] These latter two films also dealt with local topics, and were screened in Ukrainian. Denysenko and Ivanov, however, were working within tried and true genres of representing the nation, despite the innovations of the former production. The audience at the Ukraina that evening was a particular kind of elite audience, one that expected to see an unusual film. Many of them had already seen *Shadows* during free, private screenings at the October House of Culture.[30] Dziuba believed that particular texts invited pre-determined readings, perhaps generically determined readings. In broaching his political cause of defending accused Ukrainian nationalists, he needed a space, in which a particular kind of reception was already activated, while also desiring the centrality of the Ukraina's physical location, and the significance of the movie theatre's name.

Thus we find in Dziuba's choice of protest venue a peculiar desire for both visibility and exclusivity, in addition to an interest in the specific problems that Paradjanov's film raised. Several newspapers had featured *Shadows of Forgotten Ancestors* in promotional materials related to the annual 'Cinema Days' event in Kyiv that would take place on that first weekend in September. Of the supposedly 340,000 people who attended at least one screening during the three-day extravaganza, it stood to reason that some of them would want to see the most talked-about Ukrainian film of the year.[31] Upon learning that the screening was already sold out, many of them might have become angry at the system of privilege for *apparatchiks* and intellectuals, whose connections entitled them to see such a film. Central Goskino considered the possibility that spectators in Kyiv would become rowdy, warning its Ukrainian branch on Friday to enlist responsible members of the Profsoiuz organizations, the Komsomol *aktiv* and pensioners to catch ticketless spectators as they entered theatres during 'Cinema days'.[32] While Ukrainian Goskino had already initiated a campaign against ticketless spectators in the republic, efforts were oriented towards rural film points, where up to half of film audiences were getting in free in some oblasts.[33] In these cases, blame was placed on rural projectionists who either failed to collect the entrance fees or were accused of embezzling the funds.[34] The situation was different during the *Shadows* premiere: people were barred at the door, some successfully entering through the fire escape, others simply pushing their way in. Rather than constituting a problem of state finances, an official 'creative meeting with spectators' had been violated, which was only then compounded by Paradjanov's and Dziuba's transgressions. The *militsiia*'s confrontation was not with the ticketed guests at the Ukraina Theatre, some of whom stood up after Dziuba's rallying cry, nor even with Paradjanov or the protestors themselves, each of whom suffered longer-term consequences as a result.[35] Brainchenko had called the *militsiia*, rather, to disperse a violation of public order, which the ticketless spectators represented.[36] The film itself and its premiere affirmed the growing distinction in the Soviet Union between *auteur* cinema (in Russian, '*avtorskaia kino*') and cinema for the masses, a distinction both criticized and reinforced by industry and party authorities during the 1960s.[37]

On the Thursday following the premiere, the Ukrainian Filmmakers' Union met to discuss the 'unfortunate events' of 4 September. Paradjanov denied responsibility for Dziuba's speech, stating, 'I am a Soviet person and in essence I do not agree with Dziuba'. He complained of the 'poor organization' of the premiere, also alluding to the chaos of the ticketless spectators' presence that diluted the pool of intellectuals. Volodymyr Denysenko also affirmed that the problem lay not in Paradjanov's 'demagogic' speech, but in the 'hooligan behaviour' at the premiere.[38] Yet, it was no coincidence that the Ukraina event exploded at the *Shadows* premiere, within the confluence of a film intended for a particular kind of audience – the Ukrainian intelligentsia – with a festival intended for a mass audience. Dziuba's message about persecuted intellectuals, moreover, was clearly intended to garner sympathy from Paradjanov's own exclusive audience.

The audience politics surrounding Paradjanov's film were indeed complex, and not only because of the events that occurred during its premiere. That *Shadows* was intended for an elite audience was, in fact, confirmed by authorities in the film industry, who were concerned to treat Paradjanov and his crew with due respect lest they incur the enmity of other film-makers (the enmity of 'the spectator' was not yet a category of concern regarding the film). In the summer of 1963, Goskino imposed economic sanctions on Paradjanov and his crew. With the increasingly celebratory atmosphere over the film's significance from the intelligentsia by late 1964, Goskino chairman Aleksei Romanov resolved to heed his Ukrainian counterpart's warning, 'The reduction of c[omrades] Paradjanov's, Iu. Illienko's [...] pay will arouse a wide and very undesirable reaction among film-makers'. Romanov reversed sanctions on 19 January 1965.[39] Moreover, the director of *Shadows* was able to move out of the dormitory that he had resided in for the past decade to a large apartment in the prestigious neighbourhood on Ploshcha Peremohy (Victory Square).[40] Within the course of a year, Paradjanov had gone from being a 'reliable', but mediocre, director to the studio's greatest genius, respected in Kyiv for transforming Ukrainian cinema, and in Moscow for being an emerging *auteur*. Yet this occurred before a single non-elite spectator had seen the film.

After the premiere at the Ukraina, organs of distribution pulled the film once again, for fear of similar incidents and perhaps unsure of Paradjanov's future political status. In the politically charged atmosphere of 1965–6, with the recent arrests of Ukrainian intellectuals (not to mention the Siniavskii / Daniel' trial in Moscow) compounding tensions between the creative unions and the CPU, Paradjanov and his followers at the studio skirted two issues: that of individual genius and personal expression, on the one hand, and correct national representation, on the other. As Thaw-era cultural politics intersected with issues of national representation in Ukraine, questions emerged not only about who was qualified to represent the republic, but also who was qualified to consume the images thus produced. The next two chapters investigate the politics of Ukrainian authorship and the 'danger' that emerged in Paradjanov's subsequent film, *Kyiv Frescoes* (*Kyivs'ki fresky*), his cinematographer Iurii Illienko's directorial debut *A Well for the Thirsty* (*Krynytsia dlia sprahlykh*), and his young protégé Vasyl' Illiashenko's *Coordinate Your Watches* (*Perevirte svoi hodynnyky*), which also became the articulated foundations of a 'new school [*novoe napravlenie*]' in Soviet cinema, 'Ukrainian poetic cinema'.

Shadows of Forgotten Ancestors and Reception Politics

For two weeks after its premiere, there was no mention of *Shadows of Forgotten Ancestors* in the press. Finally, on 17 September, Evhen Kyryliuk, the most important Shevchenko scholar in Ukraine, proclaimed that *Shadows* was a definitive work of Socialist Realism. While admitting its complexity, he argued for the film's inclusion under a newer conception of Socialist Realism that emerged with the end of the cult of personality. Indeed, as Thomas Lahusen has noted, Socialist Realism contained little of its 'educational foundation' in post-Stalinist articulations of its 'method'. Especially after the Twentieth Party Congress, Soviet literary critics were given freer reign to define this 'historically open system of the truthful representation of life'.[41] Kyryliuk concluded that Paradjanov and Chendei had 'correctly read Kotsiubyns'kyi's story', and had removed the 'crude sociological schemes' (i.e., Zlatousov's strict socialist realist reading of the literary text) that pervaded interpretation of Kotsiubyns'kyi during the period of the cult.[42] The following Monday, the Ukraina tested the waters with another evening screening of the film. It passed without further problems, and nightly screenings occurred at the Ukraina from 27 September to 17 October.[43] On 16 October, Dmytro Shlapak in *Na ekranakh Kyieva* celebrated the film as in the same league as *Battleship Potemkin*, *Earth*, *The Cranes are Flying* and *Ballad of a Soldier*, and drew particular attention to Paradjanov's role as *auteur* in the production of the film.[44] Thereafter, *Shadows* expanded beyond central Kyiv theatres, even showing regularly at several factory clubs until late November.[45] While the film did not even see an average degree of box office success for Soviet cinema, selling under 11 million tickets throughout the USSR, it garnered enough interest to maintain its presence at theatres in major Soviet cities throughout the fall of 1965. And, while organs of distribution were wary of the film, Josephine Woll's claim that '*Shadows* barely ran in commercial theatres' is far from true.[46] Nonetheless, we cannot consider Kyiv's pattern of distribution representative of Ukraine as a whole, and certainly not of the Soviet Union as a whole. *Shadows of Forgotten Ancestors* was a festival film, functioning internationally and domestically to demonstrate the vitality of Ukrainian high culture.

As the film was leaving Kyiv theatres in November, the Ukrainian Film-makers' Union gathered in plenum, where Levchuk once again praised the film for its 'revelation of the national originality of culture, everyday life, language, and customs of our people'.[47]

Nonetheless, S. P. Ivanov's statement that 'spectators judged the film harshly' probably had more resonance in the hall that day. Indeed, one engineer from Dnipropetrovsk wrote a long and derisive letter to the Russian-language daily *Pravda Ukrainy* complaining of the film's incomprehensible 'Ukrainian atmosphere'. Addressing the (unpublished) letter directly to Dovzhenko Studio, he wrote:

> I am an ordinary movie watcher, [just] one of the consumers of your product, and if you wish to know what happened to me during a screening of *Shadows of Distant* [sic] *Ancestors*, take a bowl of good Ukrainian *borshch*, put a half kilo of honey in it and try to eat it within a half an hour...That will tell you about the condition of my brain during the next day...[48]

While it was not unusual for people writing to journals or newspapers about films to identify themselves as non-professionals or 'ordinary', this writer's further delineation of that identity with 'consumer' of a 'product' indicates how Soviet audience politics was changing in the 1960s. In his analogy to *borshch* and honey, moreover, the writer alluded to the folkloric mode of representing Ukrainians, but in Paradjanov's schema, it is mere intellectual citation, which, rather than amusing, becomes nerve-racking for spectators. The engineer continued, asking, 'For what reason do you try to mess with the spectator's psychological condition? [...] The spectator never forgets that he sits in the theatre, in a comfortable chair [...] and that he is the spectator.'

Such a notion of spectatorship was definitively at odds with what scholars have identified as the model for media consumption in the Soviet Union. The spectator was not simply a 'consumer' or 'recipient' of culture, but the 'object of reshaping', according to Evgenii Dobrenko.[49] In approaching the authorities, the engineer, however, made it clear that he did not want indoctrination, political or otherwise, during his leisure time; rather, he felt able to speak as a spectator wanting nothing more than comfort and entertainment from an engaging plot. In using the vocabulary of the 'mass spectator', moreover, he further transformed it from the 'object of reshaping' to the subject of leisure:

> For the first time in my life, I saw how spectators, not by themselves, but in rows, got up and left[...] Someone stated aloud their grandfather's aphorism, 'Cross yourself at such a strange sight'. In general, the audience revealed the rarest unanimity.

At the same time, the engineer was well versed enough in other aspects of political dogma to critique the studio on the basis of its own stated goals: first, to represent the Ukrainian ethnoscape; and second, to develop along the traditions of Alexander Dovzhenko. He went on:

> In my view, you develop only the form of Dovzhenko's art, that is to say, the most external level, and attach to this the progress of the highest technical know-how. But Dovzhenko's art reached such heights [of expression] due to the fire of patriotic feelings, and a civic pathos, that is, due to the content.

Thus, the engineer ended his critique of *Shadows* condemning its emptiness, its very inability to *affect* the spectator, to transcend the material world. 'Feelings' and 'pathos' were the stuff of 'content', while 'technique' was located in the formal dimensions of the film. This is not necessarily a 'contradiction', as he meant to reject the author's role in the film by de-emphasizing being (the film-maker's journey to Hutsulshchyna) and doing (the film-maker's talent or authorship) to return to the practical and objective question of what the film accomplished. Here, the answer was simple: the unaffected spectator left the theatre, unsatisfied. The engineer echoed Nikolai Lebedev, who wrote in the June 1964 issue of *Iskusstvo kino*, 'A film, which doesn't make it to the spectator, which isn't watched, which isn't "consumed" or is "consumed" by an insignificant number of people, is also worthless...'[50]

In practice, few would deny the filmmakers' talents, or the film's political importance for Ukrainian national cinema, but in speaking for the Ukrainian spectator, opponents of Paradjanov were able to question the film's legacy. When the union met to discuss nominating *Shadows* for the Shevchenko Prize (the highest CPU award for literature and art) on 5 January 1966, various members danced around the film, largely because it seemed from their vantage point that only foreigners and intellectuals appreciated it. While certainly a bad sign, many at the meeting stated that this did not necessarily exclude the film from consideration for the prize, due to the incredible talent of the director and cinematographer. Iurii Kondufor, the chair of the CPU Department of Culture, who had to ratify all nominations, stated very clearly, however, '[n]o one is nominating this film for the Shevchenko Prize. Argentina celebrated [*otmetila*] this film, but that in no way means that we should get behind it.'[51] Later in the meeting, Oleksandr Korniichuk made the case for the film's omission from nomination despite support from the union even clearer:

> For the Argentines who watched *Shadows of Forgotten Ancestors*, it was important how the cinematographer made the trees spin around [...] but we Ukrainians, when we evaluate such a defaced image of the Ukrainian people, it's not pleasant for us. There is a kind of wild tendency there. This is not the Ukrainian people. This film has nothing in common with Kotsiubyns'kyi.[52]

In making this claim, Korniichuk affirmed that the film was intended for a specifically Ukrainian audience, but it failed because *Shadows* instead appealed to an international festival audience.

During a March 1967 union plenum, screenwriter and Deputy Chairman of Ukrainian Goskino Oleksandr Levada pointed out its lack of a popular audience, with Carpathian spectators in particular writing 'letters of outpourings of displeasure concerning the film'.[53] Levada was able to dissect the film-makers' organic connection with the Carpathian highlanders, and thus complicate the film's claim to authenticity. Levada brought the film down from the mountain of personal expression to 'actual' Hutsuls living in 'the present [*suchasnist'*]'. The June 1967 issue of *Novyny kinoekrana* echoed Levada's concerns, publishing a letter from a self-identified Hutsul, Bohdan Chufus. He wrote,

> Dovzhenko Studio gave us *Shadows of Forgotten Ancestors* – a genuine poem about the life of the Hutsuls, about a pure and great love. But this event was in the past! We would like to see contemporary Hutsuls, who approach the glory of Communism with their labour. We are waiting, dear film-makers, for films about the contemporary Carpathians from you.[54]

In this overdetermined letter, the writer did not deny that particular landscapes produce certain types of people, and affirmed the primordial quality of ethnicity. Chufus also did not deny the talent displayed in Paradjanov's film by drawing attention to issues of 'formalism' or 'abstractionism;' rather, the problem became its very distance from actuality. Chufus still maintained '[y]ou don't see any films about our country', suggesting that Paradjanov's subject was located elsewhere. Chufus's concerns were not for the *auteur*, but for the film's relevance to the Carpathian spectator. The engineer from Dnipropetrovsk, moreover, affirmed the subject's 'distance' with his intentional mistitling. He pointed to a second problem for Kyiv filmmakers, that of Dovzhenko Studio's national and aesthetic patrimony, which framed its goals around an implicitly auteurist agenda. Like many of Paradjanov's critics who played the audience card, he demanded both customer satisfaction and a proper understanding of Dovzhenko's work; the latter could not but evoke debates from the early 1930s about Modernism and Socialist Realism. As an *auteur*, Paradjanov failed to temper his personal concerns with the proper social awareness that political authorities expected of all cultural producers.

Moving 'Outside the Collective:' Paradjanov's *Kyiv Frescoes*

As the campaign against *Shadows of Forgotten Ancestors* emerged in 1966–7, Paradjanov experienced another political defeat with his aborted production, *Kyiv Frescoes*. The latter film proved to be the beginning of the director's undoing, ending with his arrest a decade later. While he and the studio promoted *Frescoes* as a Victory Day film – an homage to Kyiv, the 'Hero City' – the film bore no similarity to parallel works released during this important anniversary year. After 1965, Brezhnev would establish what Nina Tumarkin calls the 'cult of World War II', with the naming of new 'hero-cities', the construction of the eternal flame on the side of the Kremlin wall, and a number of large monuments on the sites of major battles and Nazi atrocities.[55] While such sites were simultaneously evocative of Soviet heroism and suffering, Paradjanov's film seemed to exist entirely outside such a narrative.

In the screen test that Paradjanov shot with Oleksandr Antypenko in 1965, which essentially killed the production, we see a series of four self-contained thematic explorations, introduced and concluded with images from the Caves Monastery and Ukraine's nearby war memorial. Whereas the director was constrained by the Ukrainian literary canon with *Shadows of Forgotten Ancestors* in what he intended as a total exploration of the Hutsul ethnoscape, he used *Kyiv Frescoes* for a fuller investigation of the aesthetic possibilities of combining his disparate interests in objects and things. His justification for the apparently random assortment of thematic material contained in the *Frescoes* trial was to insist that these elements composed the very living material of a city, both nationally and historically Ukrainian and multinationally modern. Yet, in rejecting the very specific dimensions of each of these two sites of meaning production, Paradjanov's film appeared as a fractured representation, not of a space of cultural significance, but of his own aesthetic sensibilities. Moreover, in its self-reflexive juxtaposition of mass culture and high art, *Frescoes* not only appeared to celebrate Kyiv's existence between history and the contemporary, but also affirmed a supposedly bourgeois understanding of an undifferentiated culture of consumption.

The first 'fresco' is emblematic of the entire short: three soldiers pose in an empty room save for three paintings of Cossack hetmen behind them. The *mise-en-scène* of the shot, as with the screen test in general, is artless. There is even lighting; the camera sits at a 90-degree angle to the rear wall. The scene is silent, except for the ambient sound of the three soldiers who walk in. Each of them sits in a wooden chair, and removes his boots. One of the soldiers wears a cowboy hat, and has a handlebar moustache. After removing the hat, he poses with a Cossack ceremonial mace (*bulava*). While posing, water flows across the uneven hardwood floor, and the soldiers begin mopping. The second part of the trial occurs in the same barren room, the centre of which now contains a lifeless soldier lying on a bed, with a woman and child attending to his body. An ornate picture frame hangs in the foreground of the shot, composing the three in the background. We hear sounds of priests chanting.

The second half of the screen test continues in the same Soviet interior, but becomes more fragmented, mixing filmic citations from Eisenstein and Dovzhenko with Orthodox ritual, jazz, a wedding, classical mythology, children's games and Renaissance art. Paradjanov juxtaposes items on loan from the Kyiv Museum of Western and Eastern Art – vases, busts, Velázquez's *Infanta Margarita* – with objects from an Orthodox mass – incense, bells and garments. We cut to a contemporary couple in bridal costume. Their movements are slow, deliberate and histrionic. People are holding Orthodox icons as a boy dressed in angel's wings cranks an antique gramophone. A black couple dances to jazz. A nude female stands motionless in the frame, with birch logs separating her standing body from a man lying on the floor. The trial ends with a montage of churches, seemingly presented as an afterthought, reminding the spectator of the film's intentions to present an 'image of Kyiv'.

While only a screen test for a future film that was never made, James Steffen has pointed out that each of the scenes within it 'correspond more or less to passages in the shooting script'.[56] Moreover, Paradjanov edited the test as a short film for public screenings, after it became obvious that Goskino would not permit the completion of the film.[57] While a screen test was intended to test actors' abilities to play a role, here we see only parodies of acting, only self-reflection about the function of the images. Paradjanov's images were increasingly divorced from the specifics of cinema (depth, movement, montage), and approach an aesthetic of modernist metatheatre with their own self-reflexive theatricality. Rather than a screen test, the short film Paradjanov presented to the studio, Ukrainian Goskino and a select public at the Kyiv House of Culture in December and January 1965–6 was the expression of a director who by now felt entirely comfortable moving outside of the realm of Soviet aesthetic and narrative conventions. The short film's bookends of war memorials and churches are all that returns us to a cinematic commonplace. The question that emerges from this highly experimental and, indeed, *personal*, project[58] is how *Kyiv Frescoes* made it as far as it did, despite reservations about it at all levels of the Soviet film industry.

Throughout the project, the director maintained that *Kyiv Frescoes* was intended to represent Kyiv during and after the war; that he was lending his genius to 'contemporary' concerns: the memorialization of the Great Patriotic War. When it became evident to everyone that this was not Paradjanov's intention with the film, Goskino questioned his privileged position at Dovzhenko Studio. Deputy Chairman Vladimir Baskakov wrote to Ivanov in August 1965:

> We can't forget that the film's action takes place in Kyiv, a city that experienced a heavy siege, encirclement, and occupation, which became an arena for an intense battle, and in 1943, the Soviet Army's victory. All of this is missing in the screenplay.[59]

In September, Ivanov issued a statement that the shooting script could not 'be considered a completed and valuable basis for a future film about Kyivans and Kyiv'.[60] In Paradjanov's highly personal and abstract conceptions of the city, Goskino found his project divorced, not only from the ideological basis of the 1965 Victory Day celebrations, but also from the studio's identity within the framework of 'national cinemas' in the USSR.

At the same time, the director's identity as an *auteur*, who helped forge Dovzhenko Studio's movement away from the Stalinist folkloric and towards a new mode and space of national representation, provided him with a free hand in developing the project outside of the complicated bureaucratic system of double and triple levels of approval for each stage in the production process. When Paradjanov submitted his screenplay to the studio in April, for example, the screenplay editorial board urged the director to 'consider the general conception' of the future film, but issued a broader statement to industry officials to resist any 'rude interventions or rigid counsel'.[61] Iurii Illienko called the screenplay 'pure *auteur* cinema':

> Such a screenplay has appeared because it was the physiological necessity of the author to express [it]. Therefore, the screenplay cannot be bad. It can't be a failure. If it were my will, I'd get a group together and shoot a screenplay [*literaturnaia stsenariia*], even without a shooting script [*rezhiserskaia stsenariia*].[62]

Paradjanov continually asserted his intellectual independence, becoming increasingly irate about any suspicion about his intentions. To advance his unorthodox method, he called for the establishment of an 'experimental studio[...] in the quest for the new', where film-makers were allowed to 'take risks'.[63] His conception of an 'experimental studio' sought a method of film-making '*vne kollektiva* (outside of the collective)', believing that it could function as an alternative space of cultural production.

Sigismund Navrotskii, who actively fought for resolving the 'problem of cadres' in Ukrainian cinema, became an active opponent of 'youth experimentation' and perhaps the most recognizable neo-Stalinist at Dovzhenko Studio during the later 1960s. For example, Navrotskii called 'six years in prison' for Ivan Dziuba's speech at the *Shadows* premiere a 'liberal measure'.[64] Nonetheless, he too fancied himself an *auteur*, continually calling for the elimination of 'a whole series of instructions, which take root in our everyday lives and do not give us the possibility to live and work freely and creatively'.[65] In speaking against Vasyl' Tsvirkunov's regimentation of thematic plans during a union meeting, Navrotskii complained that when the studio 'pins a director' to a particular film, 'creative individuality gets lost'.[66] Speaking during a union plenum in 1962, Navrotskii attempted to explain why he had become more of a 'critic' than film-maker in recent years:

> No creative worker ... has any desire to work according to a plan [*rabotat' po planu*]; they have their own personal creative plan; they want to do such things closer to themselves [*lit.*: 'in their biography']. They don't want to be embarrassed in front of [other] people ... But there is also another working principle: the principle of working on whatever earns [money]. This doesn't suit me.[67]

He advocated that the studio provide the opportunity for a select group of talented directors to work '*ne po planu*' and '*vne kollektiva*', with only the 'Party Programme' to guide them.[68] Yet Navrotskii's 'personal' conception for a film, an 'exploration of the international character of the October Revolution', was in no way similar to that of Paradjanov's symbolist conception in *Kyiv Frescoes*, even if we accept that the latter film was in fact 'about Kyiv'.

Yet both Navrotskii and Paradjanov were uneasy with making films exclusively for an agenda that privileged 'national' representation at the expense of personal expression. After reading the shooting script in July, studio opinion on *Kyiv Frescoes* had shifted to some degree, although the leadership remained committed to promoting the film, largely because of the *auteur* behind it. The manner of critique is instructive in terms of what the studio expected from Paradjanov after his success with *Shadows*. Dmytro Pavlychko, for example, was concerned with the 'cosmopolitanism' of the imagery, of its lack of a 'Kyivan, a purely Ukrainian image'.[69] Vasyl' Zemliak stressed that, like all directors at the studio, 'Paradjanov has to think with Dovzhenko's categories'.[70] The message was clear: Paradjanov's personal expression was to be encouraged, but he had to work within the framework of Ukrainian national cinema in his choice of thematics and mode of representation, a mode for which he himself had established the precedent with *Shadows*. In its decision to pass the shooting script on to Goskino, the studio opted to emphasize 'personal expression' over 'national' representation, however, asking Moscow to pass the script into production on the basis that such a 'risky experiment' was 'possible and justified only because of the interesting and original mark of the artist who stands behind it'.[71]

When Goskino saw the results of Paradjanov's 'mark', and those results did not correspond either to the tolerated formal edginess and method of seeing nationality contained in *Shadows*, interest in the film-maker's character transformed into character assassination. In the midst of this conflict surrounding *Kyiv Frescoes*, the SKU Presidium met to discuss Paradjanov's 'conduct'. Ukrainian film critic Viacheslav Kudin noted that the director had

> dug himself into a political and moral hole, and acted uncivilly [during the production of *Kyiv Frescoes*]. We have only to listen to how he conducts conversations among students, how he used foul language around women. If we don't pay attention to all this, the issue with comrade Paradjanov can acquire a serious character.[72]

Indeed, a KGB report from the early 1970s stated: 'Many studio workers describe [Paradjanov] as a morally corrupt person who has turned his apartment into a gathering place for all kinds of dubious individuals engaged in drinking, debauchery...and sometimes anti-Soviet discussions.' Later in the report, they quoted the director telling an informant, 'I am the first to dig the grave for Socialist Realism with my films'.[73] As an *auteur*, whose work now dealt, to a greater degree, with his own interests and personality, Paradjanov's public conduct was subject to the same scrutiny as his aesthetic outlook. During the *Kyiv Frescoes* fiasco, Zemliak characterized Paradjanov as 'one of those artists who easily hypnotizes those around him', and was concerned that the director was developing an 'entourage [*otochennia*]' of young people at the studio.[74]

In essence, the director's personal character and aesthetic sensibilities had become part of a continuum that eventually led to his arrest and imprisonment several years later. On 17 December 1973, the director was charged with indecent conduct and convicted on 24 April 1974 of 'sodomy, and the manufacture, sale and distribution of pornographic materials'.[75] On the eve of the trial, *Vechirnii Kyiv* announced Paradjanov's arrest under the heading, 'In the Name of the Law', alongside other infractions for drunkenness and various violations of public order. The article, penned by the public prosecutor, stated that the film director 'led an immoral type of life, ruined his family, converted his apartment into a den [*pryton*] of depravity, and resorted to sexual corruption[...]'[76] Thus, Paradjanov's private space was implicated as a particular component of his '*vne kollektiva*' lifestyle. In Paradjanov's case, as well as that of Navrotskii, '*vne kollektiva*' implied a separation from the confines of the studio, the latter an official space invested solidly in a collective enterprise of Ukrainian national representation. Moreover, the presence of an Italian 'committee in defence of Paradjanov', along with open letters to the Soviet leadership against his arrest from French and American film-makers, in addition to a letter signed by various other Soviet *auteurs*, including Tarkovskii, to this effect, connected the dots for security organs between the director's 'genius' and his supposed crimes.[77]

'Ukrainian poetic cinema', the self-conscious movement that emerged at Dovzhenko Studio from *Shadows of Forgotten Ancestors*, was not simply a new aesthetic platform of national representation; rather, it was a means of defining 'national cinema' in relation to an individual *auteur*. The presence of an *auteur* like Paradjanov at Dovzhenko Studio was the principal means through which its management sought to escape from the Stalinist mode of representing Ukrainians without compromising the goal of national representation, and to mark off national cinema from genre production. Yet in Paradjanov's increasing refusal to participate in this collective project, with his largely superficial mobilization of local/national concerns in *Kyiv Frescoes*, his conduct, which befitted a 'cosmopolitan', grew ever more problematic to the CPU, Goskino and studio authorities.

* * *

As Vasyl' Zemliak implied during a discussion of *Kyiv Frescoes*, the director of *Shadows of Forgotten Ancestors* had tarnished his reputation as the bearer of 'Dovzhenko's categories'. The original Ukrainian *auteur*, as Lebedev suggested in his *Outline on the History of Cinema in the USSR*, Alexander Dovzhenko came to embody the discursive intentions of the studio that later bore his name.[78] One of the frequent critiques of the studio in the early 1960s was that Kyiv had failed to live up to its namesake's standards. Screenwriter Mykola Zarudnyi, for example, stated during the March 1962 SKU plenum that he felt 'Alexander Petrovich's displeasure' upon entering the studio grounds where a bust of the film-maker stood.[79] Thus, at the beginning of the decade, national embodiment was grounded particularly within Dovzhenko's individual character, perhaps to an equal degree as it was within his work.

While Paradjanov promoted himself as the hand-picked successor to Dovzhenko in his *Iskusstvo kino* article, 'Eternal Motion', he did not believe that 'poetic cinema' could be contained by 'narrowly national' concerns. Kyiv could be represented in a different manner than would have been possible before, not because of what Kyiv was or had become, but due to changes in the world of artistic representation, which touched Ukraine, the Soviet Union and Western Europe in similar ways. He told his colleagues,

> Seven years ago, when I worked with [Petro] Lubenskii [screenwriter on *The Top Guy*], I couldn't do what I wanted to. I didn't know how. I was less literate. Today, when there's Fellini, Illienko, there's *Father of a Soldier*, when there are five-six great poets in Ukraine[...] I understand how to start to make new films at the studio, when Osyka and Illienko have appeared at the studio.[80]

While Paradjanov routinely made use of the term 'poetic cinema' to define his work alongside that of Dovzhenko, the attachment to the word 'Ukrainian' was less essential for him. He was as much interested in the term as it applied to other *auteurs* like

Fellini, poet-film-maker Pier Paolo Pasolini and Andrei Tarkovskii as he was the self-conscious student of the 'poet of cinema' Alexander Dovzhenko. Yet the Soviet and Ukrainian context for 'poetic cinema' was fundamentally entangled in the life and legacy of Dovzhenko, not only because Dovzhenko Studio continually drudged up his name for emulation but also as legitimating 'poetic cinema's' aesthetic and 'political' agenda within the particular space of Ukraine.

When celebration of Paradjanov's 'authentic' image of Hutsulshchyna shifted to complaints about his film's lack of a mass audience, ostensibly because it was difficult to understand, it was not solely about accusations of 'formalism' and audience politics, just as audience politics was not solely about audience desire. After all, the average Soviet film in the mid-1960s was a box office failure.[81] For the moment, this remained a problem for the organs of distribution, and did not constitute an explicitly political problem. By contrast, those who initiated the reaction against *Shadows* beginning in early 1966 played the audience card to distance mainstream production at Dovzhenko Studio from what was soon labeled 'Ukrainian poetic cinema'. During 1965 and 1966, the most contentious two films made at Dovzhenko Studio were in production, which, combined with the Ukrainian intelligentsia's response to the arrests of August-September 1965 over the course of the following year, established a polarized atmosphere at the studio. Nonetheless, such 'poetic' films went into production on the basis of promoting personal expression and a Ukrainian national theme, two principles that emerged from the marriage of Thaw principles with an official reinvestment in the 'national character' of republican film studios.

Illienko's directorial debut, *A Well for the Thirsty* (*Krynytsia dlia sprahlykh*, 1966, released 1988), was shelved by the end of 1966, while production was halted on Vasyl' Illiashenko's *Coordinate your Watches* (*Pereverte svoi hodynyky*, 1966) around the same time. While diverse in style, both directors considered their work to be the heirs of Dovzhenko's early principles, on the one hand, and Paradjanov's *Shadows* on the other. Paradjanov, for his part, actively used his prestige to promote their work, calling on the studio to establish a conscious policy for cultivating 'poetic cinema'.[82] During this short period of two years, the idea of 'poetic cinema' became an all-important dimension of how film-makers at the studio defined their work.

Chapter 5

'UKRAINIAN POETIC CINEMA' AND THE CONSTRUCTION OF 'DOVZHENKO'S TRADITIONS'

Volodymyr Denysenko (director of *A Dream*) proclaimed in 1964 that one could divide the production of Dovzhenko Studio into two varieties: those that were merely 'imitative' of film production in Moscow, and those that contained a 'cinema poetics [*kinopoetika*]', which appealed to 'Dovzhenko's traditions'.[1] Denysenko, a student of Dovzhenko during 1954–5 at VGIK, aligned himself with the latter, but the dichotomy to which he alluded was far less clear-cut. 'Poetic cinema' in Ukraine was never a fixed aesthetic system (in the fashion of Italian Neorealism, for example). As Denysenko suggested, it functioned as a cultural trope to differentiate Ukrainian cinema, both from central productions in Moscow, and from the folkloric mode of representing Ukrainians that dominated film production during the Stalinist era. While 'poetic cinema' operated more broadly in Soviet critical discourse, its association with 'Dovzhenko's traditions' imparted a clear nationalistic value to the term in Ukraine.

Rather than a common aesthetic system, the concept of the 'poetic' pointed towards a series of shared interests that spanned multiple generations of Ukrainian film-makers. In grouping together film-makers with divergent interests who nonetheless labelled their work 'poetic cinema', however, we can identify a number of similar assumptions, within which each of them was working: first, and perhaps most important, is the question of authorship, which I explored in the last chapter. Related to the first, the second characteristic of Ukrainian poetic cinema is a shared interest in folklore and historical-mythological themes. Many scholars of nationalism have identified the re-working of folkloric material into mass-produced literary forms as a fundamental component of the nationalist project. Moreover, the Soviet culture industry constantly celebrated a folkloric image of non-Russians, read through canonical authors, the ideological assumptions of realism and injected with perceptible condescension associated with a discourse of 'national colour'. Thus, in approaching such a discourse, Ukrainian film-makers were also keen to reject its saccharine qualities, and attempted instead to both de-familiarize and re-authenticate a national folklore. Finally, film-makers who identified their work as 'poetic cinema' were interested in modernist and *avant-garde* cinemas in the Soviet Union and Western Europe – specifically, in Surrealism and Expressionism, from an earlier period, and with the more open aesthetic system that characterized, for example, the French New Wave, from a later period.

On a literal level, the films that Denysenko referenced, and those that later came to be identified with 'poetic cinema' were themselves written by poets. Denysenko's *A Dream* was written by Dmytro Pavlychko (like Denysenko, a Gulag survivor), and *Shadows* screenwriter, Ivan Chendei, was a poet and collector of Carpathian folklore. Ivan Drach and Lina Kostenko, the authors of Iurii Illienko's *A Well for the Thirsty* and Vasyl' Illiashenko's *Coordinate Your Watches*, were the two most prominent representatives of Ukraine's young poets during the 1960s. Kostenko was, moreover, the wife of studio head Vasyl' Tsvirkunov. Thus, poets and film-makers came together at Kyiv studio like nowhere else in the Soviet Union.

Yet the most important connection Denysenko made was between 'poetic cinema' and Dovzhenko's legacy at the studio in Kyiv, and in this respect, he was far from alone. One writer for the Ukrainian Komsomol newspaper, *Molod' Ukrainy*, stated deterministically, 'To show contemporary Ukraine and its people: This is the main task for the heirs of Dovzhenko's artistic treasures – Ukrainian film-makers.'[2] In fact, it seemed as though 'speaking in the language of Dovzhenko' became studio policy in the 1960s, and yet such a claim had widely varying implications. A soft claim to the film-maker's legacy meant a continued commitment to representing a local and national space, and that Dovzhenko Studio in particular had an exclusive claim to

Ukrainian thematics. To make a hard claim to Dovzhenko suggested that the only possible representation of Ukrainians was within the 'genre' of 'poetic cinema', that is, in implementation of a modernist and counter-realist 'poetics'. The difference between soft and hard claims to Dovzhenko's legacy were also contained in an understanding of film style as, in the former case, a collective mode of representation attached to the studio's 'brand', and, in the latter case, determined by personal expression and attached to the 'mark' of individual authorship.

Several remarks made during studio and union gatherings in the mid-1960s indicated the emergence of a polarized atmosphere among Ukrainian film-makers on the issue of 'poetic cinema'. Film director Oleksandr Muratov, in discussing the 'two tendencies in Ukrainian cinema' at a union plenum in late 1965, complained that 'some comrades' believed that only 'expressive' films could represent the Ukrainian ethnoscape, while films about 'real life' were somehow not national.[3] Screenwriter Oleksandr Syzonenko made a similarly polarizing remark from the other perspective during a 1962 union plenum, wherein he recalled the 'violent struggle in the Thirties' between the 'poets of cinema', which he associated with Dovzhenko, Eisenstein and Pudovkin, and the 'realists or prosaists', who rallied behind film director Sergei Iutkevich. Syzonenko continued, 'Eisenstein is no more, Pudovkin is no more, and Dovzhenko is no more, but Iutkevich remained, and it has not been the best side of our cinema that has remained.'[4]

Dovzhenko had become the embittered victim of Stalinism, who nonetheless managed to resist its influence on his work, even the work most directly associated with Stalin. Moscow film critic Efim Dobin, who wrote several articles in *Iskusstvo kino* and a monograph on the topic of 'poetic cinema', examined *Shchors* (1939) to explore Dovzhenko's mature poetics, a space where the film-maker's modernist disposition was tempered by tribute to a heroic, party-minded leader of the Civil War and his folksy, peasant sidekick, Bozhenko. In discussing this film, Dobin was able to isolate and praise Dovzhenko's anti-realist aesthetic contained in the scene of Bozhenko's funeral, affirming the importance of Dovzhenko's personal authorship in the scene's very 'constructedness [*sostroennost'*]' and stylization: 'It is completely obvious that A. Dovzhenko did not attempt at accuracy, not even at resemblance... All the scene's components are in complete harmony with its high, ceremonial, poetic construction.'[5] Thus, an attachment to poetic devices, even when the film-maker deliberately circumvented realist convention, could elicit praise during the early 1960s.

At the root of Dovzehnko's rehabilitation as a great *auteur* and as a 'son of Ukraine' was his work's ability to question the tenets of Socialist Realism. Dobin made a further point about Dovzhenko's construction of the landscape, showing that Ukrainian nature itself dictated such a construction:

> The blossoming sunflowers across the entire screen are a favourite image of his native Ukrainian nature...Nature in Dovzhenko's [work] is never a passive space of action. The landscape is itself metaphorical...In this way, it is poetic.[6]

Two primordial elements stand out in Dobin's praise of Dovzhenko's *Shchors*, both of which are irrelevant to the heroic story, and in many cases serve as counterpoints to the narrative: the peasant Bozhenko, drawn from Dovzhenko's autobiography (resembling his grandfather and uncle, according to the director), and the quality of the landscape. The funeral scene connects both elements in a transhistorical moment as young soldiers carry the peasant's body over a suddenly peaceful Ukrainian steppe. The funeral is 'poetic' not only due to questions of form – the use of visual metaphor, in particular – but more frequently encapsulates the particular content that is capable of embodying such formal properties.

Dobin's analysis of Dovzhenko's work was emblematic of the celebratory atmosphere that surrounded the late film-maker. During the 1960s and 1970s, the press constantly celebrated his achievements, conferences in Moscow brought together the most important critics and film-makers to discuss his legacy and industry leaders in Kyiv consistently drummed up his name to orient contemporary Ukrainian film-makers.

With his affirmative Ukrainian ethnoscape, which refused to domesticate national colour and placed it instead at the centre of political action, along with his films' counter-realist qualities, Dovzhenko easily played into concerns about the 'traditions' of Ukrainian cinema, while his modernism lent credence to an *auteurist* agenda. The problem remained, however, that Dovzhenko's 'poetic' influence on Kyiv Studio during this time could not shake its associations with Ukrainian nationalism. Two films in production during 1965, on the heels of *Shadows of Forgotten Ancestors*, made hard claims to Dovzhenko's legacy and to the rootedness of 'poetic cinema' in Ukraine, but were subsequently condemned as nationalist propaganda. Opposition to the films, however, emerged locally in Kyiv, from film-makers and industry leaders ostensibly sensitive to Ukraine's cultural patrimony and protective of the studio's positive, but fragile, reputation after *Shadows*.

* * *

Before his career as a cinematographer, Iurii Illienko had been to Ukraine only to visit his grandparents during the summer holidays.[7] His parents were among the 'de-nationalized Ukrainians', as Ivan Dziuba put it, engineers who had moved from eastern Ukraine to Moscow after the war. During his VGIK years, Illienko worked with his instructor Iakov Segel' on the iconic Thaw-era film, *Farewell, My Dove!* (*Proshaite, holuby!*, 1960), and with Artur Voitets'kyi on *My Son is Somewhere* (*Des' ie syn*, 1962), both at the soon-to-be closed Yalta Film Studio, before Paradjanov, upon the advice of Iurii's older brother Vadym (cinematographer on *Oleksa Dovbush*), recruited him to Kyiv in 1963.[8] The young cinematographer was unfamiliar with Ukrainian literature and knew the Ukrainian language poorly at best. Yet his work would come to be known as the foremost example of 'Ukrainian poetic cinema'. Much later, Illienko would claim that his grandparents in Cherkassy 'gave him his language', and that his teachers at Moscow School No. 461 constantly mocked his Ukrainian accent.[9]

Like Paradjanov's *Kyiv Frescoes*, Illienko's directorial debut was to fit within the framework of the 1965 anniversary year, when First Secretary Petro Shelest furthermore affirmed the unique ways that his republic suffered during the occupation.[10] Although taking place in contemporary Ukraine, *A Well for the Thirsty* was connected through several flashbacks to the period of the war. Moreover, the film was sold as a war film as Ivan Drach's literary screenplay was published in the October 1964 issue of the journal *Dnipro*, prefaced with a photo montage of Kyiv's liberation in November 1943.[11] When commenting on the film's significance to a Moscow audience in January 1966, screenplay editor Oleksandr Syzonenko noted that, once someone had seen this film, they would understand how difficult it was for the Ukrainian people to advance to victory during the war.[12] In this way, he hoped to establish the relevance of the film, both for the domestic spectator (he admitted that *Shadows of Forgotten Ancestors* functioned mostly within the realm of 'foreign distribution'), and for the political demands of the anniversary year. *A Well for the Thirsty* was to be a film on an 'actual theme', which spoke to and about the 'Ukrainian people' in their victory over Fascism.[13] In the process, however, Illienko's film risked confronting the exigencies of the developing war cult in the Soviet Union, which insisted that all Soviet citizens suffered equally, and that emphasizing the particularity of one nation's loss stank of 'bourgeois nationalism'.[14]

A Well for the Thirsty is about an old man, Levko Serdiuk, who lives alone with his memories in a dying village near Cherkassy. One day, he decides to die. The old man finds wood to build a coffin, and invites his sons and their families back to their native village to witness his death, or rather, to witness him lying in his homemade coffin until he becomes uncomfortable and gets out. His family has dinner together, and the film ends with his daughter-in-law going into labour as she picks apples.

Today, Illienko's film remains a defining moment of Ukrainian national cinema, alongside *Shadows of Forgotten Ancestors*. As with Paradjanov's film, the context of the *political* reception of *A Well for the Thirsty* has determined how Ukrainians remember the film today. Much of the contemporary response to the film seeks to place it within a Ukrainian literary canon of resistance to Tsarist / Bolshevik power.[15] Ukrainian film critic Vadym Skurativs'kyi stated that the essential conception behind *A Well*, along with *Shadows* and other examples of 'Ukrainian poetic cinema', was the destruction of the Ukrainian peasantry, which began in the late eighteenth century with the coming of serfdom and concluded with the *Holodomor* of 1932–3.[16] Of particular interest here is the fact that Skurativs'kyi viewed these symbolic and highly folkloric films as social documents, as responses to the long-term processes and results of Ukrainian social history.

Drach began writing the screenplay in 1962, for his graduation project at the Screenplay Institute (*Vysshie stsenarnye kursy*) in Moscow. While only 26 years old at the time, the poet was well-published in the early 1960s, a party member and the darling of the Ukrainian literary establishment. In his introduction to Drach's first book, also published in 1962, the important literary historian Leonid Novychenko wrote: 'There are comrades ready to see in him the essential "method" of contemporary young poetry.'[17] That year, *Voprosy literatury* (*Questions of Literature*) interviewed him as one of the most representative of young Soviet poets, alongside Voznesensky and Evtushenko. Like Paradjanov, Drach claimed influence from a diverse body of Russian, Ukrainian, West European and American writers and film-makers, mentioning in the interview Leo Tolstoy, Dostoyevsky, Federico García Lorca, Hemingway, Faulkner, 'the early [Pavlo] Tychyna', Maksym Ryl's'kyi, Dovzhenko and Fellini.[18]

Drach published his first major work, 'Shevchenko's Death (*Smert' Shevchenka*)', in the March issue of *Vitchyzna*, while Dziuba was still the literary editor. In his poem, Drach advanced two ideas regarding the poet's memorialization: first, Shevchenko was one of the few figures that eastern and western Ukrainians shared equally, even before 're-unification' in 1944; and second, the poet himself served as a harbinger of individual artistic style, which eclipsed his political significance as a 'revolutionary democrat'. Drach wrote,

> The artist does not have well-trodden norms.
>
> He himself is the norm, he himself in his own style ...
>
> In this hundred-year and hundred-coloured storm
>
> I throw myself into the troubled sorrow-waves.[19]

Here, Drach was as much interested in the legacy of the poet for a new Ukraine that encompassed both East and West, as well as the diaspora in the Russian Far East and on the Canadian plains (with his reference, 'From Winnipeg to Vladivostok'), as he was in recapturing a politics of personal expression, which, with its emphasis on 'sorrow' and 'loss', denied the affirmative politics of the 'Friendship of Peoples'.

'Shevchenko's Death' was included in his collection, *Sunflower*, where he brought both of these concerns to bear. The centrepiece of the collection is a poem entitled 'Spraha (Thirst)', published first in the May 1962 issue of *Dnipro*, which appeared at the time as a poetic response to Khrushchev's critique of the cult of personality, with its predictable sentiment of a 'thirst' for authentic life and a return to humanistic values. In imagined conversation with Walt Whitman and Aphrodite in his college dorm room, Drach wrote:

> I have sorrow – wild, insatiable,
>
> Nothing can calm it, forever unquenchable.
>
> This is the thirst of compassion [*liudianist'*] and beauty and opportunity,
>
> I am filled with this. It burns me daily
>
> A passionate thirst is human happiness,
>
> Humanity's anxiety is my anxiety.[20]

Novychenko noted that Drach came to being, like 'his generation', under the conditions of the Twentieth Party Congress. We might also relate the poem to *A Well for the Thirsty* in its allusion to the unused well of the village that emerges after the war, signalling its spiritual death. Drach moves from an aesthetic of hope in humanity's ability to quench their thirst to an ironic statement about the 'well for the thirsty', which has dried up and is no longer potable.

Novychenko defined Drach's style as 'associative', seeing in it parallels to 'Dovzhenko's film language'. While acceptable to a certain extent, Novychenko called on Drach to rein in certain aspects of his excess, especially when it created distance between the poet and reader:

> It is true that the poet has a right to expect a reader who actively 'works together' with his thoughts, but this does not at all justify the appearance in certain of Drach's verses of images that demand special puzzle-solving skills [*spetsial'ne rozhaduvannia*]. In the end, poetry is not a rebus [puzzle].[21]

Drach's response to such mild criticism would allude to theories of audience differentiation, that the reader for whom the poems were intended – a highly educated, Ukrainian-speaking public – would understand his complex 'imagery'. Nonetheless, with the Ideological Commision reports of 1962–63, Drach discovered that there was a slippery slope from his appeal to a small subset of the mass audience to accusations of 'formalism'. In April 1963, First Secretary Pidhornyi singled out Drach for criticism during a meeting with ideological workers in the CPU, stating that his work was fodder for 'Ukrainian bourgeois nationalist counter-revolutionaries abroad'.[22] Andrii Skaba moreover accused Drach in the May issue of *Kommunist Ukrainy* of having 'an unjustifiably complicated descriptive system', which he blamed on 'the disease of his age [*bolezn' vozrasta*]'.[23] Despite such high-level criticism, literary journals *Dnipro* and *Vitchyzna*, along with Dovzhenko Studio, continued to support Drach's work.

Drach had finished his screenplay, *A Well for the Thirsty*, in 1964, and the head of the Screenplay Institute asked Tsvirkunov to consider it for production at Dovzhenko Studio, on the basis that it dealt with Ukrainian themes.[24] In following the Ukrainian Ministry of Culture's 1962 directive to employ Ukrainian writers to help 'reveal Ukrainian literature, art, and culture', Tsvirkunov had hired Drach for the Screenplay Studio. His first experience at the studio was working with Paradjanov revising Chendei's literary screenplay of *Shadows*.[25] While providing Drach with a regular salary, in addition to the standard honorarium for all work accepted for production, the *masterstvo* demanded that he write exclusively for Dovzhenko Studio, providing his employer with one viable screenplay every 18 months. To maintain his full salary, Drach additionally submitted at least six reviews of other screenplays and served as the principal editor on another screenplay each year.[26] Thus, despite the Fordist style of cultural production that Tsvirkunov was attempting to institute at Dovzhenko Studio in the early 1960s in an attempt to solve the 'problem of cadres', the *masterstvo* also functioned as a haven and regular employment for non-conformist poets like Drach, Pavlychko, Kostenko and Mykola Vinhranovs'kyi.

Drach began the literary screenplay for *A Well for the Thirsty*, subtitled 'A Contemporary Parable', with an epigraph from the final lines of Plato's *Phaedo*, during which Socrates takes the hemlock and dies. Drach intended to present a similar mythology of the noble death that he did in his poem, 'Shevchenko's Death'. In the performance and reproduction of the death ritual, death was to affirm the positive quality of life itself. We soon learn, however, that Drach's screenplay functioned as a morbid parody of such a ritual, envisioning an old and lonely widower, whose many sons have either died during the war or left him to pursue a 'contemporary' lifestyle in the city. The old man, Levko, decides to build his own coffin and lie in it until death comes, inviting his family back to their native village to observe the indefinite spectacle.[27] Despite the bleak theme of loneliness and death, Drach injected several moments of light-hearted comedy, which appealed to folkloric notions of Ukrainian humour: Levko discovers the *kolkhoz* director's electric razor, which Levko attempts to use, unsuccessfully, on his own grizzled face. Later in the screenplay, Levko's daughter-in-law Solomonia presents him with a radio to communicate with his youngest son, a test pilot. The old man, more comfortable talking to his pet goat, is unable to speak to a machine, managing only an awkward cough. Other elements of comedy include the old man's prolonged quest for official approval to acquire wood for his coffin, the latter of which alludes to the comedy of Soviet bureaucracy found in Aleksandrov's *Volga Volga* (1938) among many other Soviet films.

When the studio reviewed Drach's screenplay for production, many immediately identified the work's rural setting and iconic old man as tied into a traditional Ukrainian folkloric mode. Yet they saw in *A*

Well for the Thirsty particular promise for its allusions to Dovzhenko's style and literary content. In particular, the figure of Levko recalled Dovzhenko's work through the latter's fictionalized accounts of his own grandfather, Semen Petrovych, in *The Enchanted Desna*. During a discussion of the screenplay, Drach's colleagues conflated this resemblance with the idea of maintaining Dovzhenko's 'traditions'.[28] Zemliak commented that the film would affirm the studio's return to Dovzhenko. He told the board, 'In recent years we have moved away from that knowledge, which Dovzhenko left behind'.[29] Screenplay editor, M. A. Kyrychenko, argued more adamantly for the maintenance of 'Dovzhenko's traditions' in this screenplay: 'If we're about Dovzhenko's traditions, then this screenplay[...] is a model for how we should follow those traditions.'[30] Denysenko stated that Levko represented the 'entire Ukrainian people'.[31] Thus, the studio linked writerly knowledge specifically to the film's national significance, seen in its association with the fictionalized space of Dovzhenko's childhood. Significantly, the screenplay's definitively bleak representation of the Ukrainian ethnoscape was not at issue: after all, Dovzhenko's work too focused on death and rural poverty.

The Screenplay Editorial Board (SRK) identified two problems with the screenplay: first within the folkloric quality of some of the scenes with Levko. Novelist Iakiv Bash was positive about the Dovzhenko associations, but cautioned against Levko's association with a '*khutorians'kyi*' type, predicting that non-Ukrainians 'will call him funny, an eccentric, and so on'.[32] The second complaint registered confusion about the complex 'symbolism' and predominance of metaphor contained in the work. In a sense, Drach's colleagues found fault with both the familiar stereotypes and the de-familiarized ethnoscape that the young poet imagined. Predictably, Drach answered both complaints with the implication that he had written the film for a culturally knowledgeable Ukrainian spectator in mind. In calling the work a 'film parable', he identified both the 'simplicity' and 'locality' of the 'genre'. He went on:

> That is why when they say that it is absolutely necessary to motivate the horse [a persistent image in the film], it seems to me that for Ukrainian artists, for the world-view of a Ukrainian, the horse is [already] so motivated in Dovzhenko, in Gogol' that you know what it is[...] Whoever knows this will not shrug their shoulders at this horse.[33]

This claim is interesting in the light of Novychenko's accusation that Drach engaged in writing convoluted puzzles. Whereas Drach made the claim for ethnic knowledge, Illienko made the *auteur*ist claim for ethnic discovery, in his personal search for an authenticated Ukrainian ethnoscape, one that was unfamiliar and extraordinary, but also nostalgic for the director's lost childhood.

Illienko was probably ignorant of the specific quality of the 'Dovzhenkoist' elements in the screenplay, especially since they were drawn from Dovzhenko's post-cinematic literary career, which enjoyed little success outside of Ukraine. Fresh from shooting *Shadows* on location in the Carpathians, he was keen to discover more authenticities in the Ukrainian village that would become the setting of *A Well for the Thirsty*. Sounding like Paradjanov from a year and a half earlier, he told the studio in April:

> Only when we find ourselves in the village, when we find this milieu, and the residents of this village will be speaking in their language, when we come upon the architecture, the background of the Ukrainian village, the authentic costumes, when the real thing emerges, when we avoid the make-up in this respect, as we understand it now. Only then can the screenplay be surrounded by the flesh, which makes it possible to make the film that we have conceived.

> We travelled two thousand kilometres around the villages of Ukraine. We especially picked up old men, and offered them a seat in the car and conversed. We met with analogous situations, of old men, who were in deplorable conditions [underlining in the original document]. But it's interesting that not one of them complained, they held onto their dignity in speaking about their troubles, and regarded them with a light humour. Levko is written in this way, and not bombastically. Such a method is not eclectic; it is the method of researching character [...][34]

Illienko presented himself to an amateur ethnographer, who was, in the process, coming to know himself through a type of folkloric of real life. He knew the stereotypes to which Bash referred, but denied this quality of 'colour' its lack of authenticity. When writing about the film upon its release in 1987, Illienko continued to tell the story of his journey through Ukraine to national consciousness.

> I searched for a long time. [...] And there, in the very heart of Ukraine, between Cherkassy and Chigirin, where the Tiamin River flows into the Dnieper, I found the perfect spot – hills, black earth, such a swirl

of earthly paradise. And, moreover, in the valley, I saw sand, real sand, dunes even. And there stood a village, *khaty* with thatch roofs, and on the roofs – windmills. A Ukrainian village – standing on sand. How unnatural! I felt something in myself like a flash of lightening, like a prophecy – suddenly the essence of the film was revealed. The landscape turned out to be the key, the prototype, the methodology even.[35]

Whereas Paradjanov was interested in questions of the beauty of the human object in nature, Illienko, in his interest in discovery and ethnography, was interested in discovering a scientific basis for the authentic Ukrainian. In this case, Illienko returned to a space near his own birthplace in Cherkassy. Illienko suggests that the village is not the pastoral idyll, nor does it possess a fairy-tale-like quality of tragedy, as *Shadows of Forgotten Ancestors* contained. A discovery of the primordial ethnic self demanded the labour of travel, and a struggle with the unnatural and uncanny contained within Illienko's own native ethnoscape.

The director, however, made an interesting connection to *Shadows*, stating that his debut was about 'the same people and the same culture'.[36] Illienko here indicated that the basis for exoticizing the Ukrainian people was the Hutsul. In generalizing the Hutsul to all Ukraine, however, all Ukraine becomes Hutsulshchyna, simultaneously self and Other. Illienko commented on Dmytro Miliutenko, who played Levko in the film, 'You can't tell him apart from the peasants from the surrounding villages. And the issue is not [that he's] a prototype, but in the deep truth of [his] character.' Miliutenko too commented, 'I feel a deep kinship of Levko's family with my own. There is a lot in common.'[37] Thus, we read a similar treatment of Illienko's film as we did in the Ukrainian coverage of *Shadows*, in its emphasis on associating the actor with the role as a function of 'character', and the role itself with a more general notion of Ukrainian 'character'. Unlike Mykolaichuk in *Shadows*, however, Miliutenko had the additional cachet within Ukraine's cinematic history of having starred in both *Shchors* and Savchenko's *Bohdan Khmel'nyts'kyi*, making *A Well for the Thirsty* all the more significant for studio claims about its cultural patrimony.

A Well for the Thirsty passed into production on 20 April 1965, with the prediction that it would 'undoubtedly become a significant event in Ukrainian cinema'.[38] It was decided to shoot the film in the place that Illienko claimed to have discovered while travelling through the republic, in the village of Trushivtsi in Cherkass oblast', located at the very geographic centre of the Ukrainian SSR. Illienko continued Dovzhenko's and Paradjanov's formula for authenticity, and employed peasants from the Chyhyryn district, functioning more generally as extras, but also as ethnic decoration.

In making the film, Illienko reduced the folkloric humour of the narrative to a minimum, even eliminating a number of dominant relationships between Levko and his neighbours and family to the point where spectators unfamiliar with the published screenplay would miss significant portions of the symbolic world on display. Instead, Illienko focused almost exclusively on the fuzzy boundaries between present-day reality, memory and the spatial politics of war memorialization. A major scene in the film involves the opening of a new war memorial to honour *kolkhoz* members killed during the war. To achieve 'emotional authenticity', Illienko's crew announced the unveiling ceremony on a local radio station, and filmed an actual audience during the event.[39]

The stark tonality of the film stock continually emphasizes the dream-like quality – caught between memory and the contemporary – of the world that Levko inhabits. The sky and water appear black, while the trees possess an infrared glow. Skurativs'kyi claims that Illienko used expired and poor-quality Nikron film stock from the Ukrainian factory in Shostka to achieve this look (see Figure 5.1).[40] Despite the utter lack of colour – and, indeed, of any degree of tonal range – and the further reduction of the narrative space of the film, several features of *A Well for the Thirsty* closely resemble *Shadows*. Iurii Davydov's cinematography highlights the same combination of presentational and observational styles, alternating between artless tableaux framing in the interior shots of Levko's house, assimilating his body and the wall of memories behind him into one flattened image, and the highly mobile camera that moves along a line of humans against an expressive landscape. In this latter respect, we see a similar effort to survey rural human life as Illienko presented in the Hutsul market scene at the beginning of *Shadows*.

In *A Well for the Thirsty*, however, the landscape is de-familiarized to the point of total abstraction. The spectator receives little information about the spatial connections between the well, Levko's home, the apple orchard, the mill and the cemetery, all of which constitute the film's ethnic texture. Illienko places all of these locations upon the same barren dreamscape, simultaneously existing in memory and in the present. His wife of memory and his present-day daughter-in-

Figure 5.1   Tonal minimalism in Iurii Illienko's *A Well for the Thirsty* (1965)

law are both played by actress Larysa Kadochnikova, and the war-era soldiers pass through the contemporary landscape that is already lifeless. Alongside this dreamscape, however, exist the generic features of the 'national film', present in the ethnographic images of peasants constructing a house with hay and mud, the regionalism of Levko's speech, elements of the *kolkhoz* comedy, all of which further render the film uncanny. Whereas the Carpathian landscape of *Shadows* had been definitively unfamiliar for most eastern Ukrainians, apart from the generic antecedents of Ukrainian modernism on the one hand and the rare film like Ivanov's *Oleksa Dovbush* on the other, the central and southern Ukrainian steppe of *A Well for the Thirsty* constituted a landscape already familiar from Gogol', Shevchenko and Repin, and more recently in the work of Dovzhenko, Py'rev and Savchenko. Thus, Illienko's attempt to discover and render the unfamiliar within such a known landscape became a more difficult task, eventually necessitating the cast and crew's journey to the Uzbek desert to complete the film (where the aging actor Dmytro Miliutenko died from the strain of shooting the film).

Only towards the final 20 minutes does a narrative emerge in *A Well for the Thirsty*, and the film's dreamspace recedes. As Levko lies uncomfortably in his coffin, waiting for death, his many sons, with their wives and children, arrive. The old man grows restless with his intended 'peaceful' death, clearly bored with the charade. He coughs, fidgets uncomfortably and places kopeks in his eyes before emerging to have dinner with his family. As the large family sits at the dinner table, we hear a woman in voice-over explaining the narrative thread; that the old man had resolved to die, and invited his family, via telegram, to watch. The film ends as the old man drags a living apple tree across the orchard, apples falling behind him as a smiling Solomonia attempts to retrieve them. As she bends to claim another apple, she enters labour, dropping all of them out of her dress. The final shot is of her leaning on the ground, holding her belly, framed against the sky (Figure 5.2).

Promotion of the film began in early June 1965 in the mass-circulation weekly, *Na ekranakh Kyeva*. Ilia Shatokhin featured Dmytro Miliutenko, who played Levko in the film, writing that the

Figure 5.2 Dream image in *A Well for the Thirsty* (Illienko, 1965): Levko (Miliutenko) and his wife (Kadochnikova) at the well.

veteran Ukrainian actor 'has given ample proof that his old man Levko will be filled with a humanistic and life-affirming character'.[41] In August, the film crew met with spectators to promote the film in Chernihiv while shooting on location nearby.[42] Illienko gave interviews in October 1965 and January 1966 about the film for *Na ekranakh Kyeva*. In the first interview, he affirmed Shatokhin's notion of the transmission of 'humanistic values', telling reporters that *A Well for the Thirsty* is about the 'immortality of the great human heart'. Yevhenia Semenova introduced a second interview with Illienko and Miliutenko, affirming that the film will become a 'deeply emotional and philosophical work about a person who beautifies [*prykrashaie*] the earth and labour with his love towards it, [and] about the loyalty to his native land and responsibility for its fate'.[43]

In watching the film, one realizes how completely different such expectations were from the actual product that Illienko would soon present to Goskino. We have to understand, however, that critics and journalists knew the plot; that the film was about an old man who desires to die. In this motif, however, they viewed the image of death in the screenplay, according to Dovzhenko, as a beautiful process of renewal. Because *A Well for the Thirsty* fitted into a definitive genre, the 'national film' or 'poetic cinema', the violation of convention necessitated a response that spoke to such formal and narrative transgressions. Instead of the homage to Dovzhenko other filmmakers and critics envisioned from the screenplay, we get moments of visual parody of Dovzhenko, especially *Earth*. The latter film opens with an extended scene of an old man dying with his large extended family and neighbours looking on. The scene is serene, however, and mildly humorous as the dying old man eats an apple while another peasant says light-heartedly, 'Well, die already'. Bozhenko dies in *Shchors* in a similarly solemn yet celebratory manner. Levko, on the other hand, cannot 'simply' die, honoured for the role he played in life, but is forced instead to relive painful memories (Figure 5.3). Moreover, as Larysa Briukhovets'ka points out, if in Dovzhenko's *Earth*, the land is valued by everyone, the great crisis of *A Well for the Thirsty* is its uselessness.[44] The final scene of the old man carrying the apple tree is his last attempt to recreate the scene of beautiful death found in Dovzhenko, but ends with Solomonia in labour. Instead of the transcendental death, Illienko's film presents us with an image of grief in its persistent reproduction of loss.

When official opinion had turned against the film by February 1966, Ukrainian Goskino claimed that the film had 'significantly

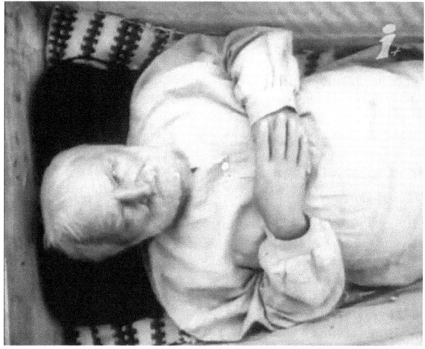

Figure 5.3 The old man dying in (top to bottom) Dovzhenko's *Earth* (1930) and Illienko's *A Well for the Thirsty* (1965)

departed from the screenplay', the contents of which were 'deeply national'.[45] As with *Kyiv Frescoes*, official reaction to the film turned from positive to negative based on the same continuum. Party officials like Andrii Skaba expected a film that represented the Ukrainian people in an affirmative manner (like Dovzhenko). In this respect, the visual flourishes were not at issue yet, nor did officials ever criticize its ethnographic mode of representing the Ukrainian 'national character'; rather, the film was problematic because of its hopelessness, something that emerges beyond the 'life-affirming' humour contained in Drach's screenplay.

Several individuals at the studio, however, remained in awe with Illienko's accomplishments, including the initially weary Bash, along with Denysenko and Paradjanov. Others, such as set designer Vladimir Agranov, told his colleagues that 'egoists', who cared nothing for the spectator, made such a film. While Vasyl' Illiashenko, who was dealing with his own problems on *Coordinate your Watches*, argued that the spectator's acceptance is not the only qualification of a film's merit, Navrotskii ironically tore into the film for its pretensions against the 'average viewer'. Tsvirkunov, however, concluded that the 'film has emerged from the source of the national character', and wholeheartedly accepted it, with certain revisions.[46] On 27 April, the studio accepted the film, concluding that it had returned to the ideas contained in Drach's screenplay, with 'the image of Ukraine, its beautiful and great nature, the diversity of landscapes, the fertile lands and wistful forests[...] appear[ing] before us'.[47] Such an affirmation, of course, was divorced entirely from the pervasive image of loss contained in the film's unfertile landscape and morose hero.

At this time, Drach was embroiled in his own controversial political activity. On the day that Dovzhenko Studio passed the completed film to Ukrainian Goskino for approval, the secretary of the Lviv Oblast Committee of the CPU issued a report on 'nationalist activity and actions against it' to his superiors in the Central Committee in Kyiv. Among those arrested in August 1965 were ten individuals in Lviv oblast. Their trial on 15 April attracted the attention of Kyiv intellectuals who were friends of several of those arrested. Drach, along with fellow poets and screenwriters Lina Kostenko and Mykola Vinhranovs'kyi, travelled to Lviv to protest outside the courthouse. The three, also accused of distributing 'ideologically vicious' unpublished works, were in the centre of a group of 30 friends of the accused. According to the report, Drach and Kostenko showered the accused with flowers as they were led to the courthouse, hailing them with 'Glory! Glory to the patriots!', while shouting at the *militsiia* and court officials, 'Shame!'.[48] The report went on, 'In a discussion with the head of the Lenin neighbourhood branch of the *militsiia* c[omrade] Saburov, Drach said, "You yourself are [only] scum, but here violence is being done to the most forward-looking Ukrainians".[49] Drach's supposed statement was unquestionably elitist in his delineation of the 'scum' from the 'forward-looking'.

Such a seemingly intimate connection between dissident politics and film production seemed to shake authorities in Ukrainian Goskino as they discussed *A Well for the Thirsty* on 4 May. Senior editor Protsenko proceeded cautiously, and suggested that they accept the film for a 'limited audience', rather than return it to the director for further revisions.[50] S. P. Ivanov agreed, stating, 'The film can only exist for a certain spectator. It's impossible to release the film on the screen.' While such a 'limited' distribution seemed to affirm Drach's own preference for the film's reception, in effect it meant that, despite no official order to 'shelve' the film, local distribution organs would not be encouraged to buy prints. The studio, however, would not have a mark against it in this case, as the film would then constitute a distribution concern. Moreover, the studio might have continued to anticipate a festival success, along the lines of *Shadows*, and the film-makers' union would have permission to screen the film at their private screening hall at the October House of Culture. During the union plenum two days later, at which Secretary Skaba made condemnatory remarks, however, Ivanov opened the event with severe words. He stated that the film was one of the recent failures of the studio for its 'canned lyricism' and fixation on death, which represented Ukraine in a negative light. A meeting of the union a week and a half later continued the argument, with Navrotskii promoting Illienko's complete repression as a 'bourgeois nationalist'. Toward the end of the month, an anonymous letter from a self-avowed 'old Bolshevik' within the Ukrainian Writers' Union accused Drach too of being a 'herald of Ukrainian nationalism', both for his appearance at the 15 April trial and for writing an 'anti-Soviet film'. He went on, 'But how much more similar trash will come out of the Ukrainian film studio, in which our Soviet life and our Soviet people are shown as caricatures.'[51] The salient critique of the film concerned its improper representation of the Ukrainian ethnic community, ostensibly due to a lack of first-hand knowledge of its 'character'.

Meanwhile, Syzonenko had suggested yet another revision, which would contain more landscapes and a 'more *even* dialogue',[52] suggesting an attempt to make the film conform to generic expectations.

To complete this new series of revisions, Drach asked for another 30,000 roubles, a sizable sum, to which Ivanov nonetheless grudgingly agreed.[53] A week later, however, a CPU Politburo decision halted production.[54] Ivanov's fears were realized as the studio was forced to repay Gosbank the 268,000 roubles spent on the production.[55] While the CPU shelved and condemned the film as bourgeois nationalist propaganda, *A Well for the Thirsty* nonetheless affirmed Illienko's and Drach's reputations as brilliant *auteurs*.

In April 1966, as Drach returned from Lviv, he met with Illienko to discuss the director's idea for a new film, this one based on Gogol's *St. John's Eve* (*Vecher na Ivana Kupala*), promoted as a mix of 'folkloric fantasy[...] with the *realia* of everyday life'.[56] At the moment when the studio was abandoning *A Well for the Thirsty* as a 'politically dangerous' project, they were approving Illienko's new film, a film completely at odds with traditional Soviet adaptations of the 'realist' Gogol of the St. Petersburg years. While Illienko had failed to produce an image of the contemporary Ukrainian ethnoscape, he returned to the safe realm of classic literary adaptation. Whereas Paradjanov's 'moral' failure with *Kyiv Frescoes* ended his directorial career in Kyiv, Illienko remained a core member of the studio collective after his political failure with *A Well for the Thirsty*, perhaps because of Illienko's legal identity as an actual Ukrainian. Nonetheless, Vasyl' Illiashenko had no such luck standing on the laurels of his nationality. *Coordinate Your Watches*, as a failed example of 'poetic cinema', in fact had the most lasting effect on its director's ability to work on future projects.

Vasyl' Illiashenko: The Failed *Auteur*

By April 1966, Illiashenko had been accused of being a fraud and would never recover his reputation in Ukrainian cinema. The reasons for this are not obvious, but indicate that the studio continued to take seriously questions of personal authorship. Paradjanov, while having failed to complete *Kyiv Frescoes*, remained an important figure at the studio, one whose words carried real weight in union and studio debates. When discussing footage of *Coordinate Your Watches* in December 1965, Paradjanov heralded the film as '*vne kollektiva*', but called the director's lack of talent 'criminal'.[57] Instead of citation of *Shadows* and Dovzhenko, he accused Illiashenko of plagiarism, along with a deployment of clichés and Ukrainian stereotypes. To Paradjanov, *Coordinate Your Watches* seemed to confirm Andrei Tarkovsky's 1962 warning that 'poetic cinema[...] easily falls into pretentiousness'.[58] Five years passed before the studio trusted

Illiashenko with another independent production, this time a mediocre industrial drama about Donbass miners entitled *Steep Horizon* (*Krutyi horyzont*, 1971). This film too became a total failure, from a creative, ideological, critical and box office standpoint.[59]

In the production drama that surrounded *Coordinate Your Watches*, Illiashenko continually mobilized Thaw-era discourses of film authorship, the cult of personality and generational division. Illiashenko intended his film as a tribute to three poets who died on the Ukrainian Front during World War II and were posthumously accepted into the Ukrainian Writers' Union in spring 1962.[60] Writer Lina Kostenko envisioned it as a 'triptych from a spiritual odyssey', the narrative moving freely among three separate stories, connected thematically. Together, the story of the poets was to explore the multiple dimensions of the Ukrainian experience during the Great Patriotic War. As a narrator explains at the beginning of the screenplay, '[These] poets are mirrors', which reflect the 'larger path'.[61] The poets' stories begin on the eve of 21 June 1941. Kyivan Leonid Levyts'kyi proposes to his girlfriend in a cemetery; peasant Volodymyr Bulaienko (played by Mykolaichuk) marries Tonia in the village church as her dictatorial father threatens to kill them and they ride off on horseback; and party poet Fedir Shvindin wakes up in a psychiatric ward after a purge hearing that leads him to attempt suicide. After the German invasion, Levyts'kyi volunteers for the Soviet Army, and dies in battle; Bulaienko joins the Ukrainian partisans, and dies while serving as a decoy as his detachment attacks a German train; Shvindin succeeds in killing himself after the Nazi 'Dr Todt' performs psychological experiments on him.

While heavy in religious and national symbolism, Illiashenko's film appears from the shooting script as a canonical example of war memorial and the horrors of the German occupation in Ukraine. While the film was remade by Leonid Osyka as *Love Awaits Those Who Return* (*Khto vernets'ia – doliubyt'*), the Shvindin and Levyts'kyi stories were removed for political and aesthetic reasons, and the entire film concerns Bulaenko, the peasant-poet-partisan. Apart from refocusing upon the most politically acceptable of the three protagonists, Osyka's name change is significant for its direct allusion to Semen Gudzenko's poem 'My Generation' (*Moe pokolenie*, 1945), which emphasizes grief and loss over war heroism:

> Love awaits those who return? No! The heart can't handle it,
> and it's not worth dying so that the living can love them.

There are no men in the family, no children, nobody in the house.
Will such grief really ease the sobs of the living?[62]

Osyka removes the question mark, perhaps appealing more to irony than the seriousness of grief. While Gudzenko was born in Kyiv and wrote many of his poems about Kyiv, he was not Ukrainian and always wrote in Russian. The change in titles had implications for how the film would be read as an example of national cinema. Osyka, too, was from Kyiv, and spoke only in Russian. During his second year at VGIK, he came to Dovzhenko Studio as an assistant director on Denysenko's *A Dream*. He took on *Love Awaits* in 1965 after authorities at VGIK failed his first graduation project, *That which Enters the Sea (Ta, shcho vkhodyt' u more)*, on the grounds of accusations of formalism.[63]

Love Awaits begins as the camera moves through the landscape along the Right Bank of the Dnieper in Kyiv. As Gudzenko's poem is heard in voice-over, we see a long pan across Kyiv factories and churches that line the Dnieper. We cut to a close-up of a marble engraver in Victory Park carving in death dates of fallen war heroes (1944, 1943, etc.). The camera pans across the thousands of graves in the cemetery, literally melding human and landscape in the context of death. Documentary voice-overs of dead soldiers' mothers recount memories of their sons, with the language switching between Russian, Ukrainian and *surzhyk*. Osyka considered this merging of oral history with fiction a completely new invention, meant to complicate the conventions of Soviet cinema's war memorialization. Moreover, in offering actual voices, Osyka believed he was authentically representing the multilingual ethnoscape of the city. While the director's colleagues at the studio generally appreciated his film, even if they considered it unlikely to attract a popular audience, many complained of Osyka's title, along with the linguistic 'dissonance' that his attempts at authenticity evoked. Bash, whose work frequently touched upon the experience of fighting on the Ukrainian front, stated that the shift between Russian and Ukrainian, instead of affirming the 'friendship of peoples',' promoted the idea of mutual incomprehensibility. He furthermore complained of the 'slippage' in the Russian voice of the mother.[64] Bash viewed Osyka's attempt at authenticity as a compromise with Russian, believing that he should have established a total Ukrainian linguistic space, the likes of which was contained in Denysenko's *A Dream*. Osyka maintained *surzhyk* as a regional particularity in his film, thus separating the literary space of poetry (always in either Russian or Ukrainian) in the film from the speech of everyday life (what Paradjanov called 'contemporary Ukrainian'). In appealing to ethnographic investigation and the personal experience of speech behaviour, Osyka, like Paradjanov, attempted to distance himself from the heated debates about linguistic policy in Ukraine taking place in both official and dissident circles.

While particular scenes resemble Paradjanov's and Illienko's work in *Shadows*, such as the exploratory pan over motionless peasants, which has the effect of locating and equating human life with a particular landscape, the look of the film relates more clearly to Illienko's *A Well for the Thirsty*, with its expressive use of tonality. Moreover, like Illienko's film, the narrative is structured loosely, with only the overriding themes of sacrifice, death and loss uniting the various movements of the plot. The narrative begins as Bulaienko's mother kisses him goodbye as he leaves for the front, changing her white headscarf to black as she watches him walk off from their thatched-roof *khata* to join his new comrades. A still cutaway to the house reveals an image identical to one of Dovzhenko's boyhood home that circulated in the early 1960s, suggesting the self-reflexive pastiche which constituted Osyka's knowledge of the Ukrainian peasant. Osyka was imagining peasant life through the lens of a reproducable mythology.

The next scene, the only one in which we see actual combat, is unusual for its stylistic distance from the rest of the film. Most of it is composed of documentary images from the front, with only the final moments showing Bulaienko arguing with his commanding officer before most of the squadron is blown away by German artillery fire. Bulaienko escapes the fray with another man, soon killed from aerial bombardment. After a series of adventures within the war-torn landscape, the poet discovers and joins a partisan group. The partisans resolve to hijack a German train, using the plain-clothes poet as a decoy to get the engineer to stop. As the partisans pick off the German soldiers as they leave the train, Bulaienko opens one of the cars to reveal one of the crimes of the occupation: the Germans had been exporting Ukrainian black earth to the West for grain production (Figure 5.4). The camera pans across thousands of gravestones in Victory Park once again as the film ends, implying without showing the poet's approaching death, as an extension of the literal abduction of Ukrainian land.

Despite Osyka's claim that he did not intend to 'imitate' Paradjanov and Illienko – that instead, he was working within a particular 'genre'

Figure 5.4   Poet Bulaienko discovers the stolen black earth in Leonid Osyka's *Love Awaits Those Who Return* (1966)

of associational poetics common to the three of them – the film lacks the sense of narrative and formal completion evident in *Shadows* and even *A Well for the Thirsty*. Instead, Osyka presents us with a series of cinematic exercises, motivated by narrative and thematic concerns such as oral history and memorialization; a play with conventions in representations of combat and violence; experimentations with rendering space and landscape; and a further exploration of aural minimalism and juxtaposition, from the linguistic 'dissonance' mentioned earlier, to the juxtaposition of jazz with Ukrainian folk songs and Soviet 'front poetry'. The final scene is the only coherent episode, perhaps getting at the essence of what Osyka intended with the film – an image of loss that positions land and people in fluid continuity. Bulaienko is positioned *within* the abducted earth. Viewed in its entirety, however, *Love Awaits* remains an essentially de-narrativized and formally eclectic project, in part due to Osyka's inexperience as a film-maker, but also emerging from the process of fixing Illiashenko's 'mistakes'. What emerges is an ostensibly apolitical but definitively *avant-garde* film, one which had no possibility of becoming either a popular film or one of the classics of 'Ukrainian poetic cinema' alongside Illienko's *A Well for the Thirsty* or Osyka's future project, *The Stone Cross* (*Kaminnyi khrest*, 1968).

*   *   *

Vasyl' Illiashenko first took up Kostenko's original screenplay for *Coordinate Your Watches* after Tsvirkunov picked the young Ukrainian VGIK student during his trip to the school in 1962. Working under the venerable Sergei Gerasimov's direction, Illiashenko made several shorts on Ukrainian themes, including an adaptation of Lesia Ukrainka's *Forest Song* (*Lesnaia pesnia*), some of Dovzhenko's war stories from *Ukraine in Flames* (*Ukraina v ogne*) and a documentary about Ukrainian craftsman that aired on Kyiv television in 1963.[65] Thus, unlike Illienko and Osyka, Illiashenko came to Dovzhenko Studio already conversant with contemporary Ukrainian identity politics.

Movement was slow on the film, with discussions and demands for revisions to Kostenko's screenplay until April of the following year. Despite such hold-ups regarding the 'cult of personality' theme in the Shvindin section, Goskino recognized the film as a major event at the studio, and that the screenplay conveyed the 'inner sincerity of the Ukrainian people' during World War II.[66] Inna Kokoreva, the head of Goskino's screenplay editorial board, stated that the work was 'original and interesting' and that 'it's necessary to support the present tendency' of presenting the 'national originality of the Ukrainian people'.[67] Goskino passed it into production, with the stipulation that some of the errors were ironed out in the process. Kokoreva and Tarasov concluded that the 'authors bravely depart from the traditional frameworks of cinema narration and resolve the screenplay in the style of poetic cinema'.[68] Thus, Illiashenko's film emerged as a work that Goskino officially represented as poetic cinema, a mode with its own generic and stylistic codes.

In December 1965, the Artistic Council viewed rushes, with Tsvirkunov, Mykola Mashchenko, Osyka and Syzonenko – the very individuals associated with, and supportive of, Ukrainian poetic cinema – expressing little faith in the film. Syzonenko, in particular, complained of the 'primitive *khutorians'ke* vision' at work in the film.[69] Osyka, who would soon take over direction of Illiashenko's film, stated that the acting was horrible (including that of Mykolaichuk!), but that the studio bore responsibility because they did not opt to view the rushes earlier. Osyka stated that he would have to shoot 80–90 per cent of the material over, if he were given the project.[70] In particular, the Artistic Council was shocked at the audacity and utter pretension of a dream sequence contained in the rushes, which imagined the three poets crucified on an embankment above the Dnieper. Zemliak, in particular, who served as a partisan commander during the war, viewed such a symbol of sacrifice as complete anathema to actual war experience, and saw the image itself as 'annoying'.[71] Ignoring these complaints about the film, Illiashenko launched into an explanation of the authorial principles at work in *Coordinate Your Watches*:

> I had faith only in myself. I had no intention to hide behind Gerasimov's wide back. I don't even follow his school. During my studies at VGIK I had my own theory: art is not a representation of life, but an allegory of life.[72]

In alluding to his supposedly non-conformist student days during a meeting to discuss what was supposed to be a mature project, Illiashenko appeared hopelessly naive and unreliable. Tsvirkunov ended the discussion, stating that the young director 'undermined our faith in him as a person'.[73] Four days later, on 25 December, shooting ended. Unlike *Kyiv Frescoes* or *A Well for the Thirsty*, the studio itself (rather than Goskino or the CPU) gave the order to halt production, suggesting a different conflict at work than with these other two banned films.

On 28 December, Gerasimov arrived from Moscow to discuss what to do with the film. Much of Illiashenko's material, he said, possessed an 'artificial sentimentality, in the tradition of Ukrainian melodrama'.[74] Paradjanov, also present at the meeting, stated: 'The director arranges [the film] incompetently.'[75] More damning, however, was screenwriter Kostenko's statement, 'I could have expected something unpleasant, but not such serious artistic miscalculations[...] It's tasteless.'[76] The poet proposed to rewrite the screenplay based on only one of the poets, and to shoot it all within the studio to save money.[77] Osyka was confirmed as the director of this remake in January.[78] Nonetheless, the budget and timetable for completing Osyka's film remained the same as *Coordinate Your Watches*, necessitating that the crew shoot exclusively on the studio grounds. Consequently, the look of *Love Awaits* resembles Paradjanov's artless *mise-en-scène* in *Kyiv Frescoes*, with a focus on medium interior shots, and frequent cutaways of objects of material culture.

Cultural politics were extremely tense in mid-to-late-1966, with the conviction of the Lviv Ten and other Kyiv intellectuals, along with the active support for the incarcerated of several poets like Drach, Kostenko and Vinhranovs'kyi, all of whom were employed at Dovzhenko Studio. The CPU Department of Science and Culture noted that Kostenko participated in a 'nationalist' meeting at the Shevchenko statue in central Kyiv on 22 May with convicted nationalist Ivan Svitlychnyi and 150 others, and personally argued that the *Kobzar* was an exclusively 'Ukrainian' document.[79] In October, Kostenko requested that the studio remove her name from Osyka's film, stating that nothing contained in the rushes resembled her original screenplay.[80] It is unclear why she did this. Perhaps she was scared of the repercussions that would come from the film, or perhaps she was genuinely annoyed with Osyka's creative licence, as she was with Illiashenko's.

Osyka's film received little acknowledgement, but Goskino approved the film for all-Union release on 1 December 1966.[81] The film premiered at the suburban Kyiv 'Dnipro' Theatre on 10 December 1967, a year after Ukrainian Goskino approved it for release.[82] The film disappeared once again until March 1968, with one week of extensive screenings in Kyiv and other major Soviet cities, to be followed with limited screenings throughout April.[83] *Iskusstvo kino* reviewed the film in March, and a final mention of it appeared during the Second Congress of the SKU on 14 November 1968, when Goskino chairman Aleksei Romanov complained of the film's poor success with Ukrainian spectators.[84]

* * *

Two issues, in particular, emerge from Illiashenko's *Coordinate Your Watches* and Osyka's remake. First, we see a political conflict between ideological authorities and the film-makers over a supposed correlation between Stalinism and Fascism. The 'cult' theme was politically dated by 1965, and the direct comparison that Illiashenko made between Stalinism and Fascism in the Shvindin story was all the more problematic after Vasilii Grossman's novel *Life and Fate* failed to pass the censors in 1962. A more pertinent conflict emerged between the war generation at the studio (Tsvirkunov, Levchuk and Zemliak) and the post-war generation (Illiashenko, Osyka and Illienko) about the meaning of the war itself. According to critics from the earlier generation, Illiashenko's film viewed the poets' deaths as a sacrifice rather than as heroic martyrdom. This conflict also manifested itself in a politics of social and cultural difference at the studio. All three of these 'war' films from 1965–6 were made by non-serving directors, whereas the studio and SKU leaderships were composed of war heroes. Each of these latter individuals supported Ukrainian poetic cinema but took fundamental issue with the way in which local and national space was situated in relation to the war and its commemoration. Personally invested in the war narrative, the older generation of Ukrainian-speakers at the studio viewed these young Russian-speaking returnees as having much too little geographic or historical experience to deal with the monumental events that their films encapsulated, despite the ethnographic and literary research that they undertook. Thus, in the final dispute over representational knowledge, nationality was conflated with generation and questions of film style. Thereafter, studio and Goskino authorities would become more critical of the *auteurist* agenda that had characterized the studio since 1964, associated as it now was with a certain youthful dilettantism with regard to the nationality question.

This same generation of Soviet Ukrainian war heroes, who now occupied the positions of leadership within the SKU and Dovzhenko Studio, had been infatuated with, and to some degree influenced by, Paradjanov's *Shadows of Forgotten Ancestors* as a model of 'authentic' national representation. Moreover, Paradjanov's film positioned Ukrainian cinema at the forefront of Ukrainian cultural politics and within a new conception of non-Russian cinema in the USSR. *Shadows* had established a consensus in Ukraine. Yet that consensus broke down, based in part on the very claims to authenticity that its film-makers made, both in public forums and within the film's formal arrangement. CPU officials and spectators alike began asking why such an 'authentic' image of the Ukrainian people need be so unusual and complex. Were representations of the Ukrainian people so 'difficult to master', as Levchuk once stated, or were Paradjanov and his followers interested in their own 'difficult' aesthetic questions more so than in Ukraine? With Ukrainian poetic cinema now implicated in dissident politics, even if only by association, the unfamiliar ethnoscape that it presented on screen to a specific public now appeared as a potential threat. If *Shadows of Forgotten Ancestors* constituted the height of 'authentic' representation, why did Ukrainian spectators not accept it as an image of themselves? In part, the fault lay in celebrating the *auteur* as the creator of national meaning, asking the spectator to see the film as its authors did. Moreover, in promotional materials, these films asked Ukrainian spectators to assimilate the unfamiliar as part of their own national identity, rather than accept the canonical objects, events and meanings contained in the 'Friendship of Peoples' mythology. Many Ukrainians, like the engineer in Dnipropetrovsk who watched *Shadows of Forgotten Ancestors,* did not see the importance of defining Ukrainians as so fundamentally different. Did this not diminish the importance of other potential identification as Ukrainian or with Ukraine?

The dispute over Dovzhenko's legacy and his artistic intentions encapsulates the problem here. Was Dovzhenko important for Ukraine because he mobilized a modernist aesthetic to reveal the essence of a unique 'national character', or was he important because he showed how and why the great events of the twentieth century – the revolution, formation of the Soviet Union, industrialization, collectivization and the Great Patriotic War – happened in Ukraine? There was general consensus among Ukrainian artists and intellectuals during the 1960s as to the film-maker's specific importance for the republic, but these questions of artistic representation touched on the very root of the problem of Ukrainian difference and how, and to whom, to show it. A film-maker's stylistic choices could be used to render a film's subject matter as familiar and comprehensible or unusual and impenetrable, which, in the present case, had implications about spatial relations between Ukraine and Russia, and between the everyday and the extraordinary. As a Ukrainian modernist film-maker, Dovzhenko rendered the everyday *as* extraordinary in his delineation of a unique Ukrainian 'national character'. As a Soviet and socialist realist film-maker, however, he was interested in showing how Ukrainians participated in the revolutionary process, albeit within their own particular cultural, social and political context. Both positions on the legacy of the film-maker and his work rejected the earlier notion of Ukrainian difference as backwardness, but the latter asserted a claim to active Ukrainian participation in modern politics and social processes, whereas the former affirmed, through Dovzhenko's role as an *auteur,* Ukraine's participation in a pan-Soviet and pan-European modernism.

During the 1960s, Dovzhenko Studio adopted an *auteurist* model for creating 'national cinema', largely because its new leadership viewed the history of Ukrainian cinema in terms of personality and the mark of talented directors, most notably that of Dovzhenko himself. The problem with this model was that it only had the traditional repressive powers of the party and state to regulate thematic content. The studio leadership gave young filmmakers like Illienko, Osyka and Illiashenko the green light based on a combination of a policy of developing young talent and a commitment to an *auteurist* agenda as a means to transform the studio's reputation. The conflict that emerged from the production of Illiashenko's and Osyka's debut was between different conceptions of authorship, and their commitment to both Modernism and the nationality question. During their work on these projects, both Drach and Kostenko became involved in dissident nationalism, and their screenplays reflected the narrative and ideological concerns of 1960s Ukrainian identity politics. By contrast, the directors were less interested in their descriptions of rural everyday life in the republic, and more so in developing a visual style that produced a de-familiarized Ukrainian ethnoscape divorced from a domesticated Stalinist folkloric and engaged with a modernist, supposedly 'Dovzhenkoist' poetics. Their lack of commitment to either a Ukrainian dissident agenda or to more mainstream questions about language policy placed these film-makers in a difficult position *vis-à-vis* CPU ideological authorities, but allowed them to continue working, provided they reconceptualize their aesthetic ambitions and relationship to a Ukrainian and broader viewing public.

Chapter 6

MAKING NATIONAL CINEMA IN THE ERA OF STAGNATION

The Ukrainian Cinematographers' Union plenum in May 1966 was a tense event for most of its members. Since the previous plenum in November, production had been halted on *Coordinate Your Watches* and *Kyiv Frescoes*, and now it seemed certain that Iurii Illienko's *A Well for the Thirsty* would also fail to reach distribution. Director Mykola Mashchenko stated that an 'unpleasant, complex and difficult atmosphere' had descended upon the studio in the past months.[1] S. P. Ivanov attempted reconciliation, stating that the 'different creative schools' emerging at Dovzhenko Studio had helped Ukrainian cinema overcome its dependence on the primitive theatricality of the 1950s and early 1960s. He denounced both 'rigid dogma' and 'haphazard experimentation'. But his denunciation of 'associationalists', as he called Paradjanov, Illienko and Osyka, made it clear that Ukrainian poetic cinema would not be, as Levchuk stated in October 1964, 'one of the prerequisites for the moulding of our product'.[2]

From Illiashenko's pretensions in particular, it was obvious to most at the studio that Ukrainian national cinema could not survive solely 'outside the collective', especially in its penchant for what Ivanov called 'formalist-roguish' qualities.[3] In the coming decade, authorities sought to reign in such excess as images of Ukrainian poets crucified on the banks of the Dnieper, while continuing to encourage such 'poetic' representations of national character, as long as they were tempered by a realist ideological pragmatism and a sympathetic eye and ear towards spectators' patience. At the same time, Dovzhenko Studio sought alternatives, both to the theatricality of the Stalinist folkloric and the 'ethnographic' tendencies of poetic cinema. With a view towards surviving in an increasingly profit-driven Soviet film industry, the Ukrainian studio had to recoup its financial losses from 1965–6 and prove to both Goskino and audiences that it too could compete with central studios without sacrificing one of its primary goals: to speak to and for the Ukrainian people.

Nonetheless, Ukrainian cinema and cultural production in the Republic more generally was becoming increasingly provincialized by the early 1970s, and this was only in part the result of new ways of thinking about media consumers. Roman Szporluk has argued that a successful campaign against the Ukrainian-language press was initiated in 1972 with the purge of Petro Shelest and his supporters in the CPU Central Committee. Under Volodymyr Shcherbytskyi, whose power base was in the same Russian-speaking, south-eastern Ukrainian industrial region as Brezhnev himself, the CPU would demand that the Ukrainian branch of Soiuzpechat' (the state printing bureau) curtail Ukrainian-language circulation of periodicals and books, having accused the organization of artificially inflating the readership for such printed material. Thereafter, a number of Ukrainian-language scholarly journals ceased publication, and the print run for such major periodicals as *Ukraina* and *Vechirnii Kyiv* shrunk, the latter reduced from 344,550 copies in 1975 to 200,000 copies five years later. The same process predictably occurred to an even greater degree in eastern Ukrainian cities like Kharkiv and Dnipropetrovsk. While the number of titles increased during the 1970s, circulation drastically declined.[4]

In the area of Ukrainian film production, we see a similar process. As the possibility of using Ukrainian-speaking actors increased during the 1970s owing to the further institutionalization of the Kyiv Theatrical Institute's film programme, a greater proportion of films were shot in the republican vernacular. At the same time, the audience for such films declined alongside distribution's increasing unwillingness to sacrifice their financial plans for a political project, in which they remained uninvested. Thus, Ukrainian-language films were pushed out of distribution in favour of Russian-language genre productions coming out of Dovzhenko Studio. Shcherbytskyi and Ideological Secretary Valentyn Malanchuk would continue to appeal to the Ukrainian-speaking intelligentsia, but only on a rudimentary level, as Szporluk's figures indicate. In many respects, the studio's promotion of an *auteurist* agenda declined during the same period. With the removal of patrons like Shelest and Ideological Secretary Fedir Ovcharenko, the appeal to the *auteur*'s genius was no longer a politically neutral question. Individuals like Paradjanov and Ilienko carried the undesirable quality of independent and unofficial influence at the studio.

This chapter explores the several interlocked causes for, and results of, the decline of a politics of national authorship as the basis for Ukrainian national cinema. Furthermore, whereas Ukrainian *auteur* cinema could survive on more limited budgets, largely because such a mode of representation marketed to audiences the spectacle of ethnic difference, genre films – adventure (*prikliuchencheskie*), science fiction and historical epics in particular – required budgets comparable to central productions. Thus, the increasing demands to make films that paid were much more difficult for the studio in Kyiv to accomplish. By the 1970s, however, the fact that films 'based on national material' did not attract large audiences mattered to Goskino under the new control of Filipp Ermash.

After CPU First Secretary Petro Shelest's ouster in 1973, the lack of industry support gave way to a lack of political support for Ukrainian films dealing with 'national themes', associated as they now were with an 'ethnographic', rather than a 'contemporary [*suchasnyi*]' conception of the Ukrainian people. Such ethnographic imagery came to be associated with an anti-modern representation and thus outside of the main current of Soviet realism. When film director Iurii Lysenko referred during a 'creative conference' in 1968 at Dovzhenko Studio to the 'national theme [as] consist[ing] of baggy trousers or something else like that', he implicitly connected poetic cinema to the folkloric spectacle of Stalinist cinema.[5] But in getting rid of the 'morons in the pictures', as Lysenko advocated, the question remained as to whether there was a method of representing a non-ethnographic Ukraine, which would answer both nationalities policy in the ways that Ukrainian film-makers understood it, and the demand for industry profits.

Even 'conservatives' like Tymofii Levchuk and his colleagues within the Union leadership feared a 'de-nationalization', which would arise from greater focus on industry profits. Kyiv film-makers were sceptical that their films could compete with central productions, and not only due to unequal budgets. The whole idea of box office competition with central production appeared to the studio leadership and the film-makers alike as incompatible with the socialist mode of production, and which discriminated in particular against films that dealt with national themes. Just as critics claimed that commercial Hollywood films were 'de-nationalizing' Western European cinema,[6] so too was 'Russian' cinema 'de-nationalizing' the cinemas of the Union republics in their hegemonic role in cultural production and over audience expectations.

In early 1971, a central Goskino report called for 'the transfer of film studios to a new system of planning, and economic and material stimulation', which sought to make production 'dependent on the economic results of distribution'. Many in Kyiv criticized this project because it would disproportionately hurt national cinema. One anonymous complaint argued that it would only justify distribution organs' single-minded concern for economic plans over political objectives. Distribution already showed as many imported genre films as was possible without arousing the suspicions of authorities in the cultural section of the Central Committee. How much worse might it become, the anonymous complainant speculated, if such explicitly bottom-line distribution planning reigned over Soviet cinema. Films from the republics, 'based on national material', could not compete with Mosfilm production, and certainly not with foreign cinema. Thus, 'national films' would be in danger of disappearing from the repertoire. The complaint continued: 'It would be criminal to deprive the 47 million people of Ukraine of a national and socialist film art.' In this allusion to the audience, however, the report did not imply that these 47 million were the intended audience; or rather, it did not suggest that such a number *only* corresponded to the size of the audience. In identifying the population of the Republic, the complaint argued that the Ukrainian film studio effectively represented this constituency, whether or not they chose to see any films that it produced. Moreover, the industry's reorientation towards profit and the size of the audience over the quality of the audience would cause a flight of cadres to the central studios. Thus, the complaint reasoned, such a *perestroika* of the industry would send Soviet cinema 'down the bourgeois path of development', and erode film-makers' 'moral' responsibility before the spectator.[7]

Nonetheless, such an exodus of personnel from Dovzhenko Studio to the central studios never occurred, largely because its staff had few desirable qualities for Mosfilm or Gorky studios. From the other direction, it became rarer for Moscow actors and directors to come to Kyiv for temporary work, in part because it became less lucrative to do so, but also due to the nepotistic practices of the studio collective, which routinely protested such import of temporary personnel. In a sense, the 'problem of cadres' at Dovzhenko Studio had been solved by the late 1960s, but only at a further cost to the studio's reputation and its ability to attract audiences.

The Search for a Ukrainian Blockbuster

What were Dovzhenko Studio's options (and those of other 'national' studios) after the rejection of 'poetic' experimentation from a political standpoint, on the one hand, and film commodity 'exploitation' on the other? Certainly, neither the industry management, nor those involved on the creative end, desired a situation in which only Ukrainians constituted the audience for republican productions, despite efforts to gear marketing and promotion towards such an imagined community of film consumers. Indeed, as industry officials made clear, they considered the limiting of films to republican distribution a punishment and insult to the work itself, not to mention a violation of Soviet nationalities policy. Dovzhenko Studio was fighting for recognition in the 1960s, and not merely to develop a Ukrainian national culture. In September 1968, for example, Tsvirkunov and Kostiantyn Kudiievs'kyi, the head of Ukrainian Goskino's editorial committee, wrote to central Goskino chairman Romanov with a complaint that Ukrainian-language films were more often distributed only within the republic. 'After all,' they stated, 'the Committee doesn't consider the republican screen to be a second or third tier screen in the country.'[8] Language itself did not limit a film's distribution to the linguistic community due to the extensive directives governing film dubbing in the Soviet Union. At issue were films whose authors believed it aesthetically necessary to shoot in Ukrainian, for the purpose of maintaining the national subject-matter's authenticity. Thus, central Goskino's decision to limit certain Ukrainian-language films probably had little to do with linguistic comprehension and more to do with what they perceived as the difficulty of comprehending a non-Russian ethnoscape and 'formalist' experimentation imbued with the mark of an 'author'.

To some degree, we can see how Paradjanov, Drach, Illienko and other Ukrainian *auteurs* brought such limits upon themselves when they continually answered critiques about their elaborate symbolic language to the effect that those for whom the film was intended would understand. Industry and party officials would interpret this notion of the knowledgeable audience, of course, as a clear sign of intellectual snobbery. The actual decision to limit certain 'national films' to 'knowledgeable' republican audiences demanded that the studio prove that Ukrainians not only understood such films but actually wanted to see them. In January 1967, Romanov reported on a 'strange situation' during a union plenum in Moscow, whereby films produced at 'national studios' performed more poorly in 'their own' republics than in the USSR as a whole.[9] During the Second Congress of the Ukrainian Cinematographers' Union in November 1968, Romanov returned to the same topic, stating that films like Osyka's *Love Awaits Those Who Return* performed better in Moscow than in Kyiv, despite the 'national theme' of the film. 'These Ukrainian films,' he stated, 'not only ran poorly in Ukraine, they ran worse [there] than in the whole Union.'[10] Romanov's reasoning was instructive: 'The success of a film in the Republic [in which it was made] provides an indication for its general success[...]'[11] The Chairman's counterclaim to the specificity of ethnic knowledge was that national difference did not exist at the level of film consumption, and he dared his Ukrainian colleagues to prove otherwise.

'National films' had to perform on two stages: they had to be successful with a particular spectator (one in the republic) and a 'mass' spectator (i.e., it had to generate profit). The search for a Ukrainian blockbuster involved several production strategies, from attempts to market a 'realist' poetic cinema, to work within established popular genres like war, melodrama and *detektiv*. For the purposes of realist narration, Ukrainian film-makers set such films within a particular republican landscape, but, in de-emphasizing the iconicity of landscape, made little attempt to produce meaning about the nature of it as an ethnic space. In such attempts to draw audiences to Ukrainian films, space was pushed into a recognizable background. Humans, meanwhile, act independently of the landscape. They are neither beholden to it nor identified with it. Several of the most popular films produced in Kyiv during the mid-1960s, however, had absolutely nothing to do with a 'national' theme. At the same time, such films could demonstrate that Dovzhenko Studio had the same production possibilities as central studios, and could shoot with its own cadres and budgetary restrictions.

* * *

After *A Dream, Shadows of Forgotten Ancestors* and his brief work on Illiashenko's *Coordinate Your Watches*, Ivan Mykolaichuk entered a different stage in his career, one seemingly at odds with what he had come to signify during his student years. After graduating from KITM in the spring of 1965, the actor immediately received a role on his instructor Viktor Ivchenko's new production, *The Viper* (*Gadiuka*, 1965), based on the 1929 civil war novella by Aleksei Tolstoi. In Ivchenko's film, Mykolaichuk played his first of only two villains during his career, this time a White officer who rapes the heroine Ol'ga Zotova. The gripping action and high production values made *The Viper* Mykolaichuk's greatest popular success. In 1966, 34 million people saw this historical film about the daughter of a merchant who, after being raped, fights in the Red cavalry. After the war, she returns to her ravaged village to find her family murdered. She has difficulty assimilating into a civilian life, trading her soldier's rifle for a bureaucrat's typewriter. In the end, Ol'ga becomes the further victim of corrupt officials, but maintains her essential idealism and ideological commitment.

Ivchenko directed the film in a classic realist manner, which stood at odds with his earlier 'theatrical' aesthetic in *Ivanna* (1959) and the Lesia Ukrainka adaptation *Forest Song* (*Lisova pisnia*, 1961).[12] Visually, nothing stands out in *The Viper* when compared to these earlier eccentricities, but production values were high and the acting was professional. *The Viper*'s narrative presents a linear, but psychologically complex story of the daughter of a class enemy. Mykolaichuk's role as the White officer, however, carries no subtlety, signifying pure evil in his sole purpose to prey on the innocent and seemingly helpless. In performing in his instructor's film, Mykolaichuk sought a degree of job security within the safe haven of a mature film-maker's work. He was not playing himself, the 'romantic Hutsul', and thus was not required to answer for the authenticity of a Russian White Guardist. He told *Novyny kinoekrana* in January 1966, 'I wanted to play the villain. Work on the role of the White Guard officer Val'ka Brykin was for me extraordinary and at the same time interesting.'[13] He did not identify with his role here, but merely found it 'interesting'. *The Viper* screened regularly in Kyiv from mid-March 1966 to early January 1967. After Ivchenko won the Shevchenko Award for the film two months later (*The Viper* was chosen instead of *Shadows of Forgotten Ancestors*, despite Ivchenko's own support for the latter), it returned for a week of screenings at the Druzhba Theatre on Khreshchatyk, and an additional private screening at the Kyiv Officer's Club.[14] *The Viper* had the longest run for a Ukrainian film during the entire 1960s, and routinely came back to movie theatres and factory clubs in honour of various anniversary events.

The fact that the film had nothing to do with Ukraine allowed Mykolaichuk to establish himself as a genuine actor, over and above his identity as a 'genuine Hutsul'. Several other Ukrainian actors starred in the film, including Ivchenko's student Raisa Nedashkivs'ka, in addition to other Kyiv Theatre Institute graduates Kostiantyn Stepankov and Oleksandr Movchan. And despite its non-Ukrainian thematics, Ivchenko shot the film in Hutsulshchyna.[15] With *The Viper*, we find a different attempt to create national cinema in Ukraine, one based on the studio's independence from borrowed personnel and landscapes, and one which competed with central productions for spectators. For his role in this film in particular, Mykolaichuk was distinguished as an Honoured Artist of the Ukrainian SSR, and won the prestigious Mykola Ostrovs'kyi Award.

Between 1964 and 1974, Dovzhenko Studio produced only 15 additional films that attracted 20 million or more spectators, and most of these productions related only marginally to Ukrainian themes. As we see in Figure 6.1, war films, specifically combat films dealing with the Great Patriotic War, achieved the most box office successes. Both Tymofii Levchuk's *Two Years above the Abyss* (*Dva gody nad propast'iu*) and Anton Tymonishyn's *They Knew Them Only by Face* (*Ikh znali tol'ko v litso*) dealt with Soviet counter-intelligence operations, during the Nazi occupation in Kyiv with the former, and in a generic 'Russian' port city in the latter (probably Sevastopol'). Tymonishyn continued his lucrative career by making *Doctor Abst's Experiment* (*Eksperiment Doktora Absta*), a non-comedic take on the theme that Kubrick explored in *Dr. Strangelove* (1964) about a mad Nazi scientist who contributed to the United States' acquisition of the atomic bomb. Despite being a director that contributed several 'leaders in distribution' to the Kyiv studio, CPU member and Kyiv Theatre Institute graduate Tymonishyn garnered little respect there or within the Ukrainian Cinematographers' Union for his continual use of non-Ukrainian actors and lack of regard for contemporary representational politics in the republic. Whether or not Tymonishyn cared to participate is beside the point; rather, the lack of interest in him and his films demonstrated that the studio collective and the Ukrainian Cinematographers' Union continued to be driven by the development of native cadres and the promotion of national authorship. Whenever possible, most film-makers attempted to integrate one or both of these concerns when approaching the problem of audiences.

Figure 6.1   List of Ukrainian 'Leaders in Distribution', 1964–1974[16]

Year	Title	Director	Screenwriter	Genre	# of tickets sold, in millions
1964	*Keys from the Sky*	V. Ivanov	I. Stadniuk	Comedy	22.3
1966	*The Viper*	V. Ivchenko	G. Koltunov	War	34
1966	*Two Years above the Abyss*	T. Levchuk	L. Trauberg	War	30.6
1966	*They Knew Them Only by Face*	A. Tymonishyn	E. Rostovtsev	War	40.7
1967	*The Gypsy*	E. Matveev	E. Mytko	Melodrama	55.6
1968	*Annychka*	B. Ivchenko	B. Zahoryl'ko	Melodrama	25.1
1968	*Doctor Abst's Experiment*	A. Tymonishyn	A. Nasibov	War	29.4
1968	*Spies*	O. Shvachko	E. Onopriienko	War	34
1969	*Long-Distance Romance*	E. Matveev	D. Khrabrovyts'kyi	Hist-Rev	21
1970	*The Prisoners of Beaumont*	Iu. Lysenko	Georges Juribida	War	20
1971	*Inspector of Criminal Investigations*	S. Tsybul'nyk	M. Makliars'kyi	Detective	40.9
1971	*Nina*	O. Shvachko	S. Smirnov	War	21.6
1973	*Everyday Criminal Investigations*	S. Tsybul'nyk	M. Makliars'kyi	Detective	27.3
1973	*Only the Old Go to Battle*	L. Bykov	E. Onopriienko	War	44.3
1973	*The Black Captain*	O. Lentsius	Iu. Lukin	War	21.9
1974	*The White Bashlik*	V. Savel'ev	Shynkuba	Hist-Rev	20.8

While Oleksii Shvachko's *Spies* (*Razvedchiki*) located his counter-intelligence film in a non-Ukrainian space – a stretch of the Danube in Hungary – he peopled it with Ukrainian intelligence officers and employed studio actors to play the major roles, including Mykolaichuk as the hero Captain Kurganov,[17] Andrii Sova as Corporal Cherniak, Stepankov as a Hungarian partisan and Leonid Bykov as Sergeant Makarenko. The film's plot, a common motif for Soviet cinema in the mid-1960s, finds Soviet intelligence officers rendering humanitarian aid to a village whose supply lines were cut off by the retreating German occupiers. Intended for the growing youth audience, *Spies* is full of action and suspense, with little of the psychological exploration of Ivchenko's *The Viper*. Here again, however, the film provided more visibility to Mykolaichuk as a Soviet actor. By 1969, he had demonstrated his ability to play in Ukrainian and Russian literary roles (Shevchenko and Val'ka), as the authentic self in Ukrainian poetic cinema productions (Ivanko), and now in a genre film as Kurganov. If, in 1964–6 we saw Mykolaichuk in neckties with embroidered folk patterns and a Hutsul *keptar'*, we now saw him on the cover of *Novyny kinoekrana* as a professional actor able to transcend his ethno-national identity, and as a machine gun-toting adventure hero (Figure 6.2–6.3). Released at the beginning of Soviet schoolchildren's summer recess, theatres sold almost 35 million tickets for *Spies*, demonstrating the Soviet film industry's growing conversance with marketing films appropriately.[18]

Of the 'leaders in distribution' listed in Figure 6.1, however, only L. Bykov's *Only the Old* and Sulamif Tsybul'nyk's *Inspector* (*Inspektor ugolovnogo rozyska*) could be considered Soviet 'blockbusters'. While other films attracted an above average number of spectators, these two films dominated movie theatres in 1971 and 1973 respectively, each sparking sequels later in the decade (Tsybul'nyk's *Everyday* [*Budni ugolovnogo rozyska*] in 1973, and Bykov's *One-Two Soldiers Went* [*Aty-baty shli soldaty*] in 1976). While the two films were shot in Russian, and in no way pretended to be 'national films', 'Ukraine' and 'Ukrainians' appeared in both.

Tsybul'nyk's well-crafted *detektiv* follows a group of Kyiv *militsiia* officers who are tracking down a murder suspect. The film concludes as the detectives' pursuit takes them to the Carpathians, after they discover that the suspect has returned to his native mountain village. They visit his mother's house on an unpeopled mountainside, where she tells them in perfect Russian that her son has just left. The detectives call in assistance from a helicopter to track his movements through the nooks and crannies of the Carpathians, where they eventually find and catch him. Here, the Carpathians functioned not so much as an ethnic fountain of youth; rather, the landscape becomes a tactical prop, whose characteristics were determined, not by a Ukrainian ethnoscape, but by the popular detective genre. The one inhabitant we see in these mountains is an old peasant woman, who represents not 'national colour' but generic backwardness.

Leonid Bykov, a popular actor at the Kharkiv Theatre during the 1950s, moved to Lenfilm in the 1960s to become famous in primarily comedic roles. In 1973, Bykov returned to Ukraine to direct

Figure 6.2 Ivan Mykolaichuk as popular action hero. Image from November 1969 in *Za Radians'kyi fil'm*

олум'яним нашим патріотам, людям великої мужності присвятили новий фільм «Розвідники» митці Київської кіностудії ім. О. П. Довженка. Твір цей належить до героїко-пригодницького жанру, і заслуга авторів у тому, що стиль жанру витриманий з початку до кінця. Режисери О. Швачко та І. Самборський зуміли донести до глядача ту складну і надзвичайно напружену обстановку, в якій доводилось діяти нашим розвідникам, розповісти про події, що не вміщуються в рамки звичайності.

Figure 6.3 Ivan Mykolaichuk as popular action hero. Image from February 1969 in *Novyny kinoekrana*

Only the Old, the story of a 'multinational' Soviet air squadron operating in German-occupied Ukraine, assigned to what they understood as a suicide mission. Bykov plays the commanding officer, Lieutenant Titarenko, who, while speaking flawless Russian, calls his comrades '*khloptsy*' rather than the Russian equivalent of '*rebiata* (guys, buddies)', and, when alone with Airman Kuznechyk (played by Kyiv Theatre Institute graduate Sergei Ivanov), speaks Ukrainian. Managing assistant director of Dovzhenko Studio Hlib Shandybin wrote to the new head of Ukrainian Goskino Vasyl' Bol'shak in September 1973 asking that the Russian original *not* be dubbed into Ukrainian, on the basis that it would tarnish the film's *multi*national character and 'ruin' the film's 'dramaturgy'.[19] While similar to Paradjanov's argument against a Russian dub for *Shadows*, the shift from a discourse of 'colour' to one of 'narrative' or 'dramaturgy' represented a new stage in the representational politics of Soviet nationalities policy, one which sought to locate nationalities outside of both folkloric and ethnographic sites of exploration, while continuing to acknowledge their existence. In this way, *Only the Old* represented the visual and aural components of line four on Soviet citizens' passports, neither condescending nor exoticizing, but merely revealing contemporary reality within a comprehensible, yet truthful, narrative about the tragedy and heroism of those who fell in the Great Patriotic War. While denying the natural connections of ethnic subjects to particular landscapes found in Ukrainian poetic cinema, the film also removed the domesticated folkloric spectacle of the non-Russian found, for example, in the opening segment of Pyr'ev's *Tractor Drivers.*

The Viper, Spies, Inspector and *Only the Old* represented successful attempts by Ukrainian filmmakers to remain relevant after the crisis of 1965–6, as Dovzhenko Studio attempted to save itself from the stigma of *Kyiv Frescoes, A Well for the Thirsty* and *Coordinate Your Watches.* At the same time, as S. P. Ivanov's statement about 'different creative schools' indicated, the studio continued to promote its *auteur* geniuses (at least while Shelest remained First Secretary), and attempted to cash in on the respect from intellectuals that Ukrainian poetic cinema had provided the studio.

During the late 1960s, republican Goskinos and studios believed that the industry was still committed to expanding production, and provided justification that such a plan made sense in terms of the successes of Paradjanov and Illienko in Ukraine, Rezo Chkheidze and Tenghiz Abuladze in Georgia, Tolomush Okeev in Kirghizia and Vytautas Žalaklavičus in Lithuania among other national *auteurs.* An increase in production would not only allow republican studios to compete economically with central studios, bringing much-needed funds to expand and modernize production facilities, but also to justify their very existence as equals, rather than as their subordinates. At the Second Congress of the Ukrainian Cinematographers' Union, several speakers mentioned increasing production by 125 per cent to 30 full-length feature films annually. Similar proposals appeared before Goskino from republican studios throughout the latter part of the decade.[20] First Secretary Shelest attempted to use his influence in the party to compel the industry to move on this issue. In a letter to the Central Committee of the CPSU in early 1969, he argued that the 'conservative programme for the release of feature films … leads, on the one hand, to a rise in the cost of producing films and, on the other hand, to the lengthy inoccupation of creative workers'. While rejecting the possibility of 30, he recommended a modest increase to 15 films per year.[21] By 1968, production on full-length feature films for non-television release at Dovzhenko Studio had already stabilized at around 12 films per year. In the 1970s, this number constituted official Goskino policy, which the studio maintained until 1993.[22] The industry saw no further need for an increase in production, and viewed 12 films per year as the top level that the market could handle. Even at this level, only one or two films annually were profitable, and the industry continued to subsidize the bulk of production.[23]

For authorities in central Goskino, then, the demand to increase production provoked questions about how many more Ukrainian-themed films Soviet audiences would pay money to see. During the decade between 1968 and 1978, authorities in Goskino promoted audience research as a way of understanding patterns of film consumption. As Hollywood had done beginning in the late 1930s, the Soviet film industry now appealed to the language of public opinion polls, rather than propaganda, as the idiom through which it understood 'the audience'.[24] Within this idiom, audiences became a multitude of 'taxonomic collectives', to whom the industry could direct its marketing. Sociologists studying film audiences determined that adventures and comedies were the films that most spectators enjoyed watching, that they preferred foreign productions to domestic and central productions to those from the Union republics.[25] In August 1972, CPSU Ideological Secretary Ermash replaced Romanov as chairman of central Goskino, and came to power with a firm policy of further reducing production budgets for studios that did not generate profits.[26] One representative of central Goskino told the Ukrainian Cinematographers' Union in 1976 that Ukrainian filmmakers had to find their 'special group of film spectators', or risk becoming irrelevant to Soviet cinema. He mentioned that the chairman wanted each studio to have 'its own form of contact with the spectator. [...] The value of this reorientation is [there is] a film for each audience.'[27]

In fact, Ukrainian Goskino along with the union was firmly committed to appealing to a Ukrainian spectator, particularly after film sociologists demanded that the industry understand audiences as 'differentiated' according to age, sex, nationality and education categories. The circulation of the Ukrainian-language film press – constituting the monthly magazine *Novyny kinoekrana* and the weekly newspaper *Na ekranakh Ukrainy* – continued to grow into the early 1970s. The latter, moreover, stated their goal as advertising the best of Soviet cinema, but 'Ukrainian cinema in particular'.[28] A sociological study conducted with spectators in the republic in 1972, however, determined that Ukrainians were largely indifferent to such promotion of Ukrainian films. Sociologists discovered that Ukrainian spectators enjoyed Bykov's *Only the Old*, but then, so did everyone else. After hearing the dismal results of the study, the head of Dovzhenko Studio's editorial board Petro Kuvyk stated that they were 'dangerous to publish', especially in light of earlier statements that republican films had to perform well at home to ensure approval for broader distribution.[29] Predictably, such promotional focus on Ukrainian production did not correspond to how distribution organs chose to act. The head of Ukrainian distribution told the Union that they needed to de-emphasize Ukrainian films during the annual Cinema Days event in 1973 to guarantee a larger turnout.[30]

Ermash's Goskino proposed that republican studios could survive only by undertaking further economic restructuring. In order to save money on personnel, Dovzhenko Studio was forced to introduce the practice of hiring directors on contract rather than paying them a salary.[31] Dovzhenko Studio, under the management of Al'bert Putintsev since 1973, tried ever harder to make films that sold, while answering the increasingly difficult political demands to make *zakaznye* films that did not. From 1965 to 1975, the average feature film released from Kyiv attracted 50 per cent fewer spectators, a drop from 11.2 million to 5.3 million people.[32]

Zemliak stated in the mid-1970s that Ukrainian films were now little different from central productions, except that the former were not as good. While attendance was declining everywhere in the Soviet Union,[33] films from Kyiv experienced this decline to an unprecedented level. Most of the post-'65 generation of studio directors moved to the growing field of television production, discovering in it more money and more creative support than in feature film-making. In late 1971, Zemliak complained that this shift to television impoverished screenwriters due to the practice of using Moscow writers for television. In a sense, Zemliak believed, television was 'de-nationalizing' for its refusal to support Ukrainian writers, the latter constituting the very essence of national culture itself.[34] In accepting this notion, however, the problem was much greater than Zemliak articulated it, as Dovzhenko Studio employed Moscow screenwriters not only for television production, but also in growing numbers for feature films. Of the screenwriters listed among the 'leaders in distribution' in Figure 6.1, only three were members of the screenplay studio. At the same time, the body of directors, actors and other creative personnel working on Dovzhenko Studio productions continued to be drawn from its permanent base of cadres, largely because this was an economically sound practice. Yet, as story and narrative became the keys to increasing attendance, Goskino found it no great expense to hand out screenplays from Moscow to the Union republics, and in the process to give up on solving the problem locally. As Larysa Briukhovets'ka writes,

> The screenplay problem was never seriously analysed or untangled. But if there is an analogy with social life, then in Ukraine the highest authorities also did not have their own 'screenwriters', but 'fulfilled the roles' behind the screenplay created in Moscow.[35]

Thus, Goskino had solved the 'problem of national cadres' superficially, with a mind towards efficiency, and without, in the end, disrupting the main line of industry policy, oriented towards profitable genre productions and *zakaznye temy*.

'National Character' Between Realism and Visuality

Despite this growing orientation away from the principle of authorship towards audience politics, the issues surrounding national cinemas in the Union republics and the problem of representing 'national character' dominated Union and industry discussion from the late-1960s to the mid-1970s. While the 'problem of national cinema' emerged in the press during the earlier part of the decade, the issue coalesced in early 1967 during a Union plenum in Moscow dedicated exclusively to the 'condition and problems in the development of national cinemas in the USSR'. In his opening address to the plenum, Kyrgyz writer Chinghiz Aitmatov told the delegates: 'Today in all the Union republics, their own cinemas are being made and are functioning.'[36] He noted that national studios made over 60 per cent of the films produced in the USSR, and that national films were appearing at international film festivals 'as the best works of the year'. From this, he concluded that '[n]ational cinema is becoming the problem number one' within the industry. Yet, in the absence of agreement or even a solid definition of 'national character' emerging from these debates, the issue was determined to be a problem of realism. This resolution was distinguished from Ukrainian poetic cinema's articulation of ethnic difference. While the discourse surrounding realism functioned within audience politics – as in, 'the masses demand a realist art' – it also served the goals of demanding a representation of non-Russians divorced from a spectacle of folkloric backwardsness or ethnographic curiosity.

Such debates about 'national character' emerged in film criticism simultaneous to the 'poetic / realist cinema' debate. In his resolution to this latter debate, Efim Dobin examined Dovzhenko's cinematic poetics in terms of a rendering of folklore and landscape, which was compatible with the heroic and patriotic narrative. The function of the image, however, worked within the realm of metaphor, assimilating the human subject with the landscape, which served to make sense of the particular Ukrainian experience during the revolution and civil war, industrialization and collectivization (Dovzhenko's subjects). The question remained as to how Soviet cinema was to interpret the ethnographic features of the human landscape as it was defined in relation to a particular people or nationality.

Soviet critics in the 1960s rejected 'faceless' cosmopolitanism, demanding that the human subject 'carry' the features of his or her nationality, lest he or she become an 'abstraction'. As I explored in Chapter 1, within the folkloric mode of representing the non-Russian, this demand worked itself out literally in the sense that Cossacks wore embroidered shirts, Khmel'nyts'kyi carried his *bulava* and his hair was cut in the iconic style of the *oseledets'*. In a February 1964 article in *Iskusstvo kino*, Ukrainian critic Borys Buriak argued that, in examining the elements of national particularity in film, Soviet film-makers and critics needed to move past outward features, that is, characteristics, and attempt to understand aspects of 'national character'. In this way, he disagreed with Mikhail Klado's earlier article on this theme, which argued that the national could be revealed only in a work's artistic texture after the generally human or the social aspects are evident.[37] Buriak stated that such a conception has led to a film being nationally 'dressed' in later directorial treatment, while not located at the work's origin. In other words, 'national character' was not simply the local expression of a mobile folkloric form of representing the non-Russian.

Buriak stated: 'The real artist sees the national above all in the spiritual, labouring, and mental spheres, and not only in the folkloric and ethnographic [ones].' Following Bulgarian philosopher Tikhomir Pavlov, Buriak argued that the nation constituted a 'collective individuality'. Although he suggested that socialist nations would begin to exhibit similar common features as they came together in harmony (*sblizhenie*), he did not accept that 'the ideal' of 'national character in our time is already corresponding to the ideal of the communist character'. In other words, Buriak stated that 'national character' (i.e., Russian, Ukrainian, etc.) and 'civil character' (i.e.,

Soviet) continued to provoke different sentiments in films, despite some convergence of the two. Just as Dobin found in his examination of Dovzhenko's poetics, so did Buriak discover 'national character' in Vasyl' Bozhenko. For the same reason, Buriak noted that one of the problems with Veronika the heroine in *The Cranes are Flying*, is that she resembled a woman of any nationality more than she embodied the specific features of a Russian woman.[38]

In this comparison between Veronika's and Bozhenko's national character, language plays a minor role. After all, Bozhenko speaks Russian in *Shchors* but 'spiritually' embodies the Ukrainian national character, while Veronika, who also speaks Russian, fails to do the same for the Russian national character. In this way, Buriak disagreed with the position that, without the Ukrainian language, Ukrainian national cinema could not exist.[39] To counter the language argument, Buriak offered the example of the early Gogol. He stated that in the Russian language of the latter, there is also 'the originality of Ukrainian speech'. Buriak did not intend to promote the use of regional dialects as Ukrainian poetic cinema did, but attempted to delineate an 'internal' dynamic of 'national' speech, its non-syntactic, and indeed, non-semantic quality.[40] As with Dobin's work, in Buriak's efforts to mediate between an excess of signification (association, metaphor, visuality, essentialization) and its denial (narrative, plot, *literaturnost'*, civic over national consciousness), his criticism loses its instructive content. Apart from mere example, he failed to demonstrate how Soviet film-makers could convey the features of national character, or even general principles of how roles could embody nationality.

Such open questions about national representation did not go away. Despite Sergei Gerasimov's advice in December 1966 not to disturb the 'swamp' that was national cinema lest it become an 'active power in the enemy's hands', the Union of Cinematographers met in a January plenum to address the issue of 'national character' specifically.[41] In Gerasimov's comments on Aitmatov's speech, he feared the barrage of complaints from republican filmmakers that would inevitably emerge from the plenum. Industry apparatchik Aleksandr Karaganov was concerned more specifically about the implications for Ukrainian nationalism after hearing Aitmatov's contentious speech in December. He blurted out at the end of the meeting that he perceived 'a minor manifestation of nationalism [in Aitmatov's speech], which might be the object of investigation at a party meeting'.[42]

Nonetheless, the central committee and Goskino permitted Aitmatov to give his speech during the January plenum, during which he took up the problem of defining and representing national character. In his distaste for films 'deprived of national features', which were 'accomplished in a faceless space, and in the atmosphere of "statistical-mean" people', Aitmatov extolled the ethnographic position, one in which land and people were inextricably and primordially linked.[43] The writer laid out the basis for a discussion of the problem, explaining that the concept of national character came down to the question of 'embodying national originality'.[44] Here, however, he took a step back, stating that 'national originality' should not become 'an end in itself [*samotsel'*]', which would take a work down the road of 'exotic stereotypes and stylizations'. He identified two incorrect positions in this debate: 'One affirms that national character is almost a doubtful concept, almost a prejudice, and another fetishizes national character, and elevates it to a dogma like an age-old and constant quality.' In attempting to answer these straw-man positions from a materialist perspective, Aitmatov, like Buriak, continued to straddle both: 'Of course, national character *exists in nature* as psychological characteristics of a people, and formulated in the movement of socio-historical development.'[45] Aitmatov took us back to square one in denying the applicability of the folkloric / ethnographic mode of representation as a 'prejudice', while affirming the 'natural' quality of nationality, which was nonetheless 'socio-historically' determined.

At this point, Aitmatov relied on example to convey his argument, stating that Rezo Chkheidze's hero in *Father of a Soldier* (*Otets soldata*, 1965) represented the height of Soviet cinema's exploration of national character. At once a plot-driven vehicle that uses a similar mechanism of travel between 'home' and 'front' as Grigorii Chukhrai's *Ballad of a Soldier* (*Ballada o soldate*, 1959) to convey the effects of war on ordinary people, Chkheidze's film was also preoccupied with the 'national originality' of the title character, elderly Georgian vintner Georgii Makharashvili. While the narrative represented little that was new to the Soviet war film during the Thaw, its novelty for spectators was the character's otherness. With Makharashvili's awkward, enormous body and thick moustache dominating almost every shot, his comically broken Russian speech and organic attachment to wine, Chkheidze's hero constituted an ethnic stereotype placed within a common Thaw-era Soviet narrative. In its method of gluing 'national colour' onto a hegemonic plot of martyrdom and victory in the Great Patriotic War, *Father of a Soldier* functioned as a Thaw-era re-working of the Stalinist folkloric. While positioning a protagonist who never sheds his ethnic otherness, Chkheidze refuses to treat this as a failure to conquer backwardness. Nonetheless, Makharashvili functions as static spectacle within the film, and a protagonist who merely watches the historical narrative of World War II play itself out. While Aitmatov celebrated this genuinely popular Georgian film, based on this union of national character with a realist plot, Mikhail Kalatozov, himself Georgian by nationality, complained of the 'essentialization' of the 'Georgian national character' in *Father*. He told Aitmatov in December that the film 'should not have become the reference point for Georgian cinema. It's evidently necessary to specify this, because otherwise a dogmatic treatment of the nature of [national] character will appear.'[46]

In an attempt to get around this problem – to deal with it practically – Aitmatov stated that 'national character had nothing in common with an idealization of a certain national trait or custom; rather, part of a film's realism necessitated a correct representation of national character'. Kyrgyz director Tolomush Okeev responded to Aitmatov's speech in affirmation of the 'realism of national character'. In this formulation, 'accuracy [*tochnost'*]' was more important than a poetic form of 'authenticity [*podlinnost'*]'. Here, Okeev stressed similarity within difference: 'We also love, we also suffer and also die, like everyone, but we take different paths to this. So allow us to talk about it. It's not necessary to cut us all with the same scissors.'[47] Yet, the principle that Aitmatov and Okeev articulated in fact denied the importance of *Father of a Soldier*, because they failed to acknowledge the contrivance of the hero's journey from periphery to centre. Moreover, Chkheidze forces his hero to embody nationality over his personality, which is then spectacularized as Makharashvili moves among an ethnically neutral Soviet people.

Much of what constituted the visuality of 'national character' was under attack for its lack of realism. In fact, national character seemed as hard to define visually, as it was to deny narratively. The January plenum shifted focus by the second day, to tangible questions of production facilities, budgets, salaries and problems with distribution. Many of the representatives from the republics spoke about the increasing impoverishment of national studios, and harangued Goskino for its 'extreme centralisation' and lack of attention and condescension to 'the periphery'.[48]

With this focus on 'realism' as the basis of national character, studio authorities demanded closer attention to screenplays. The resolutions to the January plenum complained of the 'poverty of the screenplay portfolio' at republican studios, along with the 'inoperativeness of resolving questions about including screenplays in the thematic and production plans'. The resolutions mentioned nothing about the discussion of national character, precisely because the plenum resolved nothing. Instead, republican studios were blamed for releasing 'superficial and weak films, provoking the legitimate dissatisfaction of spectators'.[49] An event initiated as a forum for republican film-makers to discuss the 'problem' of national cinemas in the USSR ended with an indictment against the very people who articulated it as such. For Goskino, if the problem was a lack of realism, the solution could only be the further scrutiny of the 'literary basis' of national cinema.

The 'screenplay problem' had its origins much earlier, and was the reason that many republican studios – Dovzhenko Studio and Gruziia-Fil'm in particular – established a staff of salaried writers in the early 1960s. Yet complaints about the exorbitant cost of maintaining these writers emerged almost instantly. Moreover, a common concern during the crisis of 1965–6 was that director-*auteurs* were diverting from the screenplays to engage with formalist poetics. In this exclusive attention to the screenplay problem, however, we see a corresponding attack on visuality. Iurii Illienko and set designer Volodymyr Tsyrlin were particularly concerned about these implications when the 'screenplay problem' re-emerged in the later part of the decade, precisely because it meant that authorities had rejected the 'visual' dimensions of representing national character. During a March 1968 studio conference, Tsyrlin broached the topic of the increasingly under-represented topic of '*izobrazitel'nost* (visuality)' in cinema. Illienko assented, saying, 'It is not cinema that has harmed film dramaturgy, but it is film dramaturgy that has harmed film art[...] They want to rob cinema of the right to be an independent art form and to make it an appendage of literature.'[50]

Tsyrlin and Illienko expanded on this 'offence' to film art in a series of articles in the studio newspaper, *Za Radians'kyi fil'm* (*For Soviet Film*), during late 1969. The former opened the debate on 8 October with 'The Problem of Visuality and the Tendency of Criticism', where he argued that, while Ukrainian cinema had become increasingly 'visual' during the 1960s, film critics continued to write about it as if it were a 'literary' form, with their examination limited to narrative and 'philosophy'. Tsyrlin contended that critics refused to discuss a film's 'visual culture' because they remained ignorant of its functioning. Moreover, film-makers and screenwriters needed to study painting and other visual arts to understand how to make interesting pictures.[51] In a somewhat self-serving gesture, Illienko continued the discussion on 22 October in his article, 'Triunity', where he referred to the profession of cinematographer as the most vital of a film's 'authors'.[52] Pointedly calling the cinematographer turned director turned screenwriter a '*samoznavets*',[53] film critic Iurii Levin countered in the 19 November issue that Illienko's idea was 'original, but not credible'. As Levin perceived, perhaps correctly, Illienko continued to adhere to a principle of '*vne kollektiva*' authorship. Illienko knew that the industry's focus on screenplay production meant not only disinterest in visual experimentation – the very basis for poetic cinema – but also greater inflexibility in relation to thematic plans and the homogenization of film narrative and structure. The delineation of a 'screenplay problem' was seen in the late 1960s as an official policy meant not only to undo the principle of film authorship of the mid-1960s, but also erode studio independence.

In 1967, Il'ia Vaisfel'd wrote – in relation to Hollywood, of course – about the 'struggle for saving cinema's national self-dependency against the expansion of capitalist film monopolies with their ideology of "commercial realism"'.[54] Within the present climate of increasing centralization and renewed appeals to realism and for consistency with the screenplay, such statements could not but strike a chord with republican film-makers. In removing visuality from the question of national character, suggesting instead that it constituted a problem of realism, authorities consciously affected the ways that film-makers could articulate nationality. While the promotion of national cinemas in the Union republics remained official policy, with articles on the topic appearing in *Iskusstvo kino* and *Voprosy kinoiskusstva* throughout the early 1970s, the content of these pieces represented little of interest on the topic, with the only significant development being a discursive shift from the plural 'national cinemas' of the 1960s to the singular 'multinational Soviet cinema'. For the most part, these articles merely conveyed the standard narrative of republican studio construction, a description of the major works within the canon of each of the republics and affirmed the party's commitment to both internationalism and 'multinationality'.[55] Multinationality would remain little more than an abstraction, and increasingly devoid of content. After all, if the social reality of

Ukraine was that the majority of Ukrainians not only knew Russian but were also conversant in it, what principle dictated the continued promotion of Ukrainian-language culture, especially when attempts to move away from language proved all too vague and self-consciously inexplicable?

'De-Nationalization' in the Post-Shelest Era?

Ivan Dziuba, in following the logic of 1920s Ukrainianization framers Oleksandr Shums'kyi and Mykola Skrypnyk, identified the problem of Russian-speaking Ukrainians as enforced de-nationalization, and argued that the purpose of vernacular culture was not to reflect contemporary reality, but to help such Russified Ukrainians come to self-consciousness. The principle that grounded these assumptions was Leninism itself, in addition to Socialist Realism in its forward-looking and pedagogical function. In fact, First Secretary Shelest, Illienko and, oddly enough, Paradjanov were individuals who came to 'national' consciousness within the particular cultural politics of Ukraine after Stalin. Each of these individuals shared the assumption that 'de-nationalization' was a real danger to Ukrainians, and accepted that promotion of national culture took precedence over the free-market principle of representing the 'reality' of national character, a component of which admitted the absence of a unique Ukrainian public.

While 1968 had definitive implications for how the party interacted with film-makers and other members of the creative intelligentsia, with Josephine Woll calling this year the end of the Thaw, Brezhnev considered the CPU under Shelest as nothing if not loyal. Shelest had been the most vocal member of the Politburo in support of intervention in Czechoslovakia, and as such, Brezhnev continued to give him some leeway in his choices for appointments in the CPU apparatus. As Andrii Skaba relinquished his position as CPU Ideological Secretary to head the Institute of History at the Ukrainian Academy of Sciences in 1968, Shelest replaced him with chemist Fedir Ovcharenko. Having heard that the new Ideological Secretary carried liberal tendencies, Paradjanov wrote to Ovcharenko in 1969 on the importance of counteracting Goskino's developing policy of sabotaging republican studios, and his own work in particular. Written in Russian, and translated into Ukrainian by Dziuba, Paradjanov identified himself as the director of *Shadows*, a film, he claimed, that was the 'first in many years to bring international prestige to Ukrainian cinema'. He stated that his film sparked the 'original Ukrainian poetic cinema of the 1960s'. Unfortunately, he claims, the 'school' was now 'paralysed' and unable to bear its 'mature fruit'. He stated, 'Such experiments (*poiski*) are oh so necessary today, because art cannot survive on mass commercial products or on the average, generally accepted level [of production…]'. Paradjanov appealed to Ukraine's poetic traditions contained in the 'experimental' work of Dovzhenko, a man who took 'risks' in his use of symbols and metaphor. In admitting that he was Armenian rather than Ukrainian, he stated that he stayed in Kyiv despite offers to work at the Armenian film studio, because he 'fell in love with Ukrainian culture, I grew with it as an artist and I cannot conceive of my work without it'.[56]

In this letter to Ovcharenko, unthinkable under Ideological Secretary Valentyn Malanchuk and First Secretary Volodymyr Shcherbytskyi, we find Paradjanov attempting to speak to both Ukrainian nationality politics of the 1960s, which increasingly found support among top-ranking members of the party, and to concerns about Soviet cinema's commercialization. Essentially, Paradjanov saw these two problems as necessarily linked. Moreover, we see the director opportunistically appealing to a Ukrainian nationality politics in 1969, something absent from a 1957 letter to the studio director and the Ukrainian Ministry of Culture. In this earlier letter, Paradjanov appealed exclusively to the cultivation of personal expression and '*vne kollektiva*' production, indicating that the nationality question was no longer linked to the Thaw-era problematic of personal authorship. Now, Paradjanov appealed to his contribution to a system of national representation, which had its origins in Dovzhenko's work.

After his letter, Shelest gave Paradjanov an audience, during which the First Secretary offered the director an opportunity to work on a *kolkhoz*-themed screenplay entitled *Earth, the Earth Once Again* (*Zemlia, shche raz zemlia*). The element of thematic repetition present even in the title must have turned off Paradjanov and he declined. After the studio finally put the skids on his adapation of *Intermezzo* in early 1972, the director left for Moscow with the hope of working with Viktor Shklovskii on a made-for-television adaptation of Hans Christian Andersen's *Miracle in Odense*. He returned to Kyiv only once more during his life, after hearing that his son, Suren, had contacted typhus in December 1973. While waiting at the station for his train back to Moscow, Kyiv *militsiia* officers arrested him. By this time, Ovcharenko had returned to life as an apolitical chemist at the

Academy of Sciences, and Shelest was living on a pension in Moscow, forced into early retirement.

In the late 1960s, Shelest too began questioning cultural policies emanating from Moscow, and as such was both fearful of Paradjanov the individual and proud of his work in and for the republic. Around the time that Paradjanov wrote to Ovcharenko, Shelest complained in his diary of certain 'political figures in Moscow, who are scared of anything non-Russian, who treat it with a certain distrust, even contempt, and reveal flagrant great-power chauvinism'.[57] In appropriating such a language directly after discussing a campaign to discredit Ivan Dziuba, we cannot help but wonder if the dissident's ideas had made an impression on the First Secretary. After all, Dziuba identified the same chauvinistic fear of the non-Russian in *Internationalism or Russification?* when he argued that any mention of 'national sentiment, consciousness and duties' necessarily entailed the label of 'bourgeois nationalism' in the Soviet Union. Yet as is evident in Shelest's implementation of Dziuba's language, 'national sentiment, consciousness and duties' remained at the root of mainstream cultural and political discourse into the late 1960s. Dziuba was attacked, not because he chose to criticize recent interpretations of Leninist nationalities policy, but because he 'played into the hands of the enemies' by airing his concerns, and refusing to acknowledge the positive work that nationalities policy had done for Ukraine. In a letter to the CPSU Central Committee, Shelest addressed the critique advanced by Dziuba and others, not with mere condemnation of the very mention of Ukrainian national sentiment, but with arguments that disputed their claims, while specifying further work in developing certain areas of cultural life in the republic that essentially would respond to the substance of his petition.[58]

In his diary, Shelest registered increasing annoyance with what he perceived as an anti-Ukrainian bias in Moscow. On one occasion, he wrote that Brezhnev had asked him why Ukrainians still insist upon speaking Ukrainian. To Shelest, Brezhnev was questioning the very basis of Ukrainian nationality in the Soviet Union, and he now believed that he had to respond in an official capacity to this claim from the centre. The result, *Oh Ukraine, My Soviet Land* (*Ukraino, nasha Radians'ka*, 1970) addressed a number of general historical and geographical sites of importance for justifying the Ukrainian nation, primarily located in a pre-revolutionary and non-Russian Ukraine.[59]

Simultaneously, Vitalii Fedorchuk was appointed Ukrainian KGB head, with the support of Shelest's rivals led by Shcherbytskyi within the CPU apparatus. According to émigré scholar Borys Lewytzkyj, Fedorchuk was responsible for spreading anti-Shelest propaganda within the central committee of the CPU and CPSU, suggesting that the First Secretary was attempting to promote the dissident and nationalist movements, in addition to agitating for the removal of Brezhnev. In April 1971, Shelest was removed from his posts as CPU First Secretary and Chairman of the Ukrainian Council of Ministers, in addition to his spot on the CPSU Politburo. Shcherbytskyi took his place in all three arenas. Brezhnev made it clear, when Shelest asked him the reason for his removal, that it was based on Fedorchuk's and Shcherbytskyi's efforts.[60] In 1973, Shelest was removed from all official duties, and retired on a pension.

While Shelest did in fact accept some of the principles of the dissident movement as he rose in his political career within the same cultural milieu, the accusations that led to his removal were preposterous. After all, Shelest lived the rest of his life in Moscow, and even refused to endorse Ukraine's declaration of independence in 1990. But Paradjanov and others involved in the Ukrainian film industry addressed Shelest and his people in the CPU Central Committee within the idiom of the development of Ukrainian culture and the assertion of a personal ideological commitment to such a project against the rising tide of 'de-nationalization' emerging in the form of Soviet cinema's commercialization.

Chapter 7

'UKRAINIAN POETIC CINEMA' BETWEEN THE COMMUNIST PARTY AND FILM AUDIENCES

The decline of a Thaw-era politics of culture, which qualitatively valued 'personal expression' in place of a focus on the quantitative dimensions of audiences, had a profound effect on Ukrainian cinema by the early 1970s. Most at the studio, in fact, remained committed to a system of national representation, and specifically one that viewed the Carpathians as the essential Ukrainian ethnoscape. During a 1972 conference, Vasyl' Zemliak tried to explain to his colleagues why the Carpathians were more important than the Donbass mines and the Dnieper: 'Things are preserved there, which are not yet destroyed, there are things there, which belong to this people.' Zemliak's position remained unchanged from the debates of 1965: the Carpathians were a Ukrainian space that was both essentially different but also essentially one's own. The writer's point took on a different tone, however, when he suggested in the same speech that Leonid Osyka and Iurii Illienko did not understand either the Ukrainian language or its customs, and pointed towards the work of fellow Zhytomyr peasant and war hero Tymofii Levchuk as the model for national representation.[1] Essential to Levchuk's style of filmmaking was its epic quality – big budget themes taken directly from party congresses and the latest celebratory event or anniversary. By the late 1960s, however, the First

Secretary of the Ukrainian Cinematographers' Union displayed a significant influence from poetic cinema's content (and to some degree, even its style), choosing to locate his films about Honoré de Balzac, the Kotsiubyns'kyi family and partisan leader Sydir Kovpak in the Carpathians, and featuring Ukrainian-speaking actors Ivan Mykolaichuk and Kostiantyn Stepankov among others.

Zemliak's transfer of loyalty from poetic cinema to Levchuk reflected the crisis of national representation at Dovzhenko Studio in 1972. Within an increasing emphasis during the previous years on profitable films, on the one hand, and ideological retrenchment regarding nationalities policy on the other, poetic cinema directors in Ukraine had to speak to broader concerns beyond the principle of national authorship. And yet, Iurii Illienko and Leonid Osyka (not to mention Paradjanov, who left for Armenia in 1966 to make his surrealist *Colour of Pomegranates*) seemed to move in the opposite direction with their superficial attempts to appease industry and ideological authorities with classical literary adaptations and 'heroic' historical themes.

After all, the principles of adaptation were mobilized to establish Ukrainian poetic cinema at the beginning of the 1960s with Denysenko's *A Dream* and Paradjanov's *Shadows*. By the same token, the 'failures' of 1965–6 all shared a uniquely non-literary origin. By emphasizing canonical literary sources like Gogol and the Ukrainian realists Vasyl' Stefanyk and Ivan Franko, Illienko and Osyka now attempted to bypass the ideological scrutiny that coincided with their 'formalist' debuts. After all, such writers were already vetted as acceptable expressions of national culture. Similarly, Illienko, along with the younger director Borys Ivchenko (son of Viktor Ivchenko), returned to the theme of the Great Patriotic War, this time in a more directly realist vein. And yet, largely due to the de-investment of national studios by 1972 for both ideological and financial reasons, even box office successes were met with certain scepticism from Moscow if they dealt with the national substance of Ukrainian poetic cinema. Only Levchuk, Bykov and a few other Stalin-era directors managed to make 'national cinema' in Kyiv by the mid-1970s, especially after First Secretary Shcherbytskyi publically denounced poetic cinema during a major party plenum in May 1974 as 'fetishistic' of the Ukrainian national character. Thereafter, the press could no longer write about this now banned school or on any of its exemplars.

The Safe Realm of Literature and History?

Illienko's adaptation of Gogol's *St. John's Eve* (*Vecher na Ivana Kupala*, 1968) constituted an eclectic mix of Ukrainian folkloric motifs and encounters with the supernatural, along with visual humour and farce, a story of forbidden love and couched political critique. Stylistically, the film contains frequent narrative lapses, jump cuts, a moving camera and tableaux images. Employing a film solarization technique that Illienko used in the fight between Ivanko and Iurko in *Shadows of Forgotten Ancestors*, *St. John's Eve* distinguishes between the 'real' and the world of the supernatural with different colour schemes. Some scenes are viewed through a negative print, and others contain only tones of blue or orange (Figures 7.1–7.2). By the second part of the film, as witches and devils possess Petro, the protagonist, the film degenerates into absurdist constructions, as if the spectator were experiencing the same delusions. In mixing the symbolic world of Ukrainian folklore and the presence of Cossacks and other historical / mythological figures with such a dynamic and defamiliarized literary terrain, Illienko's film functioned as a complex, intellectual parody of the Stalinist folkloric, along with frequent visual citations of Dovzhenko's *Zvenyhora* and other, more recent works of Ukrainian poetic cinema.

Written by Illienko himself, and shot by his older brother Vadym, *St. John's Eve* was to be a completely '*vne kollektiva*' and author-driven production. When he and Ivan Drach (who had taken the film on as screenplay editor) proposed the Gogol adaptation, they

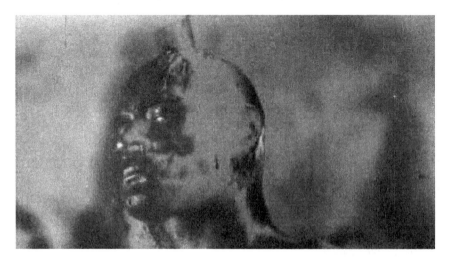

Figure 7.1　Translating the early Gogol to the screen in Iurii Illienko's *St. John's Eve* (1968)

Figure 7.2   Solarization techniques in Iurii Illienko's *St. John's Eve* (1968)

imagined it as a second chance to establish a national cinema based on the 'mark' of intellectual authorship. Couched this time in the language of classic literary adaptation, however, Illienko found an audience at the studio and within the CPU leadership largely receptive to the project, despite the director's political failure with *A Well for the Thirsty*. Critic Mikhail Bleiman, who reviewed politically questionable screenplays for central Goskino during the late 1960s and early 1970s, gave the go-ahead, stating, 'Illienko "finds" his theme in Gogol', and in my opinion, he finds it convincingly'. While discovering 'shortcomings' in the second half of the film, which significantly 'departed from Gogol's literary basis', Bleiman concluded, 'Illienko is a talented man and works seriously. It seems we see the same thing in the screenplay written by him. Thus, it is possible to have faith in its author and director.'[2] From the importance that Goskino placed on Bleiman's opinions, we may assume that the industry continued to promote the principle of individual authorship. With *St. John's Eve*, however, we begin to see the significance of the industry's drive towards selling a profitable commodity. While Illienko's 1968 production was his most experimental film before restrictions were lifted during *glasnost*, it signalled the growing divide between what critics were calling 'difficult' films and commercial productions (*kassovye fil'my*). Critics bemoaned that the Soviet film industry was losing its own claim to represent the cultured middle.[3]

Osyka too had successfully played the adaptation card to receive permission to make *The Stone Cross* (*Kaminnyi khrest*, 1968), based on two short stories by Galician novelist Vasyl' Stefanyk. The Russified Osyka initially proposed an adaptation of an Andrei Platonov story, but Tsvirkunov reportedly told Osyka, 'In Ukraine we have our own Platonov, one who is closer to us.'[4] Thereafter, the director found a Russian translation of Stefanyk, coincidentally with commentary by Platonov, believing that with this he had found the 'Ukrainian Platonov'.[5] Having discussed Stefanyk's significance for Ukrainian culture with Osyka, Drach then agreed to write the screenplay. Stefanyk's *oeuvre* included 59 short stories, many of them only a few pages long, and which attempted a description of 'slice of life' events in the lives of poor Galician peasants.[6] With his extensive merging of dialect with literary Ukrainian, Stefanyk became an ideal author to adapt in light of the success with this method in *Shadows of Forgotten Ancestors*. Drach's narrative merges two of Stefanyk's short stories, 'The Stone Cross' and 'The Thief', with the same protagonist of Ivan Didukh, which attempted a more complete literary form than the author had originally established with them. Yet, such was Osyka's penchant for stylistic eclecticism, the two stories remain noticeably cut off from each other. The overarching narrative, however, tells of an impoverished Galician peasant, who is forced in his old age to leave his home and set out with his children for Canada in search of work. The bulk of the story deals with his going away party, at which his entire village makes an appearance. In an early scene, taken from 'The Thief', Didukh discovers a thief in his barn, whom he stabs in the leg with a pitchfork before inviting him to drink with his neighbour. After drinking and discussing the reasons for Ukrainians leaving their native land, Didukh beats the thief to death. The going-away party is less realist in style, incorporating local song and other elements of ethnographic spectacle and local ritual, as a mobile camera surveys the guests wishing Ivan farewell. As the Didukh family prepares to leave at the end of the party, they change out of their 'native' clothing into urban formal wear. The film ends as they pass a stone cross on a hillside. As Vitaly Chernetsky argues, Osyka's film is preoccupied with the question of an 'identity crisis' emerging from the protagonist's desertion of the impoverished Ukrainian village, which is understood in the film as a 'symbolic death'.[7]

In keeping with a now emblematic method of Ukrainian poetic cinema, Osyka shot the film in Stefanyk's native south-west Ukrainian village of Rusiv, using actual residents in many of the roles. In a language that should be familiar, Ukrianian critic Liudmila Lemesheva wrote, 'Stefanyk's fellow countrymen did not perform in this film, but seemingly continued to live their ordinary lives'. In *The Stone Cross*, Lemesheva posited, 'Life, seen and constructed according to artistic rules, coincided with real life'.[8] Yet, as with the claim that associated contemporary Hutsuls with those represented in *Shadows*, authorities would have been hesitant to agree with such a trans-historical claim because it denied the principle of development. As the Hutsul who wrote to *Novyny kinoekrana* (cited in Chapter 4) implied, these images were 'not us'. Although Lemesheva probably did not intend to imply this, in her affirmation of the collision of the 'constructed' and the 'real', we understand that the 'not us' only became 'us' when the cameras were rolling.

In attempting to present the realism of 'national character', the first scene of *The Stone Cross* constituted a realist film, with its emphasis on dialogue and traditional framing techniques. Only the minimalism of the narrative and the seeming lack of character motivation in killing the thief stand out as elements of experimentation. The film follows a standard narrative development, in which the camera is invisible and cinematic conventions of continuity are not broken, for the most part. The scene during which the three drink together particularly accepts realist convention, even while it serves the function of colouring in the film's nationality with the use of local dialect and costume. Osyka fixates particularly on the land, but not for its beauty. In fact, the land is infinitely grey, dry and only intriguing insofar as it is uniform and inhospitable. But the hero's tragedy is not the social aspects of poverty itself, but the disconnection between land and human subject, which further posits that human misery emerges out of natural or biological conditions rather than social conditions.

As a film that addressed the problem of 'realism' and 'national character', *The Stone Cross* garnered serious accolades at the studio and in Ukrainian Goskino in February 1968. Nonetheless, Osyka's *Stone Cross*, like Illienko's very different *St. John's Eve*, remained a 'difficult' film, in part because few non-Ukrainians (or Ukrainians for that matter) were familiar with Stefanyk's work. Thus, organs of distribution were more reluctant than ever to risk regular screenings of Osyka's film. Consequently, *The Stone Cross* failed to draw even the abysmal 3.5 million spectators that Osyka's directorial debut had. In fact, both Illienko's *St. John's Eve* and Osyka's *Stone Cross* sold under 1.5 million tickets each, with less than a third of these in

Ukraine.[9] The Cinematographers' Union (Moscow) First Secretary Lev Kulidzhanov mentioned *St. John's Eve* as a film that succeeded on the 'festival circuit' but did nothing to help 'solve the problem of the spectator'.[10] One spectator wrote to the Central Committee after viewing *St. John's Eve*, calling it an 'unwholesome phenomenon'.[11]

The pattern of screening the two films, which coincided with each other in spring 1969, demonstrated that the organs of distribution had more in mind than simply limiting its time in theatres. *The Stone Cross* ran in four different theatres in Kyiv from 21 April to 4 May, and *St. John's Eve* in three theatres from 24 April to 25 May. Interestingly, the venues for both films also coincided: the Ukraina, Leningrad and Dovzhenko theatres.[12] These theatres were also the venues that showed *Shadows* and *Love Awaits Those Who Return* for the longest period. Thus, in consciously directing such 'difficult' films towards particular movie theatres, Soviet distribution was acting in accordance with Western film distribution principles of differentiated marketing of 'popular films' and 'art films'.[13]

Despite doing nothing to 'help solve the problem of the spectator', *St. John's Eve* and *The Stone Cross* were 'good' adaptations, each receiving first-category ratings and praise from major Soviet critics of all persuasions.[14] They succeeded in conveying the unique style of the early Gogol, with his mix of Ukrainian folklore, comedy and social critique, and the dismal mood of Vasyl' Stefanyk's work. While the films of 1965 came out in answer to the demand for images of the Ukrainian 'contemporary', it was in this ethnographic style of representation, which the regime understood as firmly located in the presocialist past, that they perceived an anti-Soviet position. Illienko's and Osyka's response to 1965, then, became a return to the 'actual' past, where such 'negative' imagery would be allowed, even if working on non-contemporary themes continued to be discouraged.

Yet, as Kulidzhanov suggested, Illienko and Osyka continued to refuse to participate in the new audience politics, and Ukrainian poetic cinema came to be the clearest indication that Soviet cinema more broadly was divided between '*trudnye fil'my*' and '*kassovye fil'my*'. In an article for *Sovetskii ekran*, critic Tatiana Ivanova identified in Illienko's recent work the high water mark of the 'difficult film'. According to her definition, the 'difficult film' was one in which an 'obviously high level of artistry' did not meet with a 'wide success with the spectator'.[15] In her argument, while Paradjanov's *Shadows* constituted a 'difficult' viewing experience for many spectators, *St. John's Eve* developed the 'genre' of the 'difficult film' to its extreme. Thus, while she did not deny that Illienko had adapted Gogol correctly, the results perhaps suggested that this was not a useful story to adapt in the first place. On the other hand, when writing in 'Triunity', Illienko considered Gogol's evocation of visuality in his early work to be an indication that it was ideal for adaptation, precisely due to its lack of *literaturnost'* (literary-ness). Ivanova concluded that a division now existed in Soviet cinema between the 'difficult' film and the 'commercial' film, which filmmakers needed to mend.[16]

The next films that Illienko and Osyka made – *White Bird with a Black Mark* (*Bilyi ptakh z chornoiu oznakoiu*, 1970) and *Zakhar Berkut* (1972) respectively – were historical epics, slotted to become major box office successes. In accepting that Illienko and Osyka were the two most talented directors at Dovzhenko Studio in the early 1970s, authorities in Ukrainian Goskino and the Central Committee believed that, if the two accepted that appeal to actual spectators was important, their abilities could be harnessed for the continued benefit of Ukrainian cinema. When Illienko began working on his Great Patriotic War film set in Bukovyna in late 1969, he was the youngest member of the collective to hold the prestigious position of director-producer, highest category (*rezhiser-postanovshchik vysshei kategorii*). *White Bird* was to be the showcase film from Ukraine for the 25th anniversary of Victory Day, while Osyka's story of medieval Carpathian tribes uniting against a Mongol invasion cost the studio close to 1.5 million roubles, by far the largest budget for any film made at Dovzhenko Studio to date.[17]

In many ways, Illienko's *White Bird* was his most successful and accessible film. Iurii Lysenko, no longer fed up with the 'morons in the pictures', commented that *White Bird* represented the first time that the 'new methods' were used for a 'civil theme'.[18] Iurii Novykov noted the beginning of a 'new cinematic phenomenon [of] an amalgamation of poetic and realist cinema'.[19] The Dovzhenko Studio Artistic Council called Illienko's completed film 'traditional' in terms of plot development and narration, but 'innovative' in terms of the 'directorial treatment',[20] here suggesting the positive role of its 'visual culture'. Illienko had moved away from the visual experimentation of *St. John's Eve* and made a Great Patriotic War epic about the Dzvonar' family in Bukovyna, the members of which go in different ideological directions. The screenplay's co-author, Mykolaichuk, played the role of Petro, the social hero who joins the Soviet Army, while Bohdan Stupka, a young actor at Lviv's Shevchenko Theatre, played his brother Orest, who joins the Banderists hiding out in the mountains. The third brother, Heorhii, wavers until his new bride, Vivdia, is killed by a gang of Germans and local collaborators, and afterwards becomes a committed communist. The locating of ideological divergence within the family is a persistent motif in Ukrainian literature, emerging, for example, in Gogol's *Taras Bul'ba*, Dovzhenko's *Zvenyhora* and Iurii Ianovs'kyi's novel *Riders* (*Vershnyky*), the latter most famous for Savchenko's 1939 adaptation. While such a narrative trope defines a 'good' brother and a 'bad' brother, it does so while maintaining the comprehensibility of the 'bad' brother's motives. This was the problem that was the basis of Illienko's film: Orest's character remains the most compelling personality, while Mykolaichuk's Petro is superficially drawn, almost unbelievable in his seemingly natural commitment to Communism. Members of the CPU Central Committee immediately perceived this possibility in the screenplay, and Goskino refused to approve Mykolaichuk for the role of Orest, for whom he had written it.[21] While the film won the Grand Prize at the Moscow International Film Festival in 1971, local authorities, especially the Lviv Party Committee, called the film 'socially harmful' for a scene in which Orest distinguishes the Banderists from the Germans.[22] Shelest, however, liked the film tremendously upon viewing it privately and permitted its distribution in Ukraine.[23]

The film's narrative, which takes place during World War II and the struggle between the Romanian and German occupiers, the UPA (ukrainian nationalist paramilitaries) and Soviet partisans, follows a standard plot found in many post-Stalinist Soviet war films that focus on everyday life and suffering during the war,[24] but serves to nationalize the conflict, making it specific to the particular experience of Bukovynian peasants. Apart from the narrative we find the essential questions, which the film addresses: the reconciliation of a folkloric and ahistorical past with the needs of a materialist worldview. The film is not really about ideas; rather, it is about the presentation of various facets of rural life in western Ukraine; the dialogue is frequently poetic or lyric in quality, and the characters both inhabit and perpetuate the folkloric. Objects from everyday life fill the scenes, and constitute the film's spectacle. This is emphasized by placing humans and objects self-consciously within frames, constructed out of the fabric of the scene.

White Bird possessed many of the same features as *Shadows*, evident in its emphasis on colour and camera techniques directly in line with Illienko's work on Paradjanov's film. Moreover, the film contains frequent breaks in the narrative to accommodate the presence of folkloric display (dance, diegetic music and tableaux). *White Bird*, nonetheless, remained more of a complex psychological investigation of the main characters, particularly Heorhii and Orest, than any prior work of Ukrainian poetic cinema, and its narrative followed 'classical' norms in its emphasis on continuity and motivated action. In many respects, these two aspects of the film are sharply distinguishable: spectacle is delineated from narrative content, and the rhythmic flow of the camera contrasts with the static framing devices that owe much to the style contained in *Shadows of Forgotten Ancestors.*

The authorities at Dovzhenko Studio engaged with new audience politics when attempting to find both a differentiated audience (locally in the Carpathians and nationally in Ukraine) and a mass audience for Illienko's *White Bird*. This was the first film that Ukrainian Goskino test-marketed in the republic before sending it to Moscow for all-Union release. Before the Russian-dubbed version was even completed, Dovzhenko Theatre near the studio screened the film twice in March 1971.[25] The following week, *White Bird* made its controversial appearance at the Twenty-Fourth Congress of the CPU, after which the film was pulled from distribution owing to the concerns of several west ukrainian party Secretaries about the nationalist implications of the film.[26]

Over the summer, Illienko's film was released in several spots in the republic as part of a travelling 'National Film Festival [*narodnyi kinofestival'*]' that showcased Dovzhenko Studio productions.[27] S. P. Ivanov wrote to the Cultural Section of the CPU that, during the test release of the film in Ukraine, the film performed extraordinarily well in the western oblasts, offering the 'remarkable' figure that 50 per cent of the people in Lviv Oblast' saw the film.[28] In distinction to earlier works of Ukrainian poetic cinema, letters in the studio archive were entirely positive about *White Bird*.[29] Moreover, during a 1971 sociological study conducted at the Kyiv aircraft construction plant, audiences evaluated Illienko's film highly during a private screening.[30] During the Second Congress of the Cinematographers' Union (Moscow), Kulidzhanov finished his speech about the 'problem of the spectator' with a positive word about *White Bird*, suggesting that it was a film that attempted to reconcile the growing divide between 'difficult' films and commercial cinema.[31]

Nonetheless, with Shcherbytskyi's rise to power in late 1971, the film continued to have a limited distribution. In Kyiv, *White Bird* played only at the Ukraina throughout September and October, and then briefly at Kinopanorama after the wide-screen version was released in January.[32] According to the results from test marketing, *White Bird* could have been a minor box office hit, but the Shcherbytskyi regime was clearly concerned with other problems of an exclusively ideological nature. In fact, it appears that, in this case, it was the film's potential for popular consumption that turned CPU officials against it.

Leonid Osyka's *Zakhar Berkut* (1972) represented a further attempt at melding the visual techniques and Ukrainian classic literary material of 'poetic cinema' with an objectively determined set of criteria that would appeal to Soviet audiences. Based on stories contained in the Galician-Volynian Chronicle and the 1883 short story by Ivan Franko, Osyka's film was a big budget national-historical epic about the title character who unites the Carpathian tribes against the Mongol invasion of 1241. The production of the film was incredibly taxing on both the studio's resources, and on Osyka himself (who began drinking heavily at the time). In fact, *Zakhar Berkut* did not seem to fit with his style of making small, quiet films like *Love Awaits* and *Stone Cross*. In October 1969, S. P. Ivanov wrote to Aleksei Romanov about the possibility of increasing the studio's overall production budget from 3,480,000 to 3,922,000 roubles, owing to the anniversary-year productions and the 'extremely complicated' production of Osyka's film.[33] *Zakhar Berkut* was to be a mainstream historical epic – an 'Americanization of Franko', as one contemporary critic put it[34] – along the lines of *Oleksa Dovbush* in its genre-driven iconography, but which would employ the 'new methods' of 'Ukrainian poetic cinema' to explore the Carpathian ethnoscape. In fact, the historical epic which Osyka's film most strived to emulate was the work of Romanian director Sergiu Nicolaescu, whose elaborate historical epics *The Dacians* (1966) and *Mihai Viteazul* (1970–1) offered comparable national origin myths emerging from the union of pre-national Carpathian tribes against invaders from the East (Mongols in Osyka's case and Turks in Nicolaescu's films).

Key to both Illienko's *White Bird* and Osyka's *Zakhar Berkut* was the industry's re-investment with visuality, but in the latter case only as a means to cash in on what authorities in Goskino saw as a successful model through which Hollywood recouped its profits after the losses of the late 1950s and early 1960s. The most obvious example of epic film-making in the Soviet Union was Sergei Bondarchuk's *Waterloo* (1970), a sprawling historical epic about Napoleon's final battle, which featured Rod Steiger as the title character, Orson Welles as King Louis XVIII and 20,000 extras. While it was a phenomenal box office flop upon its release in 1971, during its production Dovzhenko Studio viewed Osyka's film as a means of proving that Ukraine could be trusted to deliver a similar product for domestic and international consumption. From the very beginning, however, Kyiv film-makers realized that, despite the extraordinary budget Osyka commanded, Goskino had bigger fish to fry. Resentfully, Levchuk stated during a meeting of the studio artistic council, 'If Bondarchuk had 1,200 horses, then Osyka should have 1,500 horses!'[35] Authorities at Mosfilm, however, continually ignored Osyka's requests to use Bondarchuk's horses after he was done with them. Eventually Bondarchuk's production crew refused on the basis that they could not transport the animals to Osyka's desired location in the Carpathians. This refusal infuriated Osyka and the studio, because Bondarchuk himself was in the process of shooting a battle scene for *Waterloo* in the trans-Carpathian city of Uzhhorod around the same time.[36] In the end, they had to shoot *Zakhar Berkut* in the unlikely location of the Tian Shan mountain range of Central Asia, and Osyka had to make do with horses rented from local collective farms.[37]

Osyka was livid about such instances of the privilege that central directors received at the expense of those on the 'periphery', especially as Bondarchuk had initially made a name for himself as an actor at Kyiv Studio in the 1950s, playing such prestigious roles as Taras Shevchenko in Savchenko's 1951 production and the title character in Levchuk's *Ivan Franko* in 1956. When Bondarchuk expressed a desire to make Gogol's *Taras Bul'ba* at Dovzhenko Studio as a co-production with Mosfilm and Dino De Laurentiis studio in Italy in 1972, Osyka blurted out during a studio meeting, 'Now Bondarchuk will exploit all of us. We will work like we are in Hollywood.'[38]

While the studio and Ukrainian Goskino offered *Zakhar Berkut* praise, and audiences liked it for the most part,[39] the shifting political situation in the republic at the time of its release limited its distribution. After Ovcharenko's ouster, Fedir Malanchuk demanded a total halt to historical themes, on the basis that they had ceased to be relevant to Ukraine.[40] During a CPU plenum in May 1974, First Secretary Shcherbytskyi finally ended all discussion of Ukrainian poetic cinema:

Some time ago, examples of so-called 'poetic cinema' with its stress on abstract symbolism and sharply accented ethnographic

ornamentation were treated by individual film-makers almost as
the leading principles of the development of cinema art in Ukraine.
These views, it is necessary to say, have been overcome.[41]

The First Secretary's remarks about poetic cinema in particular were
printed in all the major Ukrainian-language newspapers and journals dedicated to literature and art. While Moscow critics continued
to discuss poetic cinema in the central press after Shcherbytskyi's
speech, the problem had been 'overcome' in Ukraine, and it was no
longer a topic in republican-level discourse. During the Malanchuk
era of the mid-to-late 1970s, both historical directors and those who
regularly worked within 'national' thematics found it difficult to
find work. Most affected was Mykolaichuk, whose health and career
took a nosedive. For five years, he played nothing except bit parts in
Ukrainian films, in addition to a few small roles at Mosfilm and in
a Bulgarian production. Central Goskino deliberately sabotaged his
career, as they halted production on an informational bulletin on
the actor, meant for popularization purposes in 1974, directly after
Shcherbytskyi's speech.[42]

In September 1974, the new Ukrainian Goskino chairman Vasyl'
Bol'shak sent an order to sovexportfilm to remove both *White Bird*
and *Zakhar Berkut* from future distribution abroad.[43] At this point,
even the possibility of generating revenue from these two celebrated
syntheses of 'poetic' and 'realist' Ukrainian cinema proved too dangerous for the mature period of Shcherbytskyi's stagnation regime.

Tymofii Levchuk and the Poetics of Stagnation

Ukrainian Goskino announced in 1972 that the studio thematic plan
for the next four years had only three 'directions [*napriamky*]' in
which filmmakers could work. The first field included the ubiquitous
yet ambiguous category of 'our contemporary'. Second, Ukrainian
directors could work in the realm of 'adaptations of Russian and
Ukrainian classics'. Finally, the Goskino report mentioned adventure films. Fresh from the trying experience of *Zakhar Berkut*, Osyka
stated that he saw nothing to work on in the next four years.[44] During
a subsequent meeting about the 1974–5 plan, Levchuk noticed that
there was only one film on a 'Ukrainian theme', his own partisan
epic, *Carpathians, Carpathians* (*Karpaty, Karpaty*, 1976).[45]

A decade before this report, in the midst of debates about poetic
cinema and praise of Paradjanov's *Shadows of Forgotten Ancestors*,
critic Mykola Berezhnyi gave the First Secretary of the Ukrainian

Cinematographers' Union a slap in the face with his statement, 'We don't need to produce Levchuks at the studio, but Dovzhenkos, because it's a bad soldier who doesn't want to be a general...'[46] In 1941, the recent graduate of the Kyiv Film Institute and assistant director on Ihor Savchenko's *Riders*, had enlisted in the Soviet Army on the day after the Germans invaded the Soviet Union. The Soviet press wrote about Levchuk's exploits on the Ukrainian Front, and he was awarded the highest medal for combat, hero of the Soviet Union. Berezhnyi's statement was not entirely fair, especially since Levchuk did in fact make a number of Ukrainian-themed films during his long career, including a three-part history of a family of Arsenal factory workers and their children, and a biopic on the life of Ivan Franko. As a member of the Verkhovna Rada, he travelled to New York, Paris, Munich and Winnipeg to speak to émigré communities, embodying a role different from that of Mykolaichuk, but nonetheless serving as an important messenger from the '*batkivshchyna* (fatherland)'. As the First Secretary of the Union, Levchuk gave strong support to both Paradjanov and the promotion of a 'Dovzhenkoist poetics' throughout 1964–7. He, nonetheless, believed in the party, and blindly accepted CPU policy, giving the order to expel Paradjanov from the union as soon as he was arrested, citing the director's lack of involvement in union activities as justification.[47]

Moreover, his work during the first half of the 1960s seemed strangely out of touch with the cultural politics and aesthetic interests of Dovzhenko Studio during this time. In 1962, he made *The Law of Antarctica* (*Zakon Antarktidy*) about Soviet Antarctic explorers who rescue a team of Belgian geologists; in 1964, *Cosmic Alloy* (*Kosmicheskii splav*) about a factory that produces rockets for space travel; and in 1966, *Two Years above the Abyss* (*Dva goda nad propast'iu*), about Ivan Kudria and the Kyiv underground during the Nazi occupation. Apart from the latter film, which dealt with a local topic and became a box office success with 30.7 million tickets sold in 1967, Levchuk appeared to his colleagues as a '*zakaznyi rezhiser*', a director who took on films that the CPSU ordered directly, without consideration of the particular goals of the studio or the potential audience for such films.

Perhaps in an attempt to reassert his relevance at the studio, Levchuk fought hard for his next project, his long-held dream of adapting novelist Natan Rybak's *Honoré de Balzac's Mistake* (*Oshibka Onere de Bal'zaka*, 1940) about the French writer's journey to the

Russian Empire to rekindle a love affair with Polish noblewoman Ewalina Hańska, whom he went on to marry five months before his death in March 1850.[48] In early 1967, Levchuk provided an explanation of the screenplay, in which he stressed Balzac's relations and knowledge of the Ukrainian people as he travelled around the countryside. He wrote that the 'film permits a spontaneous and [...] deep revelation of the picture of life of our people [...] In comparison to the novel, the screenplay has significantly expanded Balzac's acquaintance with the Ukrainian people, not only in Verkhovyna, but also in Kyiv.' The film begins in Paris, with Balzac arranging travel to the Russian Empire, as much to evade his creditors as to see Hańska. As Levchuk implied in his explanation, however, the narrative motivation for the famous writer is but a weak device to establish the fictional connection between Ukraine and the founder of 'critical realism', at once a celebrity association written upon the entire nation and a view of that nation read through the eyes of a famous tourist. As the writer passes through customs into the Empire, he is greeted with a singing troupe of four Hutsuls dressed in *keptari*. Balzac pauses to watch the spectacle, before moving on. We cut to a wide-angle mountain view as the narrator speaks: 'There she is, Ukraine, a mysterious and unknown land.' Balzac gathers Ukrainian dirt into his hands, pressing it against his face with pleasure. He immediately meets a Kyiv professor of archaeology, who shows him 'wealth under the Ukrainian earth'. The film constantly forces its hero to recognize the beauty of Ukraine's landscape, people and history, which remains unmotivated in the narrative, and furthermore absent from the Stalin-era novel, from which Levchuk adapted *Balzac's Mistake*.

In his explanation, however, Levchuk was clear to emphasize that his 'Balzac in Ukraine' story, as he called it, would not be a work of Ukrainian poetic cinema, as he stressed the strength of the actors over the 'succulence of material accessories'.[49] Balzac's relationship with Hańska *is*, in fact, de-emphasized in *Mistake*, with the man who erected the 'bridge between critical realism and Socialist Realism'[50] travelling through Ukraine as a privileged tourist, first making stops in the 'mysterious' Carpathians and heading East towards Kyiv to see St. Sofiia (Figure 7.2). While in Verkhovyna, Balzac makes friends with a young serf of the Hańska family, Levko, played by Ivan Mykolaichuk. While a minor character in both Rybak's novel and his updated 1965 screenplay, the violin-playing and highly literate prodigy Levko

Figure 7.3 Ethnographic survey of Bukovynian peasant faces in Illienko's *White Bird with a Black Mark* (1971)

took centre stage in both Levchuk's narrative and in promotional materials on the film. Rather than the hulking and rather ugly Viktor Khokhiarkov as Balzac, *Na ekranakh Ukrainy* and *Novyny kinoekrana* featured stills of Mykolaichuk in the film.[51] When the Ukrainian Cinematographers' Union nominated the film for a Shevchenko Prize, they stated that ultimately the film was 'about the Ukrainian people'.[52] Nonetheless, *Balzac's Mistake* is *not* poetic cinema, but not necessarily for the reason that Levchuk cited above, with his statement about the 'succulence' of material culture. The director made the film in a classic realist style, with its folkloric material properly motivated, if not through the narrative, then essentially through the spectator's alignment with the literary hero and his vision. The film does not present the Carpathian exotic directly to the spectator; rather, its consumption contains a diegetic origin in the figure of Balzac as a foreign tourist.

In 1973, Levchuk began work on *The Ballad of Kovpak* (*Duma pro Kovpaka*), the most extensive and expensive project of his life, which was to commemorate the heroic sacrifice of the Ukrainian partisan movement during the Great Patriotic War. General Sydir Kovpak was an ideal subject through which to explore this topic, first due to his impeccable record during the civil war, serving under the real Vasilii Chapaev, and during World War II, where he became one of the most decorated non-Russian officers, awarded hero of the Soviet Union twice, and the orders of Lenin, *Krasnoe znamia*, (Red Banner) Suvorov and Bohdan Khmel'nyts'kyi. Moreover, Kovpak was one of the few ethnic Ukrainian civilians who had led Ukrainian partisan forces during the war, the majority of whose leaders were appointed from among Red Army officers in Moscow. Thus, the image of Kovpak possessed both a legitimate political meaning during the Brezhnev era, and a safe ethnic meaning for Ukrainian cinema after the denouncement of poetic cinema in 1974. Levchuk's trilogy followed Kovpak's group from their inception in the Sumy region of north-eastern Ukraine in late 1941, to actions in the central Ukrainian Kyiv and Zhytomyr provinces in 1942, to their major raid of the Carpathians in 1943, the latter of which helped destabilize the German occupation.

The Ballad of Kovpak essentially occupied Levchuk for most of the 1970s, with the final part released in 1978. The trailer for the final part of Levchuk's film, *Carpathians, Carpathians*, is instructive for its juxtaposition of historical / mythological time grounded in the Carpathophilia of the previous decade, and 'the contemporary', the latter represented by the mobile tourist. The trailer's narrator begins in voice-over:

> Far away under the sound of the *trembita*'s (Carpathian shepherd's horn) voice. The boundless expanse of the Carpathians is opened before one's gaze. The mountaintops swim in hazy fog, the rugged forests, and the green cover of the mountain-valleys [*ukr*]. Tiny little houses in valleys [*rus*], emerald sparks of the waterfalls of the mountain streams...

We hear the distant sound of the *trembita* and then silence. The trailer cuts to the sharp bend of a contemporary highway. Cars and tourist buses fill the screen. One of the buses stops on the edge of the highway, and people dressed in modern clothing exit to get a glance at one of these 'eternal' mountain valleys. The narrator returns: 'This is the Carpathians. A colourful corner of Soviet land, a region of fairy tale beauty, and hospitable and talented people. Come and see the beauty... listen to this silence and for once recall those who obtained it for us...' Another group of tourists finds themselves in a picturesque glade, and we hear laughs, cries of delight, juxtaposed with amateur photographs and home movies. The trailer ends with an image of a monument to Kovpak located in the Bukovyna city of Chernivtsi and then cuts to the partisan leader's grave in Kyiv. Unlike the narrative teleology within Stalinist cinema, Levchuk's cinematic epic and the corresponding trailer do not end with a message of Ukrainian-Russian union, but of continuity between eastern and western Ukrainian space, the trailer offering further contextualization for the contemporary viewer with its suggestion that they owe their present consumer abundance to the generation to which its director belonged.[53]

Both *Carpathians, Carpathians* and *Balzac's Mistake* established a Carpathian imagery within an aesthetics of stagnation, an aesthetics which normalized the space as a tourist destination for an all-Union audience. At the same time, these two works, along with *Zakhar Berkut*, were pricey endeavours for Dovzhenko Studio, which lost hundreds of thousands of roubles when they failed to turn out audiences, and contributed to the impoverishment of the studio by the end of the decade.[54]

Like many directors who themselves were participants in the Great Patriotic War, Levchuk made war films for personal reasons. Illiashenko, who had an unusual soft spot for Levchuk in his ordinarily bitter heart, reads into the First Secretary the role of a new 1970s *auteur*, one who was equally concerned with personal expression as with answering the ideological demands of the Brezhnev era. 'For such artists,' Illiashenko writes in his post-Soviet *History of Ukrainian Film Art*, 'the theme of the war was an inner necessity for them, the essence of their work, and there was a continual need for them to speak about it.'[55] The attention is on the soldiers themselves, and even the leaders are hardly distinguished from the infantry. Whereas the cult of the Great Patriotic War was increasingly localized by the 30th anniversary of Victory Day in May 1975, with more monuments constructed celebrating and commemorating the local dynamics of both heroics and suffering, mainstream filmic representation was characterized by Iurii Ozerov's *Liberation* (*Osvobozhdenie*, 1970). Ozerov's epic deals with the five 'great battles' of the war: Stalingrad, Kursk, the Dnieper, Minsk and Berlin. *Kovpak* screenwriters Igor' Bolgarin and Viktor Smirnov, themselves Russians working in Moscow, perceived their film as a direct response to Ozerov, with the latter's aesthetic of placeless epicality, which narratively foregrounded the march towards victory. They viewed the Kovpak trilogy as a localized tribute to the Great

Patriotic War, in which real people – not just leaders – carried on their everyday lives in the midst of fighting behind enemy lines, initially as the losers of the conflict. While appealing to such a Thaw-era 'cult of the little guy', *The Ballad of Kovpak* also aimed at a nostalgic rehabilitation of Stalin and Stalinist culture. *Carpathians, Carpathians* begins, for example, with Kovpak and his men watching Vladimir Petrov's famous historical-biographical film *Kutuzov* (1944) about the Russian general's defeat of Napoleon in 1812. And the relationship between the folksy Kovpak and the politically knowledgeable commissar Semen Rudnev consciously evokes the central relationship in the Vasil'ev Brothers' *Chapaev* (1934). Moreover, Levchuk features Stalin himself prominently in the film, serving as the cerebral centre of the Kovpak group's activities. In its retro agenda, the film attempts at re-familiarizing Ukrainian space through a recognizable plot of Ukrainian partisan victory in the Great Patriotic War. At the same time, the film does not return to a domesticated notion of a Stalinist folkloric, as even the ethnographic textures of Ukrainian poetic cinema find their appearance in Levchuk's occasional treatment of Carpathian partisans. The camera frequently pans across partisan faces, presenting them as both Soviet soldiers and local attraction. *The Ballad of Kovpak* appeals to the classics of the war genre, but locates the conflict in a canonical Ukrainian ethnoscape. The promotion of the film returns us full-circle to the tourist view, but in this case, it is one mediated through the window of a fast-moving vehicle, with only brief spots to park and look at mountain vistas, rather than the close gaze on authentic life that *Ranok* promised its readers over a decade earlier with Camp Hutsulshchyna. The only opportunity for historical exploration is in the nostalgically familiar space of Levchuk's film.

The End of National Cinemas in the USSR

With the decline of a studio-supported *auteurism* by the early 1970s, along with a declining space for national representation, the *auteurs* themselves turned inward, and suffered a number of personal crises. Paradjanov went to prison in 1974; Illienko and Kadochnikova divorced while shooting *To Dream and To Live* (*Mriiaty i zhyty*, 1974) during the same year; and Osyka turned increasingly to the bottle, eventually abandoning experimental cinema entirely for steady work making *zakaznye fil'my*. One of the major debates of the mid-1970s in the Union Presidium was not about film at all – the union had long since determined that they would have no creative input at Dovzhenko Studio – but about their disappointment with their union hall, Budynok Kino. Film-makers complained of bad food and poor service in the cafeteria, prostitutes at the bar and a general unsightly appearance to the place. The projectionist at their exclusive theatre frequently showed up for work drunk. When the manager of Budynok Kino appeared before the union to answer for this state of affairs, he blamed the lack of funds.[56] They could not pay the standard wage for restaurant employees and projectionists, and so many of them left at the first opportunity, with only the bad apples remaining behind. With the union budget correlated to the box office performance of Ukrainian films, the Presidium had to cut costs significantly as audiences declined during the 1970s. The union continued to recoup some losses with the mild profits garnered from publication of *Novyny kinoekrana* and such blockbusters as Leonid Bykov's *Only the Old Go to Battle* and Sulamif Tsybul'nyk's *Inspector of Criminal Investigations*, but apparently not enough to maintain the respectability of the union hall.

The cynicism with which Kyiv film-makers treated 'the audience' was evident in the growing lack of involvement many of them had in public activities like the annual Cinema Days event in early September.[57] From the classic narrative style of Illienko's *White Bird with a Black Mark*, we see that he in fact attempted to approach the new audience politics of the Soviet film industry at the end of the 1960s, but political changes at the top of the CPU prevented him from being successful. It seemed evident to Illienko that popular cinema alone was not what the new studio and Goskino leadership wanted from him; rather, they expected him to start making films like everyone else, so that his very image as an *auteur* would disappear. After all, *auteurs* produced expectations with spectators, which could not be controlled by thematic, production and distribution plans. As an *auteur*-driven project, Ukrainian poetic cinema carried meaning above and beyond the films contained with its *oeuvre*, to the very people associated with it and the people associated with them. By 1972–4, this not only included a number of convicted Ukrainian nationalists, but also Paradjanov himself, whose very name disappeared from print until his return to public life in 1983. While the Shelest period included an official outlet for promoting Ukrainian difference, the Shcherbytskyi regime delineated all Ukrainian-language cultural activity as at least suspect. Nonetheless, the First Secretary continued to promote the separate status of the Ukrainian Soviet Socialist Republic, even if he also promoted the cultural status of Ukraine as Russia's 'little brother'.

By the mid-1970s Kyiv Studio had clearly become peripheral to Soviet cinema. In August 1975, the relatively young Volodymyr Denysenko said during a meeting to discuss the thematic plan: 'I read the prospective plan and thought that it's time for me to go on a pension', indicating the close of an era that he in part initiated with the production of *A Dream* in 1964.[58] During the Third Congress of the Ukrainian Cinematographers' Union in 1976, amid dutiful praise for Brezhnev and other rote speechification, the minutes of the Congress made note that union members cheered loudly for the first time as one member read a proposal to the Central Committee, which demanded for members 'the right to an additional 20 metres of living space'.[59]

During a December 1980 plenum of the Union of Cinematographers (Moscow), Chinghiz Aitmatov returned to the topic of national cinemas in the USSR. This time, however, he offered a much grimmer picture than in 1967. Instead of the excitement, mixed with caution, that he expressed 13 years earlier, now he stated:

> Today, the condition of national cinema provokes definite anxiety. Recently – during the second half of the 70s – a significant receding of the wave of cinema's development has taken shape in the provinces [*na mestakh*] [...] The brilliance, expressiveness, originality and specificity of national pictures are increasingly fading, and more often a certain general graded tendency towards leveling makes itself felt, both within the content and in the form of national art's appearance. Facelessness is knocking at the doors of the national studios... [60]

Aitmatov's words conformed to earlier anxieties about the 'de-nationalizing' effects of commercial cinema. The previous year had seen the release of the two largest box office successes in Soviet history – the adventure film, *Pirates of the 20th Century* (*Piraty XX veka*, Boris Durov, 1980), which sold 87.6 million tickets, and Vladimir Men'shov's melodrama, *Moscow Does Not Believe in Tears* (*Moskva slezam ne verit*, 1979), selling over 84 million.[61] The national studios had failed to find their brand identity in this new profit-minded industry, nor was such an industry even interested in cultivating the 'national theme'. The CPSU of the late 1970s viewed non-Russian representational politics as increasingly disconnected from a quantifiable 'mass audience', on the one hand, but also in line with the now-defeated dissident movements in the Union republics, most notably in Ukraine.

CONCLUSION: UKRAINIAN CINEMA AND THE LIMITATIONS OF NATIONAL EXPRESSION

In posing the 'national question', the Soviet regime never sufficiently resolved the tensions between particularistic identities and allegiance to a centralized state and an ideology that eschewed nationalism as a remnant of bourgeois societies. This project, which looks at the nationality question in Ukrainian cinema during the long 1960s, has had a more modest aim in addressing the problem of representing national difference. In so doing, however, I hoped to point to the ways that the Soviet Union, with its entrenched and seemingly impenetrable political culture, engendered new ways of thinking about nationality. It was during these more peaceful times that Ukrainians could consider what it meant to belong to a particular nationality, apart from the legal category on line four of Soviet internal passports. I began with the question of whether or not nationality even mattered and, if it did, how and why it mattered. The question seemed important because most scholars now affirm that nationalities policy was the principal context within which to view the national independence movements of the late 1980s. Whereas earlier scholars highlighted the history of discriminatory and repressive policies against non-Russians in the Soviet Union, historians now spoke of the state's cultivation of 'ethnic particularism'. Yuri Slezkine, for example, writes, 'In a country free from social conflict, ethnicity was the only meaningful identity. This was the legacy that Stalin bequeathed to *his* successors and that survived to haunt Gorbachev and *his* successors.'[1] In this claim, he asks us to take him at his word. After all, we know what happened to the USSR. Ron

Suny also argues for the continuity of nationalities policy between Stalin and Gorbachev, highlighting the continued presence of indigenization practices, albeit alongside Russification measures.[2] In my examination of Ukrainian cinema, however, I have discovered other questions related to nationality besides these explicitly political concerns over the nature of power between centre and periphery, and the negotiation of state concerns and national concerns, issues which arose with the formation of the Soviet Union as a federal, multinational state.

Rather than examine the level of national consciousness that Ukrainians had, or for whom identity mattered, this book has sought to investigate the very problem of representing Ukraine on film. For a new generation of Ukrainian artists, writers and intellectuals who grew up after the formation of nationalities policy, in the urban 'factories of Russification', as Ivan Dziuba called eastern Ukrainian cities, Ukrainian identity could not be assimilated unproblematically. Instead, the 1960s appear as a period during which cultural producers had less certainty about what it meant to be Ukrainian in the first place. This alienation that film-makers felt from their ascribed nationality, and their subsequent desire to rediscover an ethnic identity, contributed to the style of modernist self-expression that characterized what was called Ukrainian poetic cinema.

At the Alexander Dovzhenko Feature Film Studio in Kyiv a new leadership under Vasyl' Tsvirkunov, Vasyl' Zemliak and Sviatoslav Ivanov embarked on a project to revive a declining film production facility. To do so, they believed their task was not only to create a financially independent enterprise, with its own native-born staff, but also to renew respect for Ukrainian cinema more broadly. The studio believed that such respect would only come with a new image of the republic and its people. A legitimate 'national cinema' would only emerge if film-makers could reject the familiar image of Ukrainians as backwards peasants in folk costumes presented on the screen for popular amusement. In the studio's desire for aesthetic sophistication, Tsvirkunov sought a cohort of young Ukrainian directors, cinematographers and screenwriters educated at the All-Union Film Institute in Moscow. These young cosmopolitans – Iurii Illienko, Leonid Osyka and Ivan Drach among others – were initially more invested in the cultural politics of the Thaw more generally than they were in the particular problem of Ukrainian identity. In engaging with the Ukrainian theme, these young film-makers also had to learn what it meant to be a specifically Ukrainian film-maker and cope with the demands that such an ascribed identity placed on them.

Thus, this generation of Ukrainian film-makers and writers who worked at Dovzhenko Studio were more interested in personal expression than national independence for Ukraine, even if their cultural interests brought them into contact with dissident nationalists. And while many of these film-makers would later support the nationalist party, the Ukrainian People's Movement (*Narodnyi rukh Ukrainy*) during the late 1980s, they proudly called themselves 'Soviet' during the 1960s. Yet, in calling themselves 'Soviet', they nonetheless rejected what they considered as the homogeneity of contemporary life in the country and the repressive nature of the Soviet state and Communist Party. For them, the filmic exploration of Ukrainian nationality was an attempt to highlight the maintenance of diverse cultures within the Soviet Union. Consequently, they attempted to show, not the canonical ethnic spaces and character types – 'those notorious attributes', as one Ukrainian writer called them – that emerged in Stalinist Ukrainian cinema, but a new and unfamiliar imagery of the republic and its people, an imagery they believed was more 'authentic'.

Nonetheless, the very means through which the Stalinist state reduced the meaning of nationality to the safe space of folklore became the basis of this new interest in national identity during the 1960s. Ukrainians became knowable in Stalin-era cinema through folkloric spectacle – costumes, songs, dances, the Cossack hair lock (*oseledets'*) – and Ukraine itself through a bucolic imagery of thatched-roof houses, sunflowers, the steppe and the Dnieper River. At the same time, the Stalinist Ukrainian hero was able to transcend narrow alignment with nation and landscape to become a historical and political actor, thus firmly dividing a timeless Ukrainian space from a modern Soviet (or Russian) space. The plots and imagery of 1960s Ukrainian cinema frequently returned to folklore for their material, locating Ukraine within a simultaneously colourful and bleak rural landscape. This similarity adds considerable weight to Serhy Yekelchyk's claim that the Stalinist vision of Ukrainian history remained hegemonic throughout the Soviet period, with even dissidents mobilizing its imagery.[3] This later interest in folklore in Ukrainian cinema, however, had different intentions. Instead of Ukraine as a comedic space, filled with familiar and colourful peasants, film-makers in the 1960s sought to render rural Ukraine as an unusual space, and called attention to the specificity of Ukrainian folklore. For urban and 'Russified' sensibilities, a representation of an 'authentic' Ukraine would have to be strange, unfamiliar and somehow 'savage'.

In appealing to an ethnographic style of modernist representation, Paradjanov, Illienko, Osyka and others conceived of their audience differently than Stalinist directors like Ivan Pyr'ev. Whereas the latter's films were clearly intended for popular consumption, in its mobilization of comedic stereotypes to render non-Russians on screen, the 'poetic' directors addressed their 'difficult' films towards an educated and Ukrainian audience, one whose tastes in film dovetailed with European art cinema. But these film-makers too were implicated in new conceptions of a mass media-consuming public. These film-makers went from confidently conceiving of an elite and knowledgeable audience for their work, to cynicism over the existence of a specifically Ukrainian public at all.

This book has posited a multidimensional cause for the re-emergence of the nationality question after Stalin, which was located in Thaw-era discourse on personal expression, authenticity and resistance to conformity and social homogeneity (i.e., Russification, or the reduction of human experience to the proverbial *Homo Sovieticus*). Moreover, the search for meaning in nationality through cultural production did not aim to destroy the Soviet system; it merely made a claim for recognition of both national difference and of the artist as the producer of national meaning. In this way, we cannot look for a direct continuation from the Stalinist folkloric to Ukrainian poetic cinema to the independence movement of the late 1980s. The latter had much more to do with *political* developments in the USSR more broadly, whereas the cultural concerns of the 1960s involved a search for meaning in national categories. But what we can say about the period in Ukraine is that cinema established new expectations about the role of the individual in making nationality meaningful, outside of political negotiations. In this case, national difference, a collective identity, became encoded in the politics of individualism and authorship that characterized the cultural Thaw as a whole.

* * *

2004, the year that I began researching this topic, briefly saw Ukraine in newspaper headlines around the world, as hundreds of thousands of people gathered in Kyiv to protest an apparently fraudulent election. In what came to be known as the Orange Revolution for the colour that opposition leader Viktor Yushchenko had chosen to represent his party, the mass protest forced a re-election, which was monitored by international observers and eventually confirmed the opposition's victory. Perhaps because I had my mind on 1960s cinema, I did not have a clear conception of what seemed to me as Yushchenko's vague political platform, with its mix of free market liberalism, soft nationalism and a pro-Western populism. His campaign slogan, 'I believe I know we can', or, in its shortened form, '*Tak!* (yes)', seemed like a good youth marketing campaign, however, and the words adorned orange coffee mugs, scarves, pens and other 'revolutionary' memorabilia for sale on any block in downtown Kyiv during and after the historic events. While Yushchenko's opponent, Viktor Yanukovych, responded with his own colour (blue), the products were not forthcoming, and his vastly outnumbered supporters relied on handmade sashes to convey their allegiances. More than a consistent political ideology, Yushchenko was able to mobilize imagery attractive to young voters who considered their country to be a legitimate member of the European community. At the same time, the opposition leader's name was attached to the familiar objects of a nationalist agenda, and supporters donned *keptari* and Cossack hats, while Yanukovych's base performed their regional and ideological allegiances wearing miners' hard hats.

Some of the top names in Ukraine's nascent pop music scene contributed to the best-selling soundtrack to the revolution, *Orange Songs (Pomaranchevi pisni)*, including five-time platinum recording artist and 2004 Eurovision Song Contest winner Ruslana Lyzhychko. An avid Yushchenko fan, Ruslana's video for her hit single, 'Wild Dances (*Dyki tantsi*)', includes images of attractive and shirtless Cossacks mock-fighting and dancing with battleaxes, Hutsuls playing *trembity* against the backdrop of a Carpathian vista and protesters on the Maidan, rapidly juxtaposed with Ruslana and a group of male dancers self-consciously evoking the visual presence of Britney Spears. This updated folkloric mode of consumer culture inserted iconic images from a mythical past and present into the conventions of the music video. Moreover, in this culture of affirmative politics and fashionable abundance, Ruslana successfully resisted a reduction of the meaning of these images to the level of a national kitsch. In the lack of irony attached to their popular consumption, such iconography associated with both a Stalinist representational mode and 1960s Ukrainian poetic cinema became important elements of a contemporary Ukrainian mass culture.

Nonetheless, this work is about people who failed, and who wrote and made films about failure and loss. Dziuba's *Internationalism or Russification?* was not a nationalist rallying cry to resist Russian 'colonialism' or Soviet 'Empire;' rather, it was a melancholic and personal meditation on what he called 'de-nationalization'. None of the works of Ukrainian poetic cinema during the decade between 1964 and 1974 provide us with any sense of hope for such an affirmative Ukrainian mass culture. Even the celebratory atmosphere that surrounded *Shadows of Forgotten Ancestors* was odd, considering that it addressed a lost people, implicitly juxtaposed against the sterility of a modern and inorganic Soviet society. Ukrainian poetic cinema, as well as the dissident movement itself, was produced by people who were part of a Soviet mobile society, *auteurs* or '*samoznavtsy*' who were themselves 'de-nationalized', but who were compelled, for both personal and institutional reasons, to work within the idiom of national representation.

Within this interplay of the production and reproduction of images, Ivan Mykolaichuk was able to function as an ideal embodiment in Ukrainian cinema, wherein the nationalist potential of Cossacks and Hutsuls could be ascribed the value of personal expression. Mykolaichuk died of a 'prolonged illness' on 3 August 1987, at the young age of 47. The Ukrainian Cinematographers' Union Secretariat and Dovzhenko Studio immediately resolved to cover the costs of burial and a monument to the actor in the prestigious Baikova Cemetery in Kyiv, a space where the major political and cultural leaders of the republic were interred. The union also funded a memorial plaque to be placed on his modest apartment at 5 Serafimovych Street, and asked the Chernivtsy Oblast Party Committee to establish a school and film museum in Mykolaichuk's native Carpathian village of Chortoryiia in his honour. Finally, the union promised to provide 'personal assistance' to the actor's son, Taras Ivanovych, until he came of age, and to give an additional 5,000 roubles to Mykolaichuk's destitute wife, Marichka.[4]

Despite the desperate conditions, in which the actor seemingly spent the last years of his life, 1987 marked the re-emergence of 'Ukrainian poetic cinema' in public discourse. That year, *A Well for the Thirsty* finally screened in theatres and won a prize at the 1988 San Francisco International Film Festival. Thereafter, it routinely played on Ukraine's state-run television channel, Pershyi, to bewildered viewers. Also in 1987, Liudmila Lemesheva published the first monograph on the topic, *Ukrainian Cinema: The Problem of One*

Generation, after which followed a flurry of memoirs, critical analyses, documentaries, poetry and biographies dedicated to Mykolaichuk, Paradjanov (who died in 1990) and the other agents of poetic cinema. As the process of canonization proceeded, Paradjanov became poetic cinema's 'founder', Illienko its 'ideologue and practitioner' and Mykolaichuk its 'soul'.[5] Ukraine's foremost film scholar, Larysa Briukhovets'ka, wrote at the end of the 1990s that Mykolaichuk was 'cinema's knight [*lytsar kino*]. As a messenger, he was sent to tell those of us blinded by the vanities of everyday life of incontrovertible truths and values.'[6] Vasyl' Illiashenko, the failed director of *Coordinate Your Watches*, wrote his highly impressionistic *History of Ukrainian Film Art* in 2004, in which he argued, 'Mykolaichuk was a representation of the national idea, its colour, and the originality of [its] art... [He was] the spokesperson of all aspirations of the people and the nation... Ivan Mykolaichuk was the symbol of Ukraine and its essence.'[7] During the 1990s, film culture in Ukraine seemed to be thriving in the absence of actual films, and solely on the momentum of memorializing the 1960s-era Ukrainian *auteur*.

Despite the canonization of Ukrainian poetic cinema and its *auteurs* by the *glasnost* generation of Ukrainian films scholars, and the popularization of its imagery, the younger cohort who graduated from KITM after independence now speaks of moving away from 'shadowism [*tinizm*]', an explicit rejection of the ethnographic imagery of the 1960s. In a statement reminiscent of that very period, however, Columbia University Ukrainian literary scholar Yuri Shevchuk recently stated, 'Ukrainian cinema does not begin and end with the poetic cinema of Dovzhenko, Paradjanov, Osyka, [...] Illienko[...] There are other Ukrainian film schools, other film-makers[...]'[8] Shevchuk expressed a similar discomfort with narrowing the possibilities for Ukrainian national cinema to a rural vision of the now independent nation. While admitting that Odessa film-makers were uninterested in the politics of Ukrainian national identity during the Shelest period itself, Shevchuk now seemed all too willing to examine their work within a newer, more inclusive notion of Ukrainian national cinema, precisely because such individuals were not interested in these problems. Perhaps the mark of a modern nation, he implies, was the ability of its artists and writers to simply ignore its meaning-producing qualities and canon of national images. In the absence of a Soviet culture industry that promoted folklore as the essence of 'national character', the imagery of poetic cinema appears hopelessly outdated to contemporary art-film connoisseurs in Ukraine, even though its *auteurs* continue to be celebrated icons of a nascent Ukrainian cultural movement.

Yet, without the historical presence of Soviet Ukrainian cinema's specific visual qualities, I do not believe that Yushchenko and Ruslana could have mobilized such imagery in contemporary Ukraine. These images of Cossacks and Hutsuls remain images to be inhabited and performed, rather than lived and experienced. They continue to be exotic tropes of self-expression, rather than the basis for a long-term political project. After all, the Orange coalition quickly disintegrated after taking power in early 2005 when it became evident that within the political imaginary of the revolution there existed highly divergent ideas about Ukraine's economy, foreign policy and history. A stark example of the latter was the conflict over Yushchenko's naming UPA leader Stepan Bandera a 'hero of Ukraine' in February 2010, directly before turning over the presidency to his rival, Viktor Yanukovych.[9]

I find it striking that film-makers and critics continue to debate many of the same issues in an independent Ukraine as they did in the 1960s, not only between 'poetic' and 'realist' modes of representing the nation, but also concerning the source of financing film production and questions of linguistic policy. Most striking, however, is the question of how to maintain Ukrainian cinema in the first place, in the absence of a centralized state that had the power to maintain a certain level of production apart from the direct constraints of consumer demand, and a state that considered cinema a necessary political project, apart from the pointed mobilization of a familiar national imagery.

NOTES

Introduction

1. Richard Taylor, *The Politics of the Soviet Cinema, 1917–1929*, Cambridge 1979; Judith Mayne, *Kino and the Woman Question: Feminism and Soviet Silent Cinema*, Columbus 1989; Peter Kenez, *Cinema and Soviet Society, 1917–1953*, Cambridge 1992; Denise Youngblood, *Movies for the Masses: Popular Cinema and Soviet Society in the 1920s*, Cambridge 1992; David Gillespie, *Early Soviet Cinema: Innovation, Ideology and Propaganda*, London 2000; Emma Widdis, *Visions of a New Land: Soviet Film from the Revolution to the Second World War*, New Haven 2003; John Haynes, *New Soviet Man: Gender and Masculinity in Stalinist Soviet Cinema*, Manchester 2003.
2. For government statistics on film attendance, see Tsentral'noe statisticheskoe upravlenie pri Sovete Ministrov SSSR, *Narodnoe khoziaistvo SSSR*, Moscow 1968.
3. In a 1961 article in *Iskusstvo kino*, critic N. Klado stated that such choice posed a unique problem for the Soviet Union's goals of mass enlightenment. See, N. Klado, 'Obedniaia zhizn'', *Iskusstvo kino*, no. 8, August 1961, pp. 82–90.
4. See, Valerii Golovskoi, *Mezhdu ottepel'iu i glasnost'iu: Kinematograf 70-kh*, Moscow 2004; and Nonna Kapel'horods'ka, *Renesans vitchyznianoho kino: Notatky suchasnytsi*, Kyiv 2002. In English, Kristin Roth-Ey provides an astute analysis of film culture after Stalin in *Moscow Prime Time: How the Soviet Union Built the Media Empire That Lost the Cultural Cold War*, Ithaca 2011. See esp. pp. 25–130.
5. See, for example, Rosa Luxemburg, 'The Polish Question at the International Congress', reprinted in Horace B. Davis (ed.), *The National Question: Selected Writings*, New York 1976, pp. 49–59.
6. Yuri Slezkine, 'The USSR as a Communal Apartment, or How a Socialist State Promoted Ethnic Particularism', *Slavic Review* vol. 53, no. 2, Summer 1994, pp. 416, 418.
7. See, *Sovetskie khudozhestvennye fil'my: Annotirovannyi katalog*, vol. 3, Moscow 1961, pp. 88–103.
8. This is reported in a letter from a group of students who wrote to Dovzhenko Studio on 9 June, 1962. *Tsentral'nyi derzhavnyi arkhiv-muzei literatury i mystetstva Ukrainy* (TsDAMLMU), 670/1/1541, fol. 4–4a.
9. Leon Trotsky, 'Vodka, the Church and the Cinema', Accessed online: http://marxists.org/archive/trotsky/women/life/23_07_12.htm, 20 June 2011.
10. Anthony Smith, 'Images of the Nation: Cinema, Art and National Identity', in Hjort and MacKenzie (eds.), *Cinema and Nation*, London 2000, p. 47.
11. See especially Terry Martin, *The Affirmative Action Empire: Nations and Nationalism in the Soviet Union, 1923–1939*, Ithaca 2001, pp. 75–124.
12. TsDAMLMU, 670/1/1829, fol. 3.
13. See, Benedict Anderson, *Imagined Communities: Reflections on the Origin and Spread of Nationalism*, London 1991.
14. Serhy Yekelchyk, *Ukraine: Birth of a Modern Nation*, Oxford 2007, and Serhii Plokhy, *Unmaking Imperial Russia: Mykhailo Hrushevsky and the Writing of Ukrainian History*, Toronto 2005.

15. See, Martin, in addition to Matthew D. Pauly, 'Tending to the "Native Word": Teachers and the Soviet Campaign for Ukrainian-Language Schooling, 1923–1930', *Nationalities Papers* vol. 37, no. 3, 2010, pp. 75–93.

16. George Liber, *Alexander Dovzhenko: A Life in Soviet Film*, London 2002.

17. Stephen Bittner, *The Many Lives of Khrushchev's Thaw: Experience and Memory in Moscow's Arbat*, Ithaca 2008, Vladislav Zubok, *Zhivago's Children: The Last Soviet Intelligentsia*, Cambridge 2009, Miriam Dobson, *Khrushchev's Cold Summer: Gulag Returnees, Crime, and the Fate of Reform after Stalin*, Ithaca 2009.

18. Sergei Zhuk, *Rock and Roll in the Rocket City: The West, Identity and Ideology in Soviet Dniepropetrovsk, 1960–1985*, Baltimore 2010; William Jay Risch, *The Ukrainian West: Culture and the Fate of Empire in Soviet Lviv*, Cambridge USA 2011.

19. Amir Weiner, for example, demonstrates that as early as the 1930s, the CPSU treated the Polish and German minorities differently in western Ukraine, due to concerns with foreign espionage, even as they continued to apply undifferentiated categories of class to all national groups in the region. See, *Making Sense of War: The Second World War and the Fate of the Bolshevik Revolution*, Princeton 2001, pp. 138–149.

20. Ronald Suny, *The Revenge of the Past: Nationalism, Revolution, and the Collapse of the Soviet Union*, Stanford 1993, pp. 108–9.

21. *Tsentral'nyi derzhavnyi arkhiv vyshei orhaniv vlasti Ukrainy* (TsDAVOU), 4623/1/464, fol. 57.

22. *Tsentral'nyi derzhavnyi arkhiv hromads'kykh orhanizatsii Ukrainy* (TsDAHOU), 1/31/1678, fol. 161–3.

23. Suny, p. 109.

24. Ibid., p .117.

25. Charles Taylor, 'The Politics of Recognition', in *Multiculturalism and 'The Politics of Recognition'* Princeton 1992, pp. 25–73.

26. Evgenii Dobrenko, *The Making of the State Reader: Social and Aesthetic Contexts of the Reception of Soviet Literature*, tr., Jesse M. Savage, Stanford 1997, p. 2.

27. On the 'sociology of cinema', see Joshua First, 'From Spectator to "Differentiated" Consumer: Film Audience Research in the Era of Developed Socialism (1965–80)', *Kritika: Explorations in Russian and Eurasian History* vol. 9, no. 2, Spring 2008, pp. 317–344. Golovskoi also examines the sociology of cinema in his *Mezhdu ottepel'iu i glasnost'iu*, as does Roth-Ey in *Moscow Prime Time*.

28. I. P. Zinchenko, 'Natsional'nyi sostav i iazyk naseleniia SSSR', in G. M. Maksimov (ed.), *Vsesoiuznaia perepis' naseleniia 1970 goda*, Moscow 1976, p. 196.

29. *Rossiiskii gosudarstvennyi arkhiv literatury i iskusstva* (RGALI), 2936/4/50, fol. 38. The 'yellow banner' is a reference to the flag of the nascent Ukrainian People's Republic (1917–1918), which the current Ukrainian state adopted in 1991.

30. According to the 1970 census, only 85 per cent of ethnic Ukrainians in the USSR considered Ukrainian their 'native' language, the lowest of any nationality with a Union republic attached to it. Zinchenko, pp. 196, 200.

31. Petro Shelest, diary entry for 3 November 1969, in Iurii Shapovala, ed., *Petro Shelest: 'Spravzhnii sud istorii shche poperedu': Spohady, shchodennyky, dokumenty, materialy*, Kyiv 2003, pp. 317–8.

32. TsDAMLMU, 670/1/2158, fol. 158–9.

33. For this term, see, Marcia Landy, *The Folklore of Consensus: Theatricality in the Italian Cinema, 1930–1943*, Albany 1998.

34. Amir Weiner writes that, once the Soviet Union had incorporated the Western oblasts, its people were treated as 'natural' members of the national body. *Making Sense of War*, p. 163.

35. On the concept of ethnoscape, see Anthony Smith, *Myths and Memories of the Nation*, New York 1999, p. 16.
36. Rogers Brubaker and Frederick Cooper, 'Beyond "Identity"', *Theory and Society* vol. 29, 2000, pp. 1–47.
37. Anthony Smith, *National Identity*, New Edition, Reno 1991, p. vii.
38. Roman Szporluk, 'The Press and Soviet Nationalities: The Party Resolution of 1975 and Its Implementation' [1986], reprinted in *Russia, Ukraine, and the Breakup of the Soviet Union*, Stanford 2000, pp. 277–297.

Chapter 1. Stalinism, De-Stalinization and the Ukrainian in Soviet Cinema

1. See, Josephine Woll, *Real Images: Soviet Cinema and the Thaw*, London 2000. For Gorky's ideas about Socialist Realism, advanced at the First Congress of the Soviet Writers' Union, see Maxim Gorky, *Soviet Writers' Congress 1934: The Debate on Socialist Realism and Modernism in the Soviet Union*, H.G. Scott (ed.), London 1977, pp. 25–69.
2. *Narodnoe khoziaistvo SSSR*, Moscow 1968.
3. See, Sergei Zemlianukhin and Miroslava Segida (eds.), *Domashniaia sinematika: otechestvennoe kino, 1918–1996*, Moscow 1996.
4. TsDAMLMU, 670/1/1540, fol. 2.
5. TsDAHOU, 1/1/1691, fol. 284.
6. V. Repiakh, et al., 'Molodye za ekranom: Komsomol'tsy otvechaiut na kritiku gazetu: A chto dumaiut rukovoditeli studii imeni Dovzhenko?' *Komsomol'skaia Pravda*, 31 Jan. 1962, p. 2.
7. Sergei Paradjanov, "…chtoby ne molchat', berus' za pero': Vybrannye mesta iz perepiski s nedrugom i druz'iami', published for the first time in *Iskusstvo kino*, no. 12, Dec. 1990, pp. 332–35.
8. See Vladimir Pomerantsev, 'Ob iskrennosti v literature', *Novyi mir*, no. 12, Dec. 1953.
9. Quoted in Dmitrii Pisarevskii, 'Etapy bol'shogo puti', review of I. Korniienko, A. Zhukova, H. Zhurov and A. Romitsyn, *Ukrains'ke Radians'ke kinomystetstvo*, *Iskusstvo kino*, no. 10, Oct. 1960, p. 23.
10. Oleh Babyshkin, 'Shchob narod skazav: dobre', *Literaturna Ukraina*, 8 Jan. 1963, p. 3.
11. TsDAMLMU 670/1/1541, fol. 14. The word '*kolhospnyk*' is equivalent to the Russian '*kolkhoznik*'.
12. Richard Taylor, 'Singing on the Steppe for Stalin: Ivan Pyr'ev and the Kolkhoz Musical in Soviet Cinema', *Slavic Review*, vol. 58, no. 1, Spring 1999, p. 149.
13. TsDAMLMU, 655/1/199, fol.193. The Kuban region of the northern Caucasus has had a majority Ukrainian population since the late eighteenth century, when Catherine the Great offered the land to the Black Sea Cossack Host.
14. See, for example, Stephen V. Bittner's *The Many Lives of Khrushchev's Thaw: Experience and Memory in Moscow's Arbat*, Ithaca 2008.
15. André Bazin, 'The Stalin Myth in Soviet Cinema', reprinted in Bill Nichols (ed.), *Movies and Methods: An Anthology*, vol. 2, Berkeley 1985, pp. 29–40.
16. Il'ia Erenburg, 'Ottepel': povest'', *Znamia*, no. 5, May 1954, pp. 14–87.
17. TsDAMLMU, 655/1/199, fol. 9.
18. V. Pomerantsev, 'Ob iskrennosti v literature', *Novyi mir*, no. 12, December 1953, p. 218.

19. Ibid., pp. 228, 230.
20. Ibid., p. 219.
21. Ibid., p. 240.
22. Ibid., p. 242.
23. Quoted in Woll, pp. 21–2.
24. Viktor Nekrasov, 'Slova "velikie" i prostye', reprinted in *Sochineniia*, Moscow 2002, pp. 1121–22.
25. Ibid., p. 1122.
26. Ibid., p. 1126.
27. Katerina Clark, *The Soviet Novel: History as Ritual*, Chicago 1981, p. 15.
28. Ibid., p. 16.
29. Quoted in Evgenii Dobrenko, *Political Economy of Socialist Realism*, New Haven 2007, p. 18.
30. Quoted in Clark, p. 147.
31. Clark, p. 34.
32. Kristin Thompson, 'The Concept of Cinematic Excess', reprinted in Philip Rosen (ed.), *Narrative, Apparatus, Ideology: A Film Theory Reader*, New York 1986, pp. 130–4.
33. Pierre Bourdieu, *Language and Symbolic Power*, tr. Gino Raymond and Matthew Adamson, Cambridge 1991, p. 19.
34. Landy, *The Folklore of Consensus*, p. 4. Regina Bendix associates the use of folk-lore with the search for 'authenticity' during the Enlightenment, and connects this search with the underlying assumptions of democracy. Regina Bendix, *In Search of Authenticity: The Formation of Folklore Studies*, Madison 1997, pp. 27–44.
35. William E. Harkins, forward to Frank J. Miller, *Folklore for Stalin: Russian Folklore and Pseudofolklore of the Stalin Era*, Armonk, 1990, p. ix.
36. Widdis, *Visions of a New Land, p.* 187.
37. RGALI, 2936/4/69, fol. 11. The *lezghinka* is a traditional group dance of the northern Caucasus, predominantly involving men. Apples are believed to have originated in the mountains of Kazakhstan. *Salo* is a Ukrainian *hors d'oeuvre* made from lard, salt, and herbs. Traditionally, it is spread on bread.
38. Evgenii Margolit, 'Istoriko-biograficheskii fil'm v sovetskom kino', in *Noveishiaia istoriia otechestvennogo kino*, vol. 6, L. Arkus (ed.), St. Petersburg 2004: Accessed online, http://russiancinema.ru/template.php?dept_id=15&e_dept_id=6&text_element_id=61, 17 February 2008.
39. Vasyl' Illiashenko, *Istoriia ukrains'koho kinomystetstva*, Kyiv 2004, p. 114.
40. TsDAMLMU, 655/1/496, fol. 1.
41. Nikolai Lebedev, *Ocherk istorii kino SSSR: nemoe kino*, 2nd ed., Moscow 1965 [1947], p. 483.
42. Boris Buriak, 'Internatsional'noe – ne beznatsional'noe', *Iskusstvo kino*, no. 2 , February 1964, p.30.
43. Rostislav Iurenev, *Aleksandr Dovzhenko*, Moscow 1959, p. 25.
44. Evgenii Margolit, 'Evoliutsiia fol'klornaia traditsii v ukrainskom sovetskom kino (1920–40-e gg.)', Ph.D. diss., Leningrad Institute of Theatre, Music, and Cinema, 1979 [abstract], p. 4.
45. Bohdan Y. Nebesio, 'The Silent Films of Alexander Dovzhenko: A Historical Poetics', Ph.D. Dissertation, University of Alberta 1996, p. 86; quoted in Liber, *Alexander Dovzhenko*, p. 90.
46. See Rostislav Iurenev's critique in *Aleksandr Dovzhenko*, p. 24.
47. Ibid., p. 28.

48. Dmytro Pavlychko, 'Siiartel' vichnoho', *Literaturna Ukraina*, 15 September 1964, p. 3.
49. RGALI, 2936/1/957, fol. 124.
50. Clark, p. 37.
51. See especially Iraklii Andronikov's introduction to a series of articles about Dovzhenko in the May 1958 issue of *Iskusstvo kino* – 'Poeziia Dovzhenko', *Iskusstvo kino*, no. 5, May 1958, pp. 133–9.
52. RGALI, 2936/1/957, fol. 24.
53. Ihor Rachuk, *Oleksandr Dovzhenko*, Kyiv 1964, p. 13. The term '*khutorians'kyi*' was a word that referred exclusively to Ukrainians who had provincial ideas (like nationalism, for example) or who represented the clichés of rural Ukrainians. As Rachuk suggested, the concept of '*khutorianshchyna*' was tied into a Stalinist folkloric mode of representation.
54. See, R.W. Davies, 'Stalin as Economic Policy-Maker: Soviet Agriculture, 1931–1936', in Sarah Davies and James Harris (eds.), *Stalin: A New History*, Cambridge 2005, pp. 121–139.
55. See, Maya Turovskaya, 'The Tastes of Soviet Moviegoers during the 1930s', in Thomas Lahusen with Gene Kuperman (eds.), *Late Soviet Culture: From Perestroika to Novostroika*, Durham 1993, pp. 95–107.
56. *Narodnoe Khoziaistvo SSSR*, Moscow 1955–1968.

Chapter 2. Rebuilding a National Studio during the Early 1960s

1. After 1940, only the department of film engineering remained at the Odessa Film Institute. TsDAVOU, 4754/1/50, fol. 15.
2. Ivan Korniienko, 'Tendentsii i zavdannia', *Literaturna Ukraina*, 24 August 1962, p. 1. Korniienko repeated his criticism in 'Velinnia chasu', *Radians'ka Ukraina*, 10 January 1963, p. 3.
3. TsDAMLMU, 655/1/227, fol. 24.
4. Liudmila Pustynskaia, 'Kinematograf ottepeli v sotsial'no-politicheskom i kul'turnom kotekstakh', in Vitalii Troianovskii (ed.), *Kinematograf ottepeli: kniga vtoraia*, Moscow 2002, p. 384.
5. TsDAMLMU, 670/1/1520, fol. 82.
6. Teresa Rakowska-Harmstone, 'The Dialectics of Nationalism in the USSR', *Problems of Communism* 23, no. 3 (May-June 1974), pp. 12–3.
7. See, Shelest, 'Lyst do TsK KPRS pro pidhotovku spetsialistiv u Kyivs'komy khudozhn'omu instituti', 18 April 1964, reprinted in Iurii Shapovala (ed.), *Petro Shelest: 'Spravzhnii sud istorii shche poperedu'. Spohady, shchodennyky, dokumenty, materialy*, Kyiv 2003, pp. 427–8.
8. TsDAMLMU, 655/1/199, fol. 204.
9. RGALI, 2936/1/154, fol. 7.
10. TsDAMLMU, 670/1/1852, fol. 21–2.
11. RGALI, 2936/1/154, fol. 7–12.
12. RGALI, 2944/1/429, fol. 76–7.
13. See especially, RGALI, 2944/1/102, fol. 1–2; RGALI, 2936/4/70, fol. 19–20; and TsDAMLMU, 670/1/2523, fol. 14–6.
14. A 10 August 1962 Ministry of Culture *prikaz* set a manimum salary of 200 roubles per month for all film studio workers, before bonuses. TsDAMLMU, 670/1/1520, fol. 118.

15. TsDAMLMU, 655/1/199, fol. 186.
16. TsDAMLMU, 655/1/198, fol. 15, 48.
17. TsDAMLMU, 655/1/227, fol. 154–5.
18. Critic V. Shalunovskii, for example, expressed the opinion that Dovzhenko Studio should be closed on account of its poor output in recent years. 'Mysl', Tema, Talant', *Sovetskaia kul'tura*, 13 March 1962, p. 3.
19. TsDAMLMU, 655/1/180, fol. 47.
20. TsDAMLMU, 670/1/1640, fol. 57.
21. RGALI, 2944/1/35, fol. 73.
22. TsDAMLMU, 670/1/1856, fol. 9–10.
23. TsDAMLMU, 655/1/198, fol. 66.
24. TsDAMLMU, 655/1/198, fol. 108.
25. TsDAMLMU, 670/1/1948, fol. 57–64.
26. See, Vladimir Shlapentokh, *Soviet Public Opinion and Ideology: Mythology and Pragmatism in Interaction*, New York 1986.
27. TsDAVOU, 4623/1/468, fol. 108.
28. See, Valentyn Fomenko, 'Ne nabliudat', a voevat': zametki s kinostudii im. Dovzhenko', *Pravda Ukrainy*, 5 January 1963, p. 3.
29. V. Rybak-Akimov, 'Vypuskaty til'ky khoroshi fil'my', *Radians'ka kul'tura*, 24 July 1960, p. 2.
30. TsDAMLMU, 655/1/285, fol. 49.
31. TsDAMLMU, 655/1/539, fol. 138–140. Tymofii Levchuk was keen to mention these past box office successes in his article, 'Spilnamy silamy', in *Literaturna Ukrainy* on 28 October 1962 (pp. 2, 4).
32. Svitlana H. Zinych, *Kinokomediia: konflikt, kharacter, zhanry*, Kyiv 1966, pp. 98–101.
33. Petro Lubens'kyi, '*Koroleva benzokolonky*', *Kino Teatr*, no. 2, 2001, p. 43.
34. Ibid., pp. 42–3.
35. *Surzhyk* is a Russian/Ukrainian pidgin language spoken in the rural areas of eastern Ukraine. Typically, a Russian lexicon is used with a distinct Ukrainian pronunciation and morphology.
36. Borys Buriak, 'Internatsional'noe – ne beznatsional'noe', *Iskusstvo kino*, no. 2, February 1964, p. 30.
37. TsDAMLMU, 1127/1/83, fol. 189.
38. TsDAMLMU, 670/1/1653, fol. 71.
39. TsDAMLMU, 670/1/1442, fol. 65.
40. TsDAMLMU, 670/1/1744, fol. 59.
41. TsDAMLMU, 655/1/285, fol. 49.
42. TsDAMLMU, 655/1/203, fol. 22.
43. Vasyl' Illiashenko, *Istoriia ukrains'koho kinomystetstva*, Kyiv 2004, p. 225.
44. See, Borys Kryzhanivs'kyi and Iurii Novykov, *Viktor Ivchenko*, Kyiv 1976, pp. 21–2.
45. K. Teplyts'kyi, 'Narodu – khoroshi fil'my! Notatky z V plenumu orhbiuro Spilky pratsivnykiv kinematohrafii Ukrainy', *Radians'ka kul'tura*, 25 March 1962, p. 3.
46. Sergei Gerasimov discusses this issue of recruitment in 'Razmyshlenie o molodykh', *Iskusstvo kino*, no. 2, 1960.
47. TsDAMLMU, 655/1/180, fol. 12.
48. TsDAMLMU, 655/1/199, fol. 163.
49. TsDAMLMU, 670/1/1522, fol. 84–5.

50. TsDAMLMU, f. 655, op. 1, d. 199, l. 199.
51. See, Tsvirkunov's speech at the First Congress of the SKU: TsDAMLMU, f. 655, op. 1, d. 227, l. 89ff.
52. See, cinematographer Viktor Hres's remembrance of Tsvirkunov's trip to VGIK in 'Vin osviaiatyv liubov: spohady pro Artura Voitets'koho', *Kino Teatr*, no. 1, 2005, p. 22.
53. *Na ekranakh Kyeva*, 9 May 1965.
54. TsDAMLMU, 655/1/632, fol. 117.
55. See, for example, Oleh Babyshkin, *Ukrains'ka literatura na ekrani*, Kyiv, 1966, p. 139. See also, Leonid Osyka's comments during the June 1972 SKU Presidium meeting: TsDAMLM, 655/1/632, fol. 122.
56. Valentyn Rybak-Akymov, 'Vypuskaty til'ky khoroshi fil'my', *Radians'ka kul'tura*, 24 July 1960.
57. RGALI, 2936/1/153, fol. 95–6.
58. Syhizmund Navrots'kyi, 'Stsenarii pishche stsenariyst', *Radians'ka kul'tura*, 15 March 1962, p. 3.
59. TsDAMLMU, 670/1/1520, fol. 141.
60. See the Ukrainian Minister of Culture's comments in April 1962: TsDAMLMU, 670/1/1522, fol. 80–1.
61. B. Mykolaienko, 'Kinopasynky', *Radians'ka Ukraina*, 13 October 1962, p. 3.
62. RGALI, 2936/1/153, fol. 97.
63. TsDAMLMU, 655/1/182, fol. 191.
64. The term 'Banderist' literally meant the followers of OUN leader Stepan Bandera, but after the war, it became a derogatory term for all Ukrainians who displayed nationalist sympathies.
65. TsDAMLMU, 655/1/227, fol. 267.
66. TsDAMLMU, 670/1/1541, fol. 13; 655/1/705, fol. 87.
67. TsDAMLMU, 655/1/245, fol. 38.
68. Babyshkin, 'Shchob narod skazav: dobre', p. 3.
69. See the letter from four Dnipropetrovsk students printed in the 9 December 1956 issue of *Radians'ka kul'tura*, which stated that Kyiv needed to educate its own 'stars' for the purposes of making more films in Ukrainian. V. Shevchenko, et al., 'Vykhovuvaty svoikh aktoriv', *Radians'ka kul'tura*, 9 December 1956, p. 3.
70. TsDAMLMU, 670/1/1541, fol. 14.
71. TsDAMLMU, 655/1/245, fol. 133.
72. TsDAMLMU, 670/1/1744, fol. 46.
73. TsDAMLMU, 670/1/1750, fol. 205.
74. See, William Jay Risch, *The Ukrainian West: Culture and the Fate of Empire in Soviet Lviv*, Cambridge USA 2011, pp. 77–8.
75. Maureen Turim, *Flashbacks in Film: Memory and History*, London 1989, p. 12.
76. Kateryna Smahlii, 'Ivan Mykolaichuk u spohady Marichky', *Kino Teatr*, no. 2, 1995, p. 5.
77. TsDAMLMU, 670/1/1750, fol. 68.
78. Oles' Honchar, 'Shevchenko i suchasnist'', *Literaturna Ukraina*, 11 March 1964, p. 2.
79. Ivan Dzyuba, *Internationalism or Russification? A Study in the Soviet Nationalities Problem*, ed., M. Davies, London 1968), p. 100.
80. TsDAHOU, 1/24/6160, fol. 104.
81. TsDAMLMU, 670/1/1956, fol. 46–50.
82. TsDAMLMU, 670/1/1750, fol. 68.

Chapter 3. Sergei Paradjanov's Carpathian Journey

1. Hanna Shaburiak, '*Sonata of Hutsul'shchyny*', *Ranok*, no. 7, July 1965, p. 13.
2. David Bordwell and Kristin Thompson, *Film History: An Introduction*, 2nd ed., Boston 2003, p. 460.
3. TsDAMLMU, 670/1/1581, fol. 20–1.
4. See, Bosley Crowther, 'Film Festival: "The Hunt"', *The New York Times*, 20 Sept 1966, p. 39.
5. Theodor W. Adorno, *The Jargon of Authenticity*, tr., Knut Tarnowski and Frederic Will, Evanston 1973, p. xiii.
6. M. Malovs'kyi, 'Avtoram fil'mu "Tini zabutykh predkiv" S. Paradzhanovu, Iu. Il'ienku, Iu. Iakutovychu', *Radians'ka kul'tura*, 19 November 1964, p. 4.
7. See, Karen Kalentar, *Ocherki o Paradzhanove*, Erevan 1998, pp. 8–10; Vasilii Katanian, *Prikosnovenie k idolam*, Moscow 1997, p. 210.
8. Kalentar, p. 8.
9. Larysa Briukhovets'ka, 'Ivan Dziuba: Paradjanov bil'shyi za legendu pro Paradjanova', interview with Ivan Dziuba, *Kino Teatr*, no. 4, 2003, accessed online: http://www.ktm.ukma.kyiv.ua/show_content.php?id=129: 24 March 2005.
10. RGALI, 2936/1/528, fol. 41.
11. TsDAMLMU, 670/1/1536, fol. 40.
12. TsDAMLMU, 655/1/227, fol. 70.
13. TsDAMLMU, 670/1/1750, fol. 7.
14. TsDAMLMU, 655/1/199, fol. 14.
15. Sergei Paradjanov, 'Vechnoe dvizhenie', *Iskusstvo kino*, no. 1, January 1966, p. 61.
16. RGALI, 2936/1/528, fol. 43.
17. Patrice Dabrowski argues that Korzeniowski's play was essentially an allegory for Poland's own liberation struggle against the Russian and Hapsburg Empires. Dabrowski, ' "Discovering" the Galician Borderlands: The Case of the Eastern Carpathians', *Slavic Review* vol. 64, no. 2, 2005, pp. 380–402.
18. Anne E. Gorsuch and Diane P. Koenker, 'Introduction', in Gorsuch and Koenker (eds.), *Turizm: The Russian and East European Tourist under Capitalism and Socialism*, Ithaca 2006, p. 2.
19. N.A. Ivashkina, ed., *Turistskie marshruty*, Moscow 1977, pp. 82–4.
20. Nina Ignat'eva, 'V puti', *Iskusstvo kino*, no. 1, January 1961, pp. 90–4.
21. Paradjanov, pp. 63–4.
22. Ibid., p. 66.
23. Ibid., pp. 63–4.
24. Mykhailo Kotsiubyns'kyi, *Tini zabutykh predkiv*, Kyiv 1967, p. 9.
25. P. Zlatoustov, 'Idealizatsiia chy zhakhlyva diisnist'', *Chervonyi shliakh*, no. 4, 1929, p. 165.
26. Petro Kolesnyk, 'Kotsiubyns'kyi proty Modernizmu', *Vitchyzna*, no. 4, 1963; Olena Kravets', *M.M. Kotsiubyns'kyi pro narodnyi pobut*, Kyiv 1963; quoted in Volodymyr Zinych, 'Interes do etnohrafii', review of Kravets', *Literaturna Ukraina*, 15 September 1964, p. 3.
27. Luhovs'kyi, *Nevidomyi maestro: S. Paradzhanov*, Tini zabutykh predkiv: *Rozkadrovky*, Kyiv 1998, pp. 41, 43.
28. Ibid., p. 47.
29. See, Georgii Iakutovich, 'Khudozhnik ot boga', in Kora Tsereteli, ed., *Zhizn' – igra: Kollazh na fone avtoportreta*, Nizhnii-Novgorod 2005, pp. 83–4.

30. Iu. Bohdashevs'kyi, 'Tak trymaty'! *Novyny kinoekrana*, no. 6, June 1964, p. 8.
31. Paradjanov and Oleksii Miroshnychenko, '*Tini zabutykh predkiv*', *Novyny kinoekrana*, no. 8, 1964, pp. 4–5.
32. L. Korobchak, 'Podviinyi debiut: Aktors'ki syluety', *Radians'ka kul'tura*, 3 December 1964, p. 4.
33. Ivan Drach, 'Sviato z pryvodu ekranizatsii *Tinei zabutykh predkiv*', *Literaturna Ukraina*, 15 September 1964, p. 4.
34. TsDAMLMU 655/1/1685, fol. 2–3. '*God*' and '*rik*' are the Russian and Ukrainian (respectively) words for 'year'.
35. Ivan Mykolaichuk, 'Daleka podorozh', *Mystetstvo*, no. 4, 1965, reprinted in Mariia Ievhen'evna Mykolaichuk (ed.), *Bilyi ptakh z chornoiu oznakoiu: Ivan Mykolaichuk: spohady, interv'iu, stsenarii*, Kyiv 1991, pp. 213–5.
36. TsDAMLMU, 670/1/1750, fol. 109.
37. See, Francince Hirsch's notion of the 'virtual tourist' in 'Getting to Know the "Peoples of the USSR": Ethnographic Exhibits as Soviet Virtual Tourism, 1923–1934', *Slavic Review* 62, no. 4, 2003, pp. 683–709.
38. RGALI 2936/1/528, fol. 3–4.
39. Elena Bauman, 'Nad kem plachut trembity...' *Sovetskaia kul'tura*, 14 August 1965, p. 3.
40. Paradjanov, 'Vechnoe dvizhenie', pp. 63–64.
41. Pier Paolo Pasolini, 'The "Cinema of Poetry"', reprinted in John Orr and Olga Taxidou (eds.), *Post-War Cinema and Modernity: A Film Reader*, Edinburgh 2000, pp. 48, 51.
42. TsDAMLMU 655/1/310, fol. 13.
43. TsDAMLMU 670/1/1751, fol. 151.
44. TsDAMLMU, 655/1/400, fol. 152.

Chapter 4. Paradjanov and the Problem of Film Authorship

1. TsDAMLMU, 670/1/1539, fol. 50.
2. TsDAMLMU, 670/1/1620, fol. 14; 655/1/227, fol. 63.
3. See, TsDAMLMU, 670/1/1536, fol. 22.
4. See, Nikolai Blokhin, *Izgnanie Paradjanova*, Stavropol' 2002, p. 66.
5. Goskino chairman Sviatoslav Ivanov wrote in his memoirs (written in the mid-1970s) that even Paradjanov's enemies in the film industry considered him a 'genius'. Sviatoslav Ivanov, 'Khto takyi Paradjanov?', *Kino teatr*, no. 3, 1998, p. 3.
6. Francois Truffaut, 'A Certain Tendency of the French Cinema (1954)', in Barry Keith Grant (ed.), *Auteurs and Authorship: A Film Reader*, London 2008, pp. 9–18.
7. Alexander Dovzhenko, 'Pisatel' i kino v svete trebovanii sovremennosti', *Iskusstvo kino*, no. 2, February 1955, pp. 7–14.
8. See, Iurii Khaniutin, 'Pochtitel'nyi nepochtitel'nost'', *Iskusstvo kino*, no. 4, April 1961, pp. 69–78. The most famous articulation of a Soviet *auteur* theory came from Andrei Tarkovskii in the 1967 issue of *Voprosy kinoistusstva*. See, 'Zapechatlennoe vremia', *Voprosy kinoiskusstva*, no. 10, Moscow 1967: Accessed online, http://tarkovskiy.su/texty/Tarkovskiy/Statia1967.1.html: 13 March 2012.
9. Sergei Gerasimov, 'Razmyshleniia o molodykh', *Iskusstvo kino*, no. 2, February 1960, p. 18.

10. A much more positive assessment of '*avtorskoe kino*' from the early 1960s is contained in Zinovii Fogel's 'Izobrazitel'nost' fil'ma i khudozhnik', *Iskusstvo kino*, no. 3, March 1964, pp. 80–90.
11. On these protests, see Ann Komaromi, 'The Unofficial Field of Late Soviet Culture', *Slavic Review* vol. 66, no. 4, Winter 2007, pp. 605–29; Benjamin Nathans, 'The Dictatorship of Reason: Aleksandr Vol'pin and the Idea of Rights under "Developed Socialism"', *Slavic Review*, vol. 67, no. 4, Winter 2007, pp. 630–63.
12. See, 'Interv'iu P. Shelesta hazeti 'Moskovskie novosti'', September 10, 1989, reprinted in Iurii Shapovala (ed.), *Petro Shelest*, p. 691.
13. On west Ukrainian regional identities during the 1960s, see Risch, *The Ukrainian West.*
14. 'Sergei Parajanov's Speech in Minsk before the Creative and Scientific youth of Byelorussia on 1 December 1971', tr. James Steffen, *Armenian Review* vol. 47, nos. 3–4, vol. 48, nos. 1–2, 2001–2002, p. 17.
15. See, Marta Dziuba, 'Serhii Paradzhanov', *Kino teatr* no. 4, 2008, accessed online: http://www.ktm.ukma.kyiv.ua/show_content.php?id=796: 14 July 2011. Viacheslav Chornovil recalled that many high-ranking Ukrainian officials were also present during the premiere. See, 'Interv'iu V. Chornovola hazeti "Moloda hvardiia"', in Shapovala (ed.), p. 702.
16. Larysa Briukhovets'ka (ed.), *Poetychne kino: zaboronena shkola*, Kyiv 2001, p. 286.
17. According to the February 1965 Goskino *prikaz* on labour and finances, all literary and film material had to be translated into Russian and sent to Moscow before final approval. TsDAMLMU, 670/1/1852, fol. 166–8.
18. Ivan Dziuba, 'Sumlinnist' khudozhn'oho doslidu', *Radians'ke literaturoznavstvo*, no. 1, 1965, pp. 3–16.
19. TsDAVOU, 4754/1/50, fol. 65–6.
20. Briukhovets'ka (ed.), *Poetychne kino*, p. 269.
21. 'Interv'iu V. Chornovola', p. 702.
22. Viktoriia Skuba, '*Shadows of Forgotten Ancestors* 45 Years Later', *Den'* 23 Sept 2010: Accessed online: http://www.day.kyiv.ua/310236: 25 September 2010.
23. Ivan Dzyuba, *Internationalism or Russification? p.*14.
24. Ibid., p. 15.
25. See, Nathans, 'The Dictatorship of Reason', pp. 630–63.
26. Larysa Briukhovets'ka, 'Ivan Dziuba: Paradzhanov bil'shyi za lehendu pro Paradzhanova', interview with Ivan Dziuba, *Kino Teatr*, no. 4, 2003, accessed online: http://www.ktm.ukma.kyiv.ua/show_content.php?id=129: 24 March 2005
27. Dzyuba, p. 125.
28. Dziuba quoted the Ukrainian academic, K. D. Ushyns'kyi, with the words, 'When a language has died on the lips of a people, the people is also dead.' Ibid., p. 154.
29. TsDAMLMU, 655/1/317, fol. 6.
30. TsDAMLMU, 670/1/1852, fol. 179.
31. TsDAMLMU, 655/1/306, fol. 107. In its promotion of Den' kino-65, the Ukrainian-language weekly film newspaper, *Na ekranakh Kyieva* (after 1968, *Na ekranakh Ukrainy*), placed *Shadows* front and centre, indicating that it was the featured presentation of the festival. See, *Na ekranakh Kyieva*, 28 Aug 1965, pp. 1–2.

32. TsDAMLMU, 670/1/1852, fol. 178.
33. TsDAMLMU, 670/1/2059, fol. 65.
34. TsDAVOU, 4623/1/497, fol. 27.
35. Dziuba lost his editorial position at *Vitchyzna*, Chornovil was barred from publishing his work in *Molodaia gvardiia* and Stus was kicked out of his graduate programme at Shevchenko University.
36. Brainchenko reported to S. P. Ivanov that Dziuba once again tried to rally the spectators after the screening suggesting that he remained untouched by the *militsiia*. See, *Poetychne kino*, p. 269.
37. See, Kristen Roth-Ey, *Moscow Prime Time*, pp. 25–130; Joshua First, 'From Spectatorship to "Differentiated" Consumer', pp. 317–44.
38. TsDAMLMU, 655/1/309, fol. 244–5. Despite his renunciation of Dziuba's actions, both Ivan and Marta later recalled that Paradjanov supported the speech and that it cemented a developing friendship between the two of them. See, Briukhovets'ka, 'Ivan Dziuba', and Marta Dziuba, 'Serhii Paradzhanov'.
39. TsDAVOU, 4754/1/50, fol. 45; RGALI, 2944/4/280, fol. 30.
40. TsDAMLMU, 670/1/1581, fol. 59; 670/3/166, fol. 7.
41. Thomas Lahusen, 'Socialist Realism in Search of its Shores: Some Historical Remarks on the "Historically Open Aesthetic System of the Truthful Representation of Life"', in Lahusen and Evgeny Dobrenko (eds.), *Socialist Realism without Shores*, Durham 1997, p. 9.
42. Evhen Kyryliuk, 'Pravda, opovyta romantykoiu', *Literaturna Ukraina*, 17 September 1965, p. 3.
43. *Na ekranakh Kyieva*, 25 September, 2 October, 9 October, 16 October 1965.
44. D. Shlapak, 'Tini zabutykh predkiv', *Na ekranakh Kyieva*, 16 October 1965, p. 1.
45. *Na ekranakh Kyieva*
46. Woll, *Real Images*, p. 186.
47. TsDAMLMU, 655/1/313, fol. 22.
48. TsDAMLMU, 670/1/1829, fol. 1.
49. Dobrenko, *The Making of the State Reader*, pp. vii, 2.
50. Nikolai Lebedev, 'Kino i zritel'', *Iskusstvo kino*, no. 6, June 1964, p. 43.
51. Quoted in Blokhin, p. 68.
52. Quoted in Ibid., p. 69.
53. TsDAMLMU, 655/1/400, fol. 152.
54. Bohdan Chufus, 'Lyst do kinomyttsiv', *Novyzny kinoekrana*, no. 6, June 1967, p. 4.
55. Nina Tumarkin, *The Living and the Dead: The Rise and Fall of the Cult of World War II in Russia*, New York 1994, pp. 143–4.
56. James Steffen, '*Kyiv Frescoes*: Sergei Paradjanov's Unrealised Film Project', *KinoKultura*, Special Issue no. 9: Ukrainian Cinema, December 2009: http://www.kinokultura.com/specials/9/steffen.shtml: Accessed 12 March 2012.
57. According to Steffen, the *Kyiv Frescoes* test screened at the Kyiv House of Culture as part of a retrospective on Paradjanov's work between 3 December 1965 and 14 January 1966, along with *Flower on the Stone*. Steffen, '*Kyiv Frescoes*'. See also, Steffen's dissertation, 'A Cardiogram of the Time: Sergei Parajanov and the Politics of Nationality and Aesthetics in the Soviet Union', Ph.D. Dissertation, Emory University 2005, p. 199.
58. Svitlana Shcherbatiuk, Paradjanov's ex-wife, told Steffen in 2000 that the screen test appeared to her as a direct comment on their failed marriage. Steffen, '*Kyiv Frescoes*'.
59. TsDAMLMU, 1127/1/172, fol. 82.

60. TsDAVOU, 4754/1/47, fol. 179.

61. TsDAMLMU, 1127/1/172, fol. 4.

62. Ibid., fol. 15.

63. Ibid., fol. 16.

64. TsDAMLMU, 655/1/345, fol. 23.

65. TsDAMLMU, 655/1/198, fol. 15.

66. TsDAMLMU, 655/1/228, fol. 7.

67. TsDAMLMU, 655/1/199, fol. 67.

68. TsDAMLMU, 655/1/268, fol. 155.

69. TsDAMLMU, 1127/1/172, fol. 49.

70. Ibid., fol. 53.

71. Ibid., fol. 22.

72. TsDAMLMU, 655/1/346, fol. 32a.

73. 'KDB pro Paradzhanova: Dokumenty iz rozsekrechnoho arkhivu KDB URSR', *Kino teatr*, no. 1, 2011, accessed online: http://www.ktm.ukma.kyiv.ua/show_content.php?id=1067, 2 February 2011.

74. TsDAMLMU, 1127/1/172, fol. 51.

75. 'KDB pro Paradzhanova', *Kino teatr*, no. 2, 2011, accessed online: http://www.ktm.ukma.kyiv.ua/show_content.php?id=1123, 22 February 2012.

76. R. Dolyns'kyi, 'Imenem zakonu', *Vechirnii Kyiv*, 1 March 1974, p. 3.

77. 'KDB pro Paradzhanova', *Kino teatr*, no. 2, 2011.

78. Nikolai Lebedev, *Ocherk istorii kino SSSR*, p. 483.

79. TsDAMLMU, 655/1/199, fol. 76.

80. Ibid., fol. 64–5.

81. Marat Pavlovich Vlasov, 'Kinoiskusstvo i epokha zastoia', in Vlasov, ed., *Sovetskoe kino semidesiatykh – pervoi poloviny vos'midesiatykh godov: uchebnoe posobie*, Moscow 1997, p. 9.

82. TsDAMLMU, 670/1/1965, fol. 242.

Chapter 5. 'Ukrainian Poetic Cinema' and the Construction of 'Dovzhenko's Traditions'

1. TsDAMLMU, 670/1/1750, fol. 161.

2. Kateryna Stankenvych, 'Stsenarii chy skhemarii?', *Molod' Ukrainy*, 1 November 1964, p. 3.

3. TsDAMLMU, 655/1/313, fol. 88.

4. TsDAMLMU, 655/1/199, fol. 138.

5. Efim Dobin, *Poetika kinoiskusstva: Povestvovanie i metafora*, Moscow 1961, pp. 109–10.

6. Ibid., pp. 113–4.

7. Larysa Briukhovets'ka, *Kinosvit Iuriia Illienka*, Kyiv 2006, pp. 7–9.

8. Ibid., p. 19.

9. Ibid., p. 7.

10. TsDAHOU 1/24/5990, fol. 1.

11. K. Lishko, 'Dniv tykh chuiemo vidhomin...' *Dnipro*, no. 10, October 1964, pp. 4–5.

12. RGALI, 2944/5/136, fol. 70–1.

13. Ibid., fol. 158.

14. See, Nina Tumarkin, *The Living and the Dead*, New York 1994.

15. Bohdan Y. Nebesio, 'Questionable Foundations for a National Cinema: Ukrainian Poetic Cinema of the 1960s', *Canadian Slavonic Papers* vol. 42, no.1/2, March-June 2000, p. 43.
16. Conversations with Vadym Shurativs'kyi, June 2006.
17. Leonid Novychenko, 'Ivan Drach – novobranets' poezii', *Literaturna Ukraina*, 18 September 1962, p. 2.
18. 'Molodye – o sebe', *Voprosy literatury*, no. 9, September 1962, pp. 130–1.
19. Ivan Drach, 'Smert' Shevchenka', *Vitchyzna*, no. 3, 1962, p. 3.
20. Ivan Drach, 'Spraha', *Dnipro*, no. 5, 1962, p. 53.
21. Novychenko, 'Ivan Drach', p. 3.
22. *Radians'ka Ukraina*, 10 April 1963; quoted in Heorhii Kas'ianov, *Nezhodni*, p. 24.
23. A. Skaba, 'Kommunisticheskoe vospitanie trudiashchikhsia – vazhneishaia zadacha partiinykh organizatsii', *Kommunist Ukrainy*, no. 5, May 1963, pp. 29–30.
24. TsDAMLMU, 670/1/1781, fol. 74.
25. Vera Kandyns'ka, 'Tvorchi plany ie i, iakshchko Boh dast', ia ikh zdiisnoiu...', interview with Ivan Drach, *Kino teatr*, no. 5, 2002, p. 33.
26. TsDAMLMU, 670/1/1540, fol. 3; 670/1/1745, fol. 1–6.
27. Ivan Drach, 'Krynytsia dlia sprahlykh', *Dnipro*, no. 10, October 1964, pp. 7–42.
28. TsDAMLMU, 670/1/1780, fol. 10.
29. TsDAMLMU, 670/1/1781, fol. 64.
30. Ibid., fol. 61.
31. Ibid., fol. 26.
32. Ibid., fol. 41.
33. Ibid., fol. 47.
34. Ibid., fol. 43–5.
35. Elena Bokshitskaia, 'Iurii Illienko – pris za kompromiss', *Iunost'*, no. 9, 1987, p. 81.
36. 'Interv'iu daie Iurii Il'ienko', *Na ekranakh Kyeva*, 9 October 1965, p. 1.
37. Ye. Semenova, '*Krynytsia dlia sprahlykh*', *Na ekranakh Kyeva*, 15 January 1966, p. 2.
38. TsDAMLMU, 670/1/1781, fol. 30, 61.
39. *Molod' Ukrainy*, 27 Dec 1981, quoted in Briukhovets'ka, p. 67.
40. Conversation with Vadym Skurativs'kyi, June 2005; see also, Briukhovets'ka, p. 64.
41. I. Shatokhin, 'Novi raboty D. Miliutenka', *Na ekranakh Kyeva*, 5 June 1965, p. 2.
42. TsDAMLMU, 655/1/317, fol. 53.
43. Semenova, p. 2.
44. Briukhovets'ka, *Kinosvit Iuriia Illienka*, p. 63.
45. TsDAMLMU, 1127/1/176, fol. 33.
46. TsDAMLMU, 670/1/1965, fol. 246, 252, 259, 300–1.
47. TsDAMLMU, 670/1/1781, fol. 5–6; TsDAVOU, 4754/1/77, fol. 57–8.
48. TsDAHOU, 1/24/6160, fol. 9–11, 13.
49. Ibid., fol. 14.
50. Ibid., fol. 58.
51. TsDAHOU, 1/24/6160, fol. 108–10.
52. TsDAMLMU, 670/1/1966, fol. 3–4.
53. Ibid., fol. 8, 23.
54. TsDAMLMU, 655/1/345, fol. 54.

55. TsDAVOU, 4754/1/77, fol. 58.

56. TsDAMLMU, 670/1/1991, fol. 27.

57. TsDAMLMU, 670/1/1783, fol. 93.

58. Ibid., fol. 124–6, 129; Andrei Tarkovskii, 'Mezhdu dvum'ia fil'mami', *Iskusstvo kino*, no. 11, 1962, p. 83.

59. After viewing the completed film during a studio meeting, Denysenko, Tsvirkunov and screenwriter Evhen Onopriienko all condemned it as worthless cinema. TsDAMLMU, 670/1/2324.

60. See the shooting script: RGALI, 2944/6/503, fol. 1b.

61. Ibid., fol. 2.

62. Semen Gudzenko, *Dal'nii garnizon*, Moscow 1984, p. 32.

63. Larysa Briukhovets'ka, 'Leonid Osyka, "Shistdesiatnyk"', *Kino Teatr*, no. 2, 1995, p. 8.

64. TsDAMLMU, 670/1/2065, fol. 6.

65. TsDAMLMU, 670/1/1783, fol. 184.

66. Ibid., fol. 4.

67. Ibid., fol. 16.

68. TsDAMLMU, 1127/1/174, fol. 42.

69. TsDAMLMU, 670/1/1783, fol. 98.

70. Ibid., fol. 103.

71. TsDAMLMU, 655/1/313, fol. 60.

72. Ibid., fol. 113.

73. Ibid., fol. 118.

74. Ibid., fol. 90.

75. Ibid., fol. 93–4.

76. Ibid., fol. 95

77. Ibid., fol. 95–6.

78. TsDAVOU, 4754/1/77, fol. 49.

79. TsDAHOU, 1/24/6160, fol. 104. The *Kobzar* is Taras Shevchenko's major collection of poetry. The title means 'the bard'.

80. TsDAMLMU, 670/1/1782, fol. 2.

81. TsDAMLMU, 670/1/2065, fol. 9; 1127/1/174, fol. 206.

82. *Na ekranakh Kyieva*, 9 December 1967.

83. Ibid., 23 March 1968, 30 March 1968, 6 April 1968, 13 April 1968.

84. TsDAMLMU, 655/1/450, l. 200.

Chapter 6. Making National Cinema in the Era of Stagnation

1   TsDAMLMU, 655/1/355, fol. 212.

2. TsDAMLMU, 670/1/1750, fol. 151.

3. TsDAVOU, 4754/1/77, fol. 54.

4. Roman Szporluk, 'The Press and Soviet Nationalities: The Party Resolution of 1975 and Its Implementation', reprinted in *Russia, Ukraine, and the Breakup of the Soviet Union*, Stanford 2000, pp. 277–97.

5. TsDAMLMU, 670/1/2159, fol. 62.

6. I. Vaisfel'd wrote in 1967, 'Cinema's appeal to national aesthetic values became one of the obstacles on the path towards its subordination to a commercial standard'. I. Vaisfel'd, 'Natsional'noe – internatsional'noe', *Iskusstvo kino*, no. 9, Sept 1967, p. 19.

7. TsDAMLMU, f. 655, op. 1, d. 581, l. 22–5.

8. RGALI, 2944/1/524, fol. 126.

9. RGALI, 2936/4/70, fol. 56–7.

10. TsDAMLMU, 655/1/450, fol. 199–200.

11. Ibid., fol. 201.

12. Vasyl' Illiashenko describes *Forest Song* as on the border of theatre and cinema. Vasyl' Illiashenko, *Istoriia ukrains'koho kinomystetstva*, Kyiv 2004, p. 191.

13. Ivan Mykolaichuk, *Novyny kinoekrana*, no. 1, Jan 1966; quoted in Larysa Briukhovets'ka, *Ivan Mykolaichuk*, Kyiv 2004, p. 75.

14. *Na ekranakh Kyieva*, 14 March 1966 – 17 January 1967, 30 March, April 21, 1967; *Novyny kinoekrana*, no. 5 (May 1967).

15. RGALI, 2944/4/720, fol. 105; TsDAVOU, 4754/1/44, fol. 260.

16. Data is cited from Raisa Prokopenko (ed.), *Natsional'na kinostudiia khudozhnikh fil'miv imeni Oleksandra Dovzhenka: Anotovanyi kataloh fil'miv, 1928–1998*, Kyiv 1998.

17. When Shvachko took over the production from Ihor Sambors'kyi in February 1968, he replaced a Russian actor with Mykolaichuk, crediting the latter with more 'skill' in such a role. See, TsDAMLMU, 670/1/2151, fol. 81.

18. See, *Na ekranakh Ukrainy*, 21 April-9 June 1969. V. Poltavtsev, 'Prokatnaia zhizn' fil'ma', *Iskusstvo kino*, no. 10, Oct 1972, p. 115.

19. TsDAMLMU, 670/1/2574, fol. 23.

20. TsDAMLMU, 655/1/450, fol. 123.

21. TsDAHOU, 1/31/3689, fol. 60–1.

22. TsDAMLMU, 655/1/788, fol. 15.

23. Marat Vlasov, 'Kinoiskusstvo i epokha zastoia', in Vlasov (ed.), *Sovetskoe kino semidesiatykh – pervoi poloviny vos'midesiatykh godov: uchebnoe posobie*, Moscow 1997, p. 9.

24. See, First, 'From Spectator to "Differentiated" Consumer', pp. 317–44; Roth-Ey, *Moscow Prime Time*, pp. 71–130.

25. See, Lev Kogan, *Kino i zritel': Opyt konkretno-sotsiologicheskogo issledovaniia*, Moscow 1968.

26. See, Filipp Ermash, 'O khode vypolneniia reshenii XXV s'ezda KPSS', *Iskusstvo kino*, no. 7, 1978, p. 20.

27. TsDAMLMU, 655/1/788, fol. 182–3.

28. TsDAVOU, 4623/1/925, fol. 19.

29. TsDAMLMU, 670/1/2536, fol. 7–19, 127.

30. TsDAMLMU, 655/1/665, fol. 60.

31. TsDAMLMU, 670/1/2806, fol. 8–9.

32. Vlasov, p. 9.

33. See First, 'From Spectator to 'Differentiated' Consumer', p. 327.

34. TsDAMLMU, 670/1/2426, fol. 11–2.

35. Larysa Briukhovets'ka, *Prykhovani fil'my: Ukrains'ke kino 1990-kh*, Kyiv 2003, pp. 28–9.

36. RGALI, 2936/4/67, fol. 11.

37. M. Klado, 'Natsional'noe – v konkretnom', *Druzhba narodov*, no. 6, June 1959, pp. 169–80.

38. Buriak, 'Internatsional'noe – ne beznatsional'noe', pp. 26–36.

39. See, Mykola Makarenko, 'Gliadia v koren'', *Sovetskaia Ukraina*, no. 1, 1961, pp. 115.

40. Buriak, 26–36.

41. RGALI, 2936/4/50, fol. 17.

42. RGALI, 2936/4/50, fol. 38.
43. RGALI, 2936/4/67, fol. 14.
44. Ibid., fol. 7.
45. Ibid., 38–39.
46. RGALI, 2935/4/50, fol. 22–3.
47. RGALI, 2936/4/70, fol. 5.
48. Ibid., fol. 20.
49. RGALI, 2936/4/71, fol. 2.
50. TsDAMLMU, 670/1/2159, fol. 92.
51. V. Tsyrlin, 'Problema zobrazhennia i tendentsiia krytyky', *Za Radians'kyi fil'm*, 8 October 1969, p. 2.
52. Iurii Illienko, 'Tryiednist'', *Za Radians'kyi fil'm*, 22 October 1969, p. 2.
53. The Ukrainian word '*samoznavets*" literally means 'a scholar of oneself'.
54. I. Vaisfel'd, 'Natsional'noe – internatsional'noe', *Iskusstvo kino*, no. 9, September 1967, p. 21.
55. L. Mamatova, 'Letopis' bratstva', *Iskusstvo kino*, no. 12, December 1972, pp. 104–33; Armen Medvedev, 'Veter veka: Zametki o problemakh i fil'makh mnogonatsional'noi sovetskoi kinematografii', *Iskusstvo kino*, no. 6, June 1973, pp. 1–25.
56. 'Lyst Serhiia Paradzhanova Ovcharenku', in L. Briukhovets'ka (ed.), *Poetychne kino*, pp. 270–72.
57. 'Spohady i shchodennykovi zapysy Petra Shelesta', in Iurii Shapovala (ed.), *Petro Shelest*, p. 310.
58. TsDAHOU, 1/24/5991, fol. 118–9.
59. Petro Shelest, *Ukraino, nasha Radians'ka*, Kyiv 1970.
60. Quoted in Iurii Shapovala, 'Petro Shelest u konteksti politychnoi istorii Ukrainy XX stolittia', in Shapovala (ed.), *Petro Shelest*, p. 13.

Chapter 7. 'Ukrainian Poetic Cinema' between the Communist Party and Film Audiences

1. TsDAMLMU, 670/1/2536, fol. 81.
2. RGALI, 2944/4/1206, fol. 9.
3. See Aleksandr Karaganov, 'Kino i zritel'', *Sovetskii ekran*, no. 14, July 1965, p. 3.
4. TsDAMLMU, 655/1/400, fol. 176.
5. Ivan Drach, 'Tvorchi plany ie i, iakshcho Boh dast', ia ikh zdiisniu ...' *Kino teatr*, no. 5, 2002, p. 34.
6. See, D. S. Struk, *A Study of Vasyl' Stefanyk: The Pain at the Heart of Existence*, Littleton 1973.
7. Vitaly Chernetsky, 'Visual Language and Identity Performance in Leonid Osyka's *A Stone Cross*: The Roots and the Uprooting', *Studies in Russian and Soviet Cinema* vol. 2, no. 3, 2008, pp. 269–80.
8. Liudmila Lemesheva, *Ukrainskoe kino: Problemy odnogo pokoleniia*, Moscow 1987, p. 42.
9. TsDAMLMU, 655/1/539, fol. 143.
10. RGALI, 2936/4/305, fol. 61.
11. TsDAMLMU, 670/1/2354, fol. 8.
12. *Na ekranakh Ukrainy*, 24 April-25 May 1969.
13. See, Douglas Gomery, *Shared Pleasures: A History of Movie Presentation in the United States*, Madison 1992, pp. 183–95.

14. TsDAMLMU, 670/1/1991, fol. 14; 670/1/1992, fol. 38; TsDAVOU, 4754/1/137, fol. 99.
15. T. Ivanova, 'Trudnoe – eshche trudnee – sovsem trudno ...' *Ekran 69–70,* Moscow 1970, p. 90.
16. Ibid., p. 95.
17. TsDAMLMU, 670/1/2322, fol. 43; RGALI, 2944/4/1931, fol. 34–5.
18. TsDAMLMU, 670/1/2324, fol. 106.
19. TsDAMLMU, 670/1/2262, fol. 38.
20. TsDAMLMU, 670/1/2324, fol. 91
21. Vitalli Borshchov, 'Pid tiaharom 'serpa i molota': tvoryv svoi naikrashchi fil'my Iurii Illenko', *Na ekranakh Ukrainy,*18 April 1996, p. 3.
22. 'Protokol vid 22 bereznia 1971 roku', in Briukhovets'ka (ed.), *Poetychne kino: Zaboronena shkola,* p. 291.
23. See, Illiashenko, pp. 186, 206.
24. See, Denise Youngblood, *Russian War Films: On the Cinema Front, 1914–2000,* Lawrence 2007, pp. 107–41.
25. *Na ekranakh Ukrainy,* 13 March 1971.
26. 'Protokol', p. 291.
27. TsDAMLMU, 670/1/2262, fol. 5.
28. TsDAHOU, 1/32/585, fol. 148.
29. TsDAMLMU, 670/1/2605, fol. 58–9.
30. TsDAMLMU, 670/1/2536, fol. 12.
31. RGALI, 2936/4/305, fol. 62.
32. *Na ekranakh Ukrainy,* 30 August-27 October 1971; TsDAHOU, 1/32/585, fol. 148.
33. RGALI, 2944/4/1931, fol. 7.
34. Serhii Trymbach, 'Chomu zh ne nashym dniam sudylosia'? *Kino Teatr,* no. 1, 1997, p. 30.
35. TsDAMLMU, 670/1/2324, fol. 40.
36. RGALI, 2944/1/609, fol. 13.
37. RGALI, 2944/4/1931, fol. 19–29.
38. TsDAMLMU, 670/1/2426, fol. 14.
39. TsDAMLMU, 670/1/2454, fol. 52–3.
40. TsDAMLMU, 670/1/2997, fol. 31.
41. TsDAHOU, 1/2/101, fol. 37–8.
42. Liudmyla Lemesheva, 'Deshcho z osobystoho zhyttia krytyka', in Briukhovets'ka (ed.), *Poetychne kino,* p. 306.
43. TsDAHOU, 1/32/878, fol. 156.
44. TsDAMLMU, 655/1/632, fol. 120.
45. TsDAMLMU, 655/1/705, fol. 28.
46. TsDAMLMU, 655/1/285, fol. 49.
47. TsDAMLMU, 655/1/738, fol. 7–8.
48. Levchuk and Rybak first proposed the film in 1956. See, TsDAMLMU, 670/1/777.
49. TsDAMLMU, 670/1/1889, fol. 17–25.
50. Natan Rybak, interview in *Ekran-67,* Moscow 1967, p. 159.
51. *Novyzny kinoekrana,* no. 1, Jan 1969; *Na ekranakh Ukrainy,* 11 Jan 1969.
52. TsDAMLMU, 655/1/442, fol. 206.
53. A transcript of the trailer is in TsDAMLMU, 670/1/2580, fol. 34–8.
54. *Carpathians, Carpathians* alone cost the studio 900,000 roubles. TsDAMLMU, 670/1/2580, fol. 47.

55. Illiashenko, p. 233.
56. TsDAMLMU, 655/1/788, fol. 1–7.
57. TsDAMLMU, 655/1/665, fol. 56
58. TsDAMLMU, 670/1/2997, fol. 62.
59. TsDAMLMU, 655/1/932, fol. 69.
60. Quoted in Golovskoi, *Mezhdu ottepel'iu i glasnost'iu*, p. 80.
61. First, 'From Spectator to "Differentiated" Consumer', p. 342.

Conclusion: Ukrainian Cinema and the Limitations of National Expression

1. Yuri Slezkine, 'The USSR as a Communal Apartment, or How a Socialist State Promoted Ethnic Particularism', *Slavic Review* vol. 53, no. 2, Summer 1994, p. 449.
2. Suny, *The Revenge of the Past*, pp. 102–24.
3. Serhy Yekelchyk, *Stalin's Empire of Memory: Russian-Ukrainian Relations in the Soviet Historical Imagination*, Toronto 2004, p. 160.
4. TsDAMLMU, 655/1/1685, fol. 15–6.
5. Larysa Briukhovets'ka, 'Zirka nespodivana i nemynucha: Ekranni obrazy Larysy Kadochnykovoi', *Kino teatr*, no. 5, 1996, p. 53.
6. Briukhovets'ka, 'Reabilitatsiia dukhovnosti: Paradoks Ivana Mykolaichuka', *Kino teatr*, no. 2, 1998, p. 24.
7. Illiashenko, p. 267.
8. Yuri Shevchuk, 'The Bold Vision of Kira Muratova and Its Distorted Reflection in New York', *Maidan: An Internet Hub for Citizens Action Network in Ukraine*, accessed online: http://eng.maidanua.org/node/235: 1 June 2008.
9. For an analysis of this event, see Andrii Mokrousov, et al., 'Dyskusiia: Bandera iak problema', *Krytyka: Prostir nezalezhnoi dumky*, 14 June 2010: http://krytyka.com/cms/front_content.php?idart=208, accessed 1 May 2012.

BIBLIOGRAPHY

This bibliography does not aim to be comprehensive. It includes a list of archival materials, books and articles that may be of interest to those who wish to pursue further research on the subject.

Archival Materials

Rossiiskii gosudarstvennyi arkhiv literatury i iskusstva (RGALI)
Fond 2936 (*Soiuz kinematografistov SSSR*)
Fond 2944 (*Gosudarstvennyi komitet po kinematografii pri Sovete Ministrov SSSR*)
Tsentral'nyi derzhavnyi arkhiv hromads'kykh orhanizatsii Ukrainy (TsDAHOU)
Fond 1 (*Tsentral'nyi komitet Kompartii Ukrainy*)
Tsentral'nyi derzhavnyi arkhiv vyshykh orhaniv vlasti Ukrainy (TsDAVOU)
Fond 4623 (*Glavnoe Upravlenie kinofikatsii i kinoprokata pri Derzhkomitete po kinematografii*)
Fond 4754 (*Komitet Kinematohrafii*)
Tsentral'nyi derzhavnyi muzei-arkhiv literatury i mystetstva Ukrainy (TsDAMLMU)
Fond 655 (*Spilka kinematohrafistiv Ukrainy RSR*)
Fond 670 (*Kyivs'ka kinostudiia khudozhnykh fil'miv im. O. P. Dovzhenka*)
Fond 1127 (*Stsenarno-redaktsionnaia kollegiia Komiteta Kinematografii Ukrainy*)

Books and Articles

Anninskii, L., 'Tri zvena', *Iskusstvo kino*, no 9, 1971, pp. 134–152
Babyshkin, O., *Ukrains'ka literatura na ekrani*. Radians 'kyĭ pys'mennyk, Kyiv, 1966
Bauman, E., 'Nad kem plachut trembity ...', *Sovetskaia kul'tura*, 14 August 1965, p. 3
Bilinskii, M., 'Puti ukrainskogo kinoiskusstva', *Iskusstvo kino*, no 10, 1958, pp. 111–114
Bokshitskaia, E., 'Iurii Illienko – pris za kompromiss', *Iunost'*, no 9, 1987, pp. 80–83
Buriak, B., 'Internatsional'noe – ne beznatsional'noe', *Iskusstvo kino*, no 2, 1964, pp. 26–36
Chabanenko, I., 'Puti ukrainskogo kinoiskusstva', *Iskusstvo kino*, no 10, 1958, pp. 111–13
Crowther, Bosley, 'Film Festival: *The Hunt*', *New York Times*, 20 September 1966, p. 39
Dobin, E., 'Poeticheskoe i prozoicheskoe v kino', *Iskusstvo kino*, no 8, 1960, pp. 88–107
——— *Poetika kinoiskusstva: Povestvovanie i metafora*, Moscow, 1961
——— 'Sud'ba metafora v kino', *Iskusstvo kino*, no 2, 1964, pp. 13–25
Dovzhenko, A., 'Pisatel' i kino v svete trebovanii sovremennosti', *Iskusstvo kino*, no 2, 1955, pp. 7–14.
Drach, I., 'Krynytsia dlia sprahlykh', *Dnipro*, no 10, 1964, pp. 7–42
——— 'Sviato z pryvodu ekranizatsii *Tini zabutykh predkiv*', *Literaturna Ukraina*, 15 September 1964, p. 4
——— 'Spasibo!' *Literaturnaia Rossiia*, 26 February 1965, p. 17
Dziuba, I., 'Den' poiska', *Iskusstvo kino*, no 5, 1965, pp. 73–82

Dziuba [Dzyuba], Ivan. *Internationalism or Russification? A Study in the Soviet Nationalities Problem*, ed., M. Davies, Weidenfeld and Nicolson, London, 1968

Fomenko, V., 'Ne nabliudat', a voevat': zametki s kinostudii im. Dovzhenko', *Pravda Ukrainy*, 5 January 1963, p. 3

Honchar, O., 'Shevchenko i suchasnist'', *Literaturna Ukraina*, 11 March, 1964, pp. 2

Illienko, Iu., 'Tryiednist'', *Za Radians'kyi fil'm*, 22 October 1969, p. 2

'Interv"iu daie Iurii Il'ienko', *Na ekranakh Kyeva*, 9 October 1965, p. 1

Iurenev, R., *Aleksandr Dovzhenko*, Moscow, 1959

Ivanov, T., 'Trudnoe – eshche trudnee – sovsem trudno ...' *Ekran 69–70*, Moscow, 1970, pp. 90–95

Karaganov, A., 'Kino i zritel'', *Sovetskii ekran*, no 14, 1965, p. 3

'KDB pro Paradzhanova: Dokumenty iz rozsekrechnoho arkhivu KDB URSR', *Kino teatr*, no 1, 2011, accessed online: http://www.ktm.ukma.kyiv.ua/show_content. php?id=1067, 2 Feb 2011

'KDB pro Paradzhanova: Dokumenty iz rozsekrechnoho arkhivu KDB URSR', *Kino teatr*, no 2, 2011, accessed online: http://www.ktm.ukma.kyiv.ua/show_content. php?id=1123, 22 Feb 2012

Khaniutin, Iu., 'Pochtitel'naia nepochtitel'nost'', *Iskusstvo kino*, no 4, 1961, pp. 69–78

Klado, M., 'Natsional'noe – v konkretnom', *Druzhba narodov*, no 6, 1959, pp. 169–180

Kogan, L., *Kino i zritel': Opyt konkretno-sotsiologicheskogo issledovaniia*, Iskusstvo, Moscow, 1968

Kolesnikova, N., 'Po doroge na ekran', *Komsomol'skaia pravda*, 12 December 1961, p. 4

Korniienko, I., 'Tendentsii i zavdannia', *Literaturna Ukraina*, 24 August 1962, p. 1

——— 'Velinnia chasu', *Radians'ka Ukraina* 10 January 1963, p. 3

Korobchak, L., 'Podviinyi debiut: Aktors'ki syluety', *Radians'ka kul'tura*, 3 December 1964, p. 4

Kostenko, L. and A. Dobrovol's'kyi, 'Perevirte svoi hodynnyky', *Dnipro*, no 2, 1963, pp. 2–43

Kotsiubyns'kyi, M., *Tini zabutykh predkiv*, Derzhavne vydavnytstro, Kyiv, 1929

——— *Tini zabutykh predkiv*, Dnipro, Kyiv, 1967

Kravets', O., *M.M. Kotsiubyns'kyi pro narodnyi pobut*, Naukova dumka, Kyiv, 1963

Kryzhanivs'kyi, B. and Iu. Novykov, *Viktor Ivchenko*, Mystetstvo, Kyiv, 1976

Kyryliuk, E., 'Pravda, opovyta romantykoiu', *Literaturna Ukraina*, 17 September 1965, p. 3

Lebedev, N., *Ocherk istorii kino SSSR: Nemoe kino*, Goskinoizdat, Moscow, 1947

Lemesheva, L., *Ukrainskoe kino: Problemy odnogo pokoleniia*, Soiuz kinematografistov SSSR Biuro propogandy kinoiskusstva, Moscow, 1987

Levchuk, T., 'Rik tvorchykh shukan'', *Novyny kinoekrana*, no 1, 1965, p. 1

Makarenko, N., 'Gliadia v koren'', *Sovetskaia Ukraina*, no 1, 1961, pp. 109–135

Mamatova, L., 'Letopis' bratstva', *Iskusstvo kino*, no 12, 1972, pp. 104–133

Medvedev, A., 'Veter veka: Zametki o problemakh i fil'makh mnogonatsional'noi sovetskoi kinematografii', *Iskusstvo kino*, no 6, 1973, pp. 1–25

Navrots'kyi, S., 'Stsenarii pishche stsenaryst', *Radians'ka kul'tura*, 15 March 1962, p. 3

Nekrasov, V., 'Slova "velikie" i prostye', in *Sochineniia*, Knizhnaia palata, Moscow, 2002, pp. 1121–1126

Novychenko, L., 'Ivan Drach – novobranets' poezii', *Literaturna Ukraina*, 18 September 1962, p. 2.

Paradzhanov, S. and O. Miroshnychenko, '*Tini zabutykh predkiv*', *Novyny kinoekrana*, no 8, 1964, pp. 4–5

Paradzhanov, S., 'Vechnoe dvizhenie', *Iskusstvo kino*, no 1, 1966, pp. 60–66

———— ' "…chtoby ne molchat', berus' za pero": Vybrannye mesta iz perepiski s nedrugami i druz'iami', *Iskusstvo kino*, no 12, 1990, pp. 32–41

———— 'Sergei Parajanov's Speech in Minsk before the Creative and Scientific Youth

of Belorussia on 1 December 1971', tr. Nora Seligman Favorov and P. Elana Pick, *Armenian Review* 47, nos 3–4, 48, nos 1–2, 2001–2002, pp. 11–33

Pavlychko, D., 'Siiartel' vichnoho', *Literaturna Ukraina*, 15 September 1964, pp. 3–4

Poltavtsev V., 'Prokatnaia zhizn' fil'ma', *Iskusstvo kino*, no 10, 1972, pp. 111–118

Rachuk, I., *Oleksandr Dovzhenko*, Mystetstovo, Kyiv, 1964

Repiakh, V., et al., 'Molodye za ekranom: Komsomol'tsy otvechaiut na kritiku gazety. A chto dumaiut rukovoditeli studii imeni Dovzhenko'? *Komsomol'skaia Pravda* 31 January 1962, p. 2

Romitsyn, A., *Ukrains'ke radians'ke kinomystetstvo: narysy*, vol. 3: 1941–1954, Vydavnytstvo Akademii nauk Ukrains'koi RSR, Kyiv, 1959

———— 'Novatorstvo, traditsii, nasliduvannia', in *Kino i suchasnist'*, ed. O. Stryzhevs'kyi, Kyiv, Mystetstvo, 1961, pp. 57–87

Rybak-Akimov, V., 'Vypuskaty til'ky khoroshi fil'my', *Radians'ka kul'tura*, 24 July 1960, p. 2

Semenova, Ye., 'Krynytsia dlia sprahlykh', *Na ekranakh Kyeva*, 15 January, 1966, p. 2

Shelest, P., *Ukraino, nashe Radians'ka*, Politychna literatura Ukrainy, Kyiv, 1970

Shapovala, Iu., ed., *"Spravzhnii sud istorii shche poperedy": Spohady, shchodennyk, dokumenty, materially*, Heneza, Kyiv, 2003, pp. 427–428

Shevchenko, V., et al., 'Vykhovuvaty svoikh aktoriv', *Radians'ka kul'tura*, 9 December 1956, p. 3

Shklovskii, Viktor, "Poetry and Prose in Cinema', in *The Poetics of Cinema*, ed. B. M. Eikhenbaum and Richard Taylor, tr. Taylor. RPT Publications, Oxford, 1982, pp. 87–89

Skaba, A., 'Kommunisticheskoe vospitanie trudiashchikhsia – vazhneishaia zadacha partiinykh organizatsii', *Kommunist Ukrainy*, no 5, 1963, pp. 24–34

Sovetskie khudozhestvennye fil'my: Annotirovannyi katalog (1917–1965), 5 vol., Iskusstvo, Moscow, 1961–1979

Stalin, Joseph, 'Marxism and the National Question' (1913), Accessed online: http://www.marxists.org/reference/archive/stalin/works/1913/03.htm: July 14, 2008.

Tarkovskii, A., 'Mezhdu dvum'ia fil'mami', *Iskusstvo kino*, no 11, 1962, pp. 82–84

Tsyrlin, V., 'Problema zobrazhennia i tendentsiia krytyky', *Za Radians'kyi fil'm*, 8 October 1969, p. 2

Vaisfel'd, I., 'Natsional'noe – internatsional'noe', *Iskusstvo kino*, no 9, 1967, pp. 19–29

Varshavskii, L., 'Pravda narodnykh kharakterov', *Kazakhstanskaia Pravda*, 8 June 1965

Zinych, S., *Kinokomediia: konflikt, kharacter, zhanry*, Mystetstvo, Kyiv, 1966

Secondary Literature

Anderson, Benedict, *Imagined Communities: Reflections on the Origin and Spread of Nationalism*, 2nd ed., Verso, London, 1991

Armstrong, John A., 'Myth and History in the Evolution of Ukrainian Consciousness', in ed., Peter J Potichnyj, *Ukraine and Russia in Their Historical Encounter*, Canadian Institute of Ukrainian Studies Press, University of Alberta, Edmonton, 1992, pp. 125–139

Bausinger, Hermann, *Folk Culture in a World of Technology*, tr., Elke Dettmer, Indiana University Press, Bloomington, 1990

Bendix, Regina, *In Search of Authenticity: The Formation of Folklore Studies*, University of Wisconsin Press, Madison, 1997

Blitstein, Peter, 'Stalin's Nations: Soviet Nationality Policy between Planning and Primordialism, 1936–1953', Ph.D. dissertation, University of California, Berkeley, 1999

Blokhin, Nikolai, *Izgnanie Paradzhanova*, Stavropol', s.n. 2002

Bordwell, David, *Narration in Fiction Film*, Wisconsin University Press, Madison, 1985

Borshchov, Vitalii, 'Pid tiaharom "serpa i molota": tvoryv svoi naikrashchi fil'my Iurii Illenko', *Na ekranakh Ukrainy*, 18 April, 1996, pp. 1, 3

Bourdieu, Pierre, *Language and Symbolic Power*, tr., Gino Raymond and Matthew Adamson, Polity Press, Cambridge, 1991

———, *The Field of Cultural Production: Essays on Art and Literature*, ed., Randal Jackson, Columbia University Press, New York, 1993

Brandenberger, David, *National Bolshevism: Stalinist Mass Culture and the Formation of Modern Russian National Identity, 1931–1956*, Harvard University Press, Cambridge, MA, 2003

Briukhovets'ka, Larysa, ed., *Poetychne kino: zaboronena shkola*, ArtEk, Kyiv, 2001

——— 'Ivan Dziuba: Paradzhanov bil'shyi za legendu pro Paradzhanova', interview with Ivan Dziuba, *Kino Teatr*, no 4,2003, accessed online: http://www.ktm.ukma.kiev.ua/show_content.php?id=129: March 24, 2005

——— *Prykhovani fil'my: Ukrains'ke kino 1990-kh*, ArtEk, Kyiv, 2003

——— *Ivan Mykolaichuk*, Kino Teatr, Kyiv, 2004

——— *Kinosvit Iuriia Illienka*, Kino Teatr, Kyiv, 2006

Brubaker, Rogers, and Frederick Cooper, 'Beyond "Identity"', *Theory and Society* 21, no 1, 2000, pp. 1–47

Clark, Katerina, *The Soviet Novel: History as Ritual*, University of Chicago Press, Chicago, 1981

Dabrowski, Patrice, '"Discovering" the Galician Borderlands: The Case of the Eastern Carpathians', *Slavic Review* 64, no 2, 2005, pp. 380–402

Dobrenko, Evgenii, *The Making of the State Reader: Social and Aesthetic Contexts of the Reception of Soviet Literature*, tr., Jesse M. Savage, Stanford University Press, Stanford, 1997

Ely, Christopher, *This Meager Nature: Landscape and National Identity in Imperial Russia*, Northern Illinois University Press, DeKalb, 2002

Farmer, Kenneth, *Ukrainian Nationalism in the Post-Stalin Era: Myths, Symbols and Ideology in Soviet Nationalities Policy*, Martinus Nijhoff Publishers, The Hague, 1980

First, Joshua, 'From Spectator to "Differentiated" Consumer: Film Audience Research in the Era of Developed Socialism (1965–80)', *Kritika: Explorations in Russian and Eurasian History* 9, no 2, 2008, pp. 317–344

Gellner, Ernest, *Nations and Nationalism*, Blackwell, Oxford, 1983

Gledhill, Christine, 'Rethinking Genre', in *Reinventing Film Studies*, ed., Gledhill and Linda Williams, Arnold, London, 2000, pp. 221–243

Golovskoi, Valerii, *Mezhdu ottepel'iu i glasnost'iu: Kinematograf 70-kh*, Materik, Moscow, 2004

Gorsuch, Anne and Diane Koenker, eds., *Turizm: The Russian and East European Tourist under Capitalism and Socialism*, Cornell University Press, Ithaca, 2006

Hess, John, 'La Politique des Auteurs (Part One): World View as Aesthetics', *Jump Cut: A Review of Contemporary Media*, no 1, 1974: Accessed online: http://www.ejumpcut.org/archive/onlinessays/JC01folder/auturism1.html: 13 May 2008

Higson, Andrew, *Waving the Flag: Constructing a National Cinema in Britain*, Clarendon Press, Oxford, 1995

Hirsch, Francine, 'Getting to Know the "Peoples of the USSR": Ethnographic Exhibits as Soviet Virtual Tourism, 1923–1934', *Slavic Review* 62, no 4, 2003, pp. 683–709

—— *Empire of Nations: Ethnographic Knowledge and the Making of the Soviet Union*, Cornell University Press, Ithaca, 2005

Hobsbawm, Eric J., *The Age of Extremes: The Short Twentieth Century, 1914–1991*, Michael Joseph, London, 1994

Hoseiko, Liubomyr, *Istoriia ukrains'koho kinematohrafa*, tr., Stanislav Dovhaniuk and Hoseiko, Kino-Kolo, Kyiv, 2005

Hroch, Miroslav, 'From National Movement to Fully-Formed Nation: The Nation-Building Process in Europe', in *Becoming National: A Reader*, ed., Geoff Eley and Ronald Grigor Suny, Oxford University Press, Oxford, 1996, pp. 60–77

Iakutovich, Georgii, 'Khudozhnik ot boga', in *Zhizn' – igra: Kollazh na fone Avtoportreta*, ed., Kora Tsereteli, DEKOM, Nizhnii-Novgorod, 2005, pp. 83–84

Illiashenko, Vasyl', *Istoriia ukrains'koho kinomystetstva*, Vik, Kyiv, 2004

Illienko, Iurii, *Aostolovi Petru: Avtoportret al'ter eho (sebe inshoho): Roman-khatatan v odnii knyzi*, Bohdan, Ternopil', 2011

Kalentar, Karen, *Ocherki o Paradzhanove*, Hitutiun, Erevan, 1998

Kapel'horods'ka, Nonna, *Renesans vitchyznianoho kino: Notatky suchasnytsi*, Avdi, Kyiv, 2002

Kas'ianov, Heorhii, *Nezhodni: ukrains'ka intelihentsiia v rusi oporu 1960–80-kh Rokiv*, Lybid', Kyiv, 1995

Katanian, Vasilii, *Prikosnovenie k idolam*, Vagrius, Moscow, 1997

Katz, Abraham, *The Politics of Economic Reform in the Soviet Union*, Praeger, New York, 1972

Kenez, Peter, *Cinema and Soviet Society, 1917–1953*, Cambridge University Press, Cambridge, 1992

Komaromi, Ann, 'The Unofficial Field of Late Soviet Culture', *Slavic Review* 66, no 4, 2007, pp. 605–629

Kozlov, Denis, 'The Readers of *Novyi mir*, 1945–1970: Twentieth-Century Experience and Soviet Historical Consciousness', Ph.D. Dissertation, University of Toronto, 2005

Krawchenko, Bohdan, *Social Change and National Consciousness in Twentieth-Century Ukraine*, Macmillan Press, London, 1985

Landy, Marcia, *The Folklore of Consensus: Theatricality in the Italian Cinema, 1930–1943*, SUNY Press, Albany, 1998

Lewytzyj, Borys, *Politics and Society in Soviet Ukraine, 1953–1980*, Canadian Institute of Ukrainian Studies, University of Alberta, Edmonton, 1984

Liber, George O., *Alexander Dovzhenko: A Life in Soviet Film*. BFI Publications, London, 2002

Lubens'kyi, Petro, 'Koroleva benzokolonky', *Kino Teatr*, no 2, 2001, p. 43

Luckyj, George S. N., *Literary Politics in the Soviet Ukraine, 1917–1934*, rev. ed., Duke University Press, Durham, 1990

Luhovs'kyi, Volodymyr, *Nevidomyi maestro: S. Paradzhanov*, Tini zabutykh predkiv: Rozkadrovky, Kino-Teatr, Kyiv, 1998

Mace, James, *Communism and the Dilemmas of National Liberation*, Harvard Ukrainian Research Institute, Cambridge, MA, 1983

Magocsi, Paul Robert, *A History of Ukraine*, University of Toronto Press, Toronto,1996

Margolit, Evgenii, 'Evoliutsiia fol'klornaia traditsiia v ukrainskom sovetskom kino (1920–40-e gg.)', Ph.D. Dissertation, Leningrad Institute of Theater, Music, and Cinema, 1979

––––– 'Istoriko-biograficheskii fil'm v sovetskom kino', in *Noveishiaia istoriia otechestvennogo kino*, vol. 6, ed. L. Arkus, Seans, St. Petersburg, 2004, accessed online, http://russiancinema.ru/template.php?dept_id=15&e_dept_id=6&text_element_id=61, 17 February 2008

Martin, Terry, *The Affirmative Action Empire: Nations and Nationalism in the Soviet Union, 1923–1939*, Cornell University Press, Ithaca, 2001

Miller, Frank J, *Folklore for Stalin: Russian Folklore and Pseudofolklore of the Stalin Era*, M. E. Sharpe, Armonk, NY, 1990

Mykolaichuk, Mariia Ievhen'evna, ed., *Bilyi ptakh z chornoiu oznakoiu: Ivan Mykolaichuk: spohady, interv"iu, stsenarii*, Mystetstvo, Kyiv, 1991

Natsional'na kinostudiia khudozhnikh fil'miv imeni Oleksandra Dovzhenka: Anotovanyi kataloh fil'miv, 1928–1998, Kyiv, 1998

Nebesio, Bohdan, 'The Silent Films of Aleksandr Dovzhenko: A Historical Poetics', Ph.D. Dissertation, University of Alberta, 1996

Pasolini, Pier Paolo, 'The "Cinema of Poetry"', in *Post-War Cinema and Modernity: A Film Reader*, ed., John Orr and Olga Taxidou. Edinburgh University Press, Edinburgh, 2000, pp. 37–53

Payne, Robert, 'The Storm of the Eye: Culture, Spectacle, Paradzhanov', *Spectator* 10, no 1, 1990, pp. 32–45

Pelenski, Jaroslaw, 'Shelest and His Period in Soviet Ukraine (1963–1972): A Revival of Controlled Ukrainian Autonomism', in *Ukraine in the Seventies: Papers and Proceedings of the McMaster Conference on Contemporary Ukraine, October 1974*, ed., Peter J. Potychnyj, Mosaic Press, Oakville, Ont, 1975, pp. 283–305

Troianovskii, Vitalii, ed., *Kinematograf ottepeli: kniga vtoraia*, Materik, Moscow, 2002

Rakowska-Harmstone, Teresa, 'The Dialectics of Nationalism in the Soviet Union', *Problems of Communism* 22, 1974, pp. 1–22

Rosen, Philip, 'History, Textuality, Nation: Kracauer, Burch, and Some Problems in the Study of National Cinema', in *Theorising National Cinema*, ed., Valentina Vitali and Paul Willemen, BFI, London, 2006, pp. 17–28

Roth-Ey, Kristin, *Moscow Prime Time: How the Soviet Union Built the Media Empire that Lost the Cultural Cold War*, Cornell University Press, Ithaca, 2011

Rubchak, Bohdan, 'The Music of Satan and the Bedeviled World: An Essay on Mykhailo Kotsiubynsky', in Mikhailo Kotsiubynsky, *Shadows of Forgotten Ancestors*, Canadian Institute of Ukrainian Studies by Ukrainian Academic Press, Littleton, CO, 1981, pp. 79–121

Shapovala, Iurii, ed., *Petro Shelest: "Spravzhnii sud istorii shche poperedy": Spohady, shchodennyk, dokumenty, materially*, Heneza, Kyiv, 2003

Shevchuk, Yuri, 'The Bold Vision of Kira Muratova and Its Distorted Reflection in New York', *Maidan: An Internet Hub for Citizens Action Network in Ukraine*, accessed online: http://eng.maidanua.org/node/235: 1 June 2008

Slezkine, Yuri, 'The USSR as a Communal Apartment, or How a Socialist State Promoted Ethnic Particularism', *Slavic Review* 53, no 2, 1994, pp. 415–452

Smith, Anthony, *The Ethnic Origins of Nations*, Blackwell, Oxford, 1986

––––– *National Identity*, University of Nevada Press, Reno, 1991

—— 'Ethnic Identity and Territorial Nationalism in Comparative Perspective', in *Thinking Theoretically about Soviet Nationalities: History and Comparison in the Study of the USSR*, ed., Alexander J. Motyl', Columbia University Press, New York, 1992, pp. 45–65

—— 'Images of the Nation: Cinema, Art and National Identity', in Mette Hjort and Scott MacKenzie, eds., *Cinema and Nation*, Routledge, London, 2000, pp. 49–59.

Steffen, James, 'A Cardiogram of the Time: Sergei Parajanov and the Politics of Nationality and Aesthetics in the Soviet Union', Ph.D. Dissertation, Emory University, 2005

—— *The Cinema of Sergei Parajanov*, University of Wisconsin Press, Madison, 2013

Stites, Richard, *Russian Popular Culture: Entertainment and Society since 1900*, Cambridge University Press, Cambridge, 1992

Struk, D. S., *A Study of Vasyl' Stefanyk: The Pain at the Heart of Existence*, Ukrainian Academic Press, Littleton, CO, 1973

Suny, Ronald Grigor, *Revenge of the Past: Nationalism, Revolution, and the Collapse of the Soviet Union*, Stanford University Press, Stanford, 1993

—— *The Soviet Experiment: Russia, the USSR, and the Successor States*, Oxford University Press, Oxford, 1998

Suny, Ronald Grigor, and Terry Martin, eds., *A State of Nations: Empire and Nation-Making in the Age of Lenin and Stalin*, Oxford University Press, Oxford, 2001

Szporluk, Roman, 'The Press and Soviet Nationalities: The Party Resolution of 1975 and Its Implementation', in *Russia, Ukraine, and the Breakup of the Soviet Union*, Hoover Institution Press, Stanford, 2000, pp. 277–297

Taylor, Charles, *Multiculturalism and 'The Politics of Recognition'*, Princeton University Press, Princeton, 1992

Taylor, Richard, *The Politics of the Soviet Cinema, 1917–1929*, Cambridge University Press, Cambridge, 1979

—— 'Singing on the Steppe for Stalin: Ivan Pyr'ev and the Kolkhoz Musical in Soviet Cinema', *Slavic Review* 58, no 1, 1999, pp. 143–159

Thompson, Kristin, 'The Concept of Cinematic Excess', in *Narrative, Apparatus, Ideology: A Film Theory Reader*, ed., Philip Rosen. Columbia University Press, New York, 1986, pp. 130–142

Todorova, Maria, 'The Trap of Backwardness: Modernity, Temporality, and the Study of Eastern European Nationalism', *Slavic Review* 64, no 1, 2005, pp. 140–164

Troianovskii, Vitalii, ed., *Kinematograf ottepeli: k 100-letiiu mirovogo kino*, Materik, Moscow, 1996

—— *Kinematograf ottepeli: kniga vtoraia*, Materik, Moscow, 2002

Trymbach, Serhii, 'Chomu zh ne nashym sudylosia'? *Kino Teatr*, no 1, 1997, pp. 30–34

Tsel'tner, V. P., *F. Manailo*, Sovetskii khudozhnik, Moscow, 1986

Tumarkin, Nina, *The Living and the Dead: The Rise and Fall of the Cult of World War II in Russia*, Basic Books, New York, 1994

'Vin osviaiatyv liubov: spohady pro Artura Voitets'koho', *Kino Teatr*, no 1, 2005, pp. 19–23

Vlasov, Marat, *Sovetskoe kino semidesiatykh – pervoi poloviny vos'midesiatykh godov: uchebnoe posobie*, VGIK, Moscow, 1997, pp. 3–14 von Hagen, Mark, 'Does Ukraine Have a History'? *Slavic Review* 54, no 3, 1995, pp. 658–73

von Moltke, Johannes, *No Place Like Home: Locations of Heimat in German Cinema*, University of California Press, Berkeley, 2005

Weiner, Amir, *Making Sense of War: The Second World War and the Fate of the Bolshevik Revolution*, Princeton University Press, Princeton, 2001

Widdis, Emma, *Visions of a New Land: Soviet Cinema from the Revolution to the Second World War*, Yale University Press, New Haven, 2003

Woll, Josephine, *Real Images: Soviet Cinema and the Thaw*, I.B.Tauris, London, 2000

Yekelchyk, Serhy, *Stalin's Empire of Memory: Russian-Ukrainian Relations in the Soviet Historical Imagination*, University of Toronto Press, Toronto, 2004

—— *Ukraine: Birth of a Modern Nation*, Oxford University Press, Oxford, 2007

Youngblood, Denise, *Movies for the Masses: Popular Cinema and Soviet Society in the 1920s*, Cambridge University Press, Cambridge, 1992

—— *Russian War Films: On the Cinema Front, 1914–2000*, University of Kansas Press, Lawrence, 2007

Yurchak, Alexei, *Everything Was Forever Until It Was No More: The Last Soviet Generation*, Princeton University Press, Princeton, 2005

Zemlianukhin, Sergei, and Miroslava Segida, eds., *Domashniaia sinematika: otechest-vennoe kino, 1918–1996*, Dubl'-D, Moscow, 1996

INDEX

Lightning Source UK Ltd.
Milton Keynes UK
UKHW020607170123
415485UK00006B/519